D0177383

IT'S ALL ABOUT THE BIKE

www.transworldbooks.co.uk

IT'S ALL ABOUT THE BIKE

My Autobiography

Sean Yates

with
John Deering

CORGI BOOKS

TRANSWORLD PUBLISHERS
61–63 Uxbridge Road, London W5 5SA
A Random House Group Company
www.transworldbooks.co.uk

IT'S ALL ABOUT THE BIKE
A CORGI BOOK: 9780552169301

First published in Great Britain
in 2013 by Bantam Press
an imprint of Transworld Publishers
Corgi edition published 2014

Copyright © Sean Yates 2013

Sean Yates has asserted his right under the Copyright,
Designs and Patents Act 1988 to be identified as the author of this work.

A CIP catalogue record for this book
is available from the British Library.

This book is sold subject to the condition that it shall not,
by way of trade or otherwise, be lent, resold, hired out,
or otherwise circulated without the publisher's prior
consent in any form of binding or cover other than that
in which it is published and without a similar condition,
including this condition, being imposed on the
subsequent purchaser.

Addresses for Random House Group Ltd companies outside the UK
can be found at: www.randomhouse.co.uk
The Random House Group Ltd Reg. No. 954009

The Random House Group Limited supports the Forest Stewardship
Council® (FSC®), the leading international forest-certification organisation.
Our books carrying the FSC label are printed on FSC®-certified paper.
FSC is the only forest-certification scheme supported by the leading
environmental organisations, including Greenpeace. Our paper procurement
policy can be found at www.randomhouse.co.uk/environment

Typeset in 12½/15pt Ehrhardt by
Kestrel Data, Exeter, Devon.
Printed and bound by
CPI Group (UK) Ltd, Croydon, CR0 4YY.

2 4 6 8 10 9 7 5 3 1

For Mum and Dad

LLYFRGELLOEDD SIR DDINBYCH	
C46 0000 0540 239	
Askews & Holts	10-Mar-2015
796.626092	£9.99
RU	

In memory of Brian Phillips
1960–2011

Chapter One

It's 7 July 2012, and this is my twentieth time at the Tour de France. I was a competitor a dozen times, and this is my eighth as a *directeur sportif*. The automatic Jaguar gearbox is revving high in a low gear to keep us in position behind the bunch. Every time it changes up, it changes back down again as we're constantly adjusting our speed while the line of cyclists and cars concertinas on the climb. I glance down at the little TV screen set into the dash to get a better idea of what's going on up in front. With 20 kilometres remaining to the finish at La Planche des Belles Filles, there are seven labouring riders clear of the rest of the Tour. The main pack is closing in on them fast. This is the seventh stage, and our plan to take control of the race is about to take wings.

We've been sitting on our hands for a week waiting for this moment. Every time there has been a yell or the sound of bikes hitting the tarmac in the last seven days, my heart has been in my mouth: please, not us. Don't let anything happen to the plan. Just let us get through to stage seven unscathed. All year, whenever we've tried something, it's come off. We've been charmed. How long can it last? But the tension of the last few days has been almost unbearable, like sitting in a dentist's reception waiting to have a tooth out.

I glance in the mirror and catch the eye of Diego in the back seat, my only companion in the car. Most days I have my boss, the team principal Dave Brailsford, in the passenger seat, but today I'm alone in the front. Dave gets frustrated by not being able to see what's happening, so he's opted for the comfort of the Sky bus and the TV.

As mechanic in Sky's first team car, Diego's fingers are flexing and unflexing around a rear wheel, ready to leap out of the car at a moment's notice if one of our riders suffers a flat. Next to him on the seat is a front wheel, the second most likely mechanical necessity, then there is a tool box open with the various implements he might need, stored in order of what might be required first.

'Twenty klicks left, stay calm. Eight until our marker,' I say into the team radio. There is no reply from any of the eight men who can hear it. This is the business end of the day and they are all concentrating on the job in hand. The second radio in the car, the race radio linking us to the chief *commissaire*'s car, crackles into life, reminding us that the Garmin team are leading the bunch at present, giving the numbers of David Millar and David Zabriskie. I'm not really sure why they're working so hard: Garmin have suffered more than anyone in the string of crashes that have littered the first week of this race. Their leader, Ryder Hesjedal, was unable to start today after a smash yesterday, the biggest casualty of this race so far, as he won the Giro d'Italia in May. Two other Garmin riders have also gone home, leaving them with just six men. Sky have lost one ourselves, Kanstantsin Sivtsov, or Kosta as we call him, to a broken leg in a massive pile-up the other day. It's meant a little bit more work and a little bit more pressure for the eight guys we've still got, but you wouldn't notice from the way they've been working. And if Garmin want to ride on the front, then that's all the better for us.

Fabian Cancellara has been leading the Tour since he won the prologue last weekend, and so Nissan–RadioShack have been controlling the race to protect his yellow jersey. He's not expected to keep it through the mountains, though, and the other teams know that Sky, with our leader Bradley Wiggins poised to take the race lead if Cancellara falters, have the most to lose.

Some teams wouldn't bother protecting what they're unlikely to keep, but there are a few factors affecting Nissan–RadioShack's tactics. Firstly, their season hasn't brought them much so far, with Cancellara falling and breaking his collarbone in the Tour of Flanders to keep him out of his favourite spring Classics, then their Tour leader Andy Schleck battling the poor form and injury that have left him at home in Luxembourg for this race. That's one big name that Bradley won't have to see off if he's to become the first British Tour de France winner.

A week, or even longer, with the yellow jersey in their ranks is a massive fillip in a difficult year, and is worth fighting for.

Then there is the protocol of yellow. Yellow rules. All bow to the yellow. It is an unwritten rule in cycling that the yellow jersey is the ace of trumps in the whole of our sport. Olympic golds, World Championship rainbow stripes, a trophy cabinet full of cups, trophies, shields and cobblestones are all wonderful things, but the *maillot jaune* flies proudly above them all on the highest flagpole on the tallest tower of the castle. Protocol demands that all other considerations take second place to the golden fleece.

Finally, my Nissan–RadioShack counterpart, Alain Gallopin, is a traditionalist, and a French traditionalist at that. He understands the meaning of the jersey and is going to treat it properly. I know Alain well, he and his brother Guy were both professional riders and contemporaries of mine, and our management careers have covered similar timeframes. I know what he's likely to do, and he knows what I'm likely to do too. He could call Sky's bluff and tell his team to stop working to protect the lead, but I don't think he will. If they have a great day, Cancellara could still be in yellow tomorrow, and if he wears it tomorrow, then the day after and so on and so on until . . . well, until Paris in theory.

There was a chance that we would have had to ride on the front more than we have, but the proud traditionalist would always want to honour the jersey with strong riding, and that's how it's panned out. We've had to do our fair share of pulling, and if we do take the overall lead that workload is going to grow exponentially. From day one when we started planning this Tour de France, the most important person to have in Sky's armoury – if Brad was going to challenge – was Christian Knees. Some people in the organization couldn't see it, pointed out that he wasn't a sprinter, wasn't a climber. However, amongst our large roster of riders, he was the only man for the job of the horse: the man that never says no to a job, the rider who can tow the whole race at high speed for hours at a time, who never tires, who is always at Bradley's side. There will be a lot of work for him in the next fortnight. Bernie Eisel has been great all week, a revelation, proving to be much more than Mark Cavendish's personal assistant and happy to get his hands dirty. A great leader on the road, a rock for the team. These two have been worth their weight in gold all week, and they've worked extra hard today, especially in the absence of Kosta. Knees led the bunch on to the climb with Edvald Boasson Hagen on his shoulder, but Garmin's willingness to work has made things a little bit easier.

This is the third time I've been here this year. After the Tour of Romandie which we won with Bradley Wiggins, I drove here and rode these roads. They've not been used in the Tour de France before so it was important to get a look. Then, after we'd won the Critérium du Dauphiné, with Bradley again, I came back with the riders to let them ride the course for themselves and explain my plan for today.

I picked five stages to personally recon for this year's race: today's stage with its short but steep finishing climb, tomorrow's ride into Switzerland, both time-trial stages, and then a little-known Pyrenean stage that is finishing at Peyragudes, a climb that has never been used before in the Tour, much like this one. I've been a rider in teams where the *directeur sportif* didn't know his stuff and it spreads negativity like a disease . . . 'Here he goes again, what's he on about this time?' It's my job to know what's going to happen. I want the riders to assume, to just accept, that I'm always right, so they can concentrate on what they're doing and have one less thing to worry about.

Right now the race is pulling hard up the climb. We know that it's not going to be like this all the way to the line. There's a little peak and then a descent of about three kilometres, then the last five kilometres or so up-hill is pretty steep. This is where the plan comes into operation. Edvald has been lurking with the rest of the Sky team just on the shoulders of those Garmin riders. There is an exact spot I've pinpointed for us to make the move and I've flagged it on the satnav. It's about 100 metres shy of the summit, designed to catch out the op-position and give them as little time as possible to react. I haven't given Eddy the precise spot as I want the element of surprise to be maximized. Eddy is the ideal rider for this job: so strong, so willing to help the team, yet one of the best riders in the world in his own right. A *directeur*'s dream.

'Get ready, Eddy,' I say into the radio as we close on that mini-summit. 'OK . . . go!'

'Attaque, Team Sky,' comes out of the race radio. It must have looked like an attack to the *commissaire*, but what Eddy is actually doing is nailing it flat out for three kilometres downhill and then two more on the flat. Edvald has launched the move at the precise point on the road we had selected. 'Come on!' I shout, Diego whooping in the back. Game on.

One of Brad's rivals for the yellow jersey, Lotto's Jurgen Van Den Broeck chooses this moment to drop his chain. The long drag up to this point and the gradual accumulation of constant pressure has stretched the bunch to snapping point even before Edvald's injection of pace. Van Den Broeck couldn't have had worse luck and we see him trying to fix his own bike at the side of the road then chasing frantically to get back.

Edvald gives it full gas over the top and down the short twisting descent. ASO (Amaury Sport Organization) have had the corners repaved since our recon mission, so he is able to make even better use of his insider knowledge and lean his Pinarello even more aggressively into the snaking bends. This is the first mountain stage of the Tour, people have been waiting for this day for the best part of the year. The feeling that something is erupting, something that has been suppressed for months – pressure growing until it is intolerable – is impossible to ignore. There are motorbikes everywhere, fans screaming in riders' faces, people leaping into and out of the road between the *motos*, bikes and cars like a surreal, insane hokey-cokey. It's absolute pandemonium.

We've tried pre-planned moves like this on several occasions this year and it's always paid off. I'm hoping that all the other teams are going, 'Shit, here we go again.'

The pace Edvald sets on the flattish section before the final ascent is intense, and I weave the Jag in and out of exhausted *domestiques* as they drop back from the action. We're number two in the line of cars – Nissan–RadioShack are first by virtue of the yellow jersey on Cancellara's back – which gives us as good a view of the action as you can expect, but when the shit hits the fan at moments like these, you have to rely on Radio Tour for updates. Even our funky TV isn't much use in these more remote spots as the digital signal break-up just shuts the screen down. I preferred the old analogue version we had a couple of years back. OK, the picture wasn't as good, but when the signal got crap it just went grainy, and you could still make out what was happening. No wonder Dave prefers watching it from the bus.

It's too fast for anyone to move up what has now become a long, thin line of riders doing everything they can to hang on to the wheel in front. People often think that setting a high pace is all about dissuading other people from attacking, but there's much more to it than that. When you're hanging on for grim death to the wheel in front, 30th place in a line of eighty, there's no way you can affect the race. You can't move up to 29th, let alone first. You pray that the rider in 15th or 20th doesn't blow up and lose the wheel in front . . . you're breathing out of your arse just to hang on to the wheel in front . . . you've done that, but you've all been dropped. A rider who can do this to a race in the closing stages is a valuable rider indeed.

Riders are cracking all over the place. Jurgen Van Den Broeck manages to skirt the dropped men and get back on to the line, but he's a fraction too late. The front of the race has hit the final climb and somebody has let that wheel go. The bunch has split, leaving Van Den Broeck stuck at the back of the wrong half. He is unlikely to win the Tour de France from there. Shit happens.

The climb from here goes through a section of massive redwood trees. The Vosges Mountains are beautiful and largely unknown outside of France; even in France you don't hear many people talking about the region. Cyclists know it, though: I saw loads of people riding here on my trip in April after Romandie. On that day, a sculptor, with a selection of chainsaws like a quiver full of painter's brushes, was shaping a huge tree trunk into an astonishingly detailed wooden impression of a bear cradling a baby. I'd stopped to watch him carving away with an enormous petrol-driven power tool like it was a soft charcoal pencil, creating light and shade. Now we pass the finished work, towering over the Tour as the race flies underneath the roaring brown bear at the side of the road.

We're on the climb with just over five kilometres to go and now it's Mick Rogers's turn to take it up. Edvald has done a great job in thinning the bunch and putting us firmly in control. From here there is a Sky quartet of Mick, Richie Porte, Chris Froome and Bradley Wiggins that will aim to grab the race by the throat and take pole position for the rest of the Tour. We went over the plan again this morning: it's a four-point plan before we deliver the final blow. First Eddy, then Mick, then Richie and Froomey, before Brad plants himself into the jersey. Mick knows that he has to deliver two kilometres at threshold. For him, that means a sustained effort putting out around 460 watts. He's one of the bigger riders, a 72-kilo unit, and knowing the shape he's in, I'm confident that nobody will be able to beat that and hopefully he will cause some real problems for the other contenders. I'm working on the old Miguel Indurain masterplan. Take the initiative on the first hard stage and put as much time as possible into as many people as possible. If we can get some time gaps today it will make the next couple of weeks a lot less difficult.

This part of road under the canopy of the massive trees is very steep. People are leaping into the road in front of the riders, but the cyclists keep their heads down, concentrating on the numbers from their power meters as if they're doing a ramp test in the gym or following a programme on a home trainer.

Mick's effort is creating havoc in the front group. First they catch and pass the exhausted riders who have led for most of today's 199 kilometres, totally spent. Then the names start to crack. Alejandro Valverde has had similar luck to Jurgen Van Den Broeck and punctured at a bad time. Diego starts to shout out the names of riders who had high hopes going into today but are now falling away from the front: Dan Martin, who may have been the point of Garmin's lead-up work is dropped; World Time Trial Champion Tony Martin; Olympic Road Champion Sammy Sánchez. It's so steep, I would say about 20% here. The leaders are going visibly slowly, turning over gears of 39 x 28 and giving it everything. Tejay Van Garderen, Robert Gesink, Philippe Gilbert, Andreas Klöden, Rui Costa are all losing ground. Fabian Cancellara sees his yellow jersey floating off his back as he loses contact. Chris Horner, Frank Schleck, Janez Brajkovič, Sylvain Chavanel and Levi Leipheimer all pop. Mick turns a slightly bigger gear with Brad, two wheels back, spinning as if he is on a Sunday club run. The biggest names in the Tour are cracking left, right and centre, but Brad isn't breathing hard enough to blow out a candle. Cruising.

'Come on, Richie, this is your moment!' I shout down the radio to Richie Porte, and he slips past Mick to take it up. 'You can see the damage you're doing, just keep turning the screw.' Right now, with the race spread-eagled behind, we could ease up, make someone else do the work. But I feel that this is the moment to stick the knife in, to put some money in the bank. Anything can happen on the Tour and a buffer of a minute or two could make all the difference in the coming fortnight. I tell the boys at the front to keep at it and go hell for leather. Make hay while the sun shines, as my dad used to say. 'It's carnage behind, you're blowing them away. *Car! Nage!*'

Denis Menchov is the latest to struggle. The hill has eased and this bit is actually almost flat, but the attrition and constant pressure of the last hour have left him completely empty. The only serious rivals remaining at the front are Cadel Evans and Vincenzo Nibali; the Sky team effort has put time into everybody else worth worrying about.

Chris Froome, our best climber, takes it up for the steepening final part of the ascent. Some voices have been tipping Froomey as the best bet for overall victory, but our strategy is firmly behind Brad, proven leader, winner, and ideally suited to this year's *parcours* of fewer steep kilometres and longer individual time-trialling miles. Froomey's job is to stay at the front with Brad in the mountains and help him when needed, making sure we're never isolated at the front end of the race.

Evans fancies the super-steep ramp up to the finish line as it's reminiscent of one of his favourite race finishes, the Mur de Huy at the finale of the Flèche Wallonne in Belgium. Evans has been deserted by his team today, no other BMC riders were able to stay at the front, but he hasn't let that bother him, concentrating on matching Edvald, Mick, Richie and now Froomey, to make sure he doesn't lose sight of Brad. Thinking of victory, he pulls out into the centre of the road from Froome's wheel and makes his bid for the stage. He's such a fighter, it's hard to know if he's really got the form to pull it off or whether he's just running on pure distilled guts.

If it ends like this I will be more than satisfied. We've controlled the race completely, executed a carefully drawn-up plan with real panache, distanced any number of potential rivals and will probably take the leader's jersey as long as Brad can follow Evans for the last few yards.

But it's better than that. With Brad glued to Evans's rear wheel, Froomey finds another gear on the last gradient and hammers round the pair of them for an epic stage win. Hopefully he won't have lost his hearing from me bellowing encouragement in his earpiece over the radio over that last frantic, painful hundred metres. We'd written the script and acted it out to perfection.

This team has proved itself again to be a mighty unit. We've won virtually every race we've been to this year – from the Volta ao Algarve to Paris–Nice, the Tour of Romandie and the Critérium du Dauphiné – with the same riders and crew. We see ourselves as the elite regiment at the heart of the Sky army. Now we need to prove ourselves one more time and make history at the Tour. Today we've taken a massive stride towards making it real.

The road up to here is tiny; the local authority actually had to extend it up to this point to allow the Tour to get here. We couldn't get the bus up the narrow strip;

it's waiting for us down on the bigger road in the valley below. Instead, we've brought two *soigneur*'s cars with turbo-trainers for the warm-down, a Sky innovation that had the other teams scratching their heads when we started it. Now everybody does it.

Everybody is hugging, back-slapping and laughing at the cars while Brad goes up to the podium to pull on the jersey and my mind drifts back eighteen years to the day when I won the *maillot jaune*. It was a fantastic moment, but a very different one. While I was intensely proud to be one of the few British riders to wear it, there was never a chance of holding on to it – I was just keeping it warm for the big names. The difference is that Bradley is here with the intention of taking it all the way to Paris and being the first British cyclist in history to take it home afterwards. There's two weeks to go, but we couldn't have hoped for a better position at this stage in the race. 'He's won this, he's won that, but can he win the Tour?' is a question we've been asked all year as the victories piled up; it's a question we've asked ourselves within the team. We thought he could win it. Now we're beginning to make other people believe too.

We swap a few words of congratulation then set about the business of getting off this crowded little mountain top and back down to the bus, parked down the valley. The road is clogged with fans and the enormous apparatus of the Tour de France, and will be for hours yet. It would be easiest for the riders to just ride down, but amongst the pandemonium of fans and vehicles it's dangerous. The last thing I want is an accident, so I don't let them, ordering them into the cars like some kind of sergeant major. I must sound like Brian Clough sometimes, throwing my weight around. It's all part of the Sky dogma. Controlling the controllables. Marginal gains. Attention to detail.

The second *directeur sportif*, Servais Knaven, who is driving team car 2, and I grab bikes from the roofs of our cars and leave the vehicles with the mechanics. We make our way through the throng, twisting in and out of the queuing vehicles and walking fans, some in fancy dress, many carrying huge flags that reveal this crowd has descended on the Vosges from every part of the world. This is, unbelievably, my fourth decade at the Tour de France, and I can say with confidence that I have never seen so many Union Jacks as this year. There are a good number of Sky replica jerseys walking back down the mountain with a spring in their step, and we get a share of whoops and shouts from the masses as we weave between them.

Nearer the bottom the road widens slightly and we're able to make up some ground. We find ourselves along-side a motorbike with a pillion rider and I recognize him as Patrick, the guy who interviews managers in the team cars from that seat during the race. He seizes the opportunity to grab a quick interview in French live on France 3. We roll along next to each other, him asking me about the day, and, as I go over the events of the last couple of hours, the euphoria starts to break over me. We'd written the script, we'd directed the movie, and acted the parts to perfection. I ride in front and with a roar of pure joy I pull my shirt off, whirling it over my head like Ian Wright celebrating an injury-time winner at the old Clock End at Highbury. *'On a gagné!'* I shout, like a French football fan, live on TV with the tattoo of an American Indian across my back for all to see. My kids will die of shame if they catch this.

We're going to win the Tour de France.

Chapter Two

I always said I'd never write a book. But here we are.

Cycling has never been higher in the minds of the Great British Public, thanks to the class, perseverance and dedication of Bradley Wiggins, Mark Cavendish, Victoria Pendleton and many others. Who would have believed a decade ago that cyclists would win the BBC Sports Personality of the Year in three of the last five years? Three different cyclists at that? All three were deserved as well, all three topping what had been done by anybody else in the sport at that point: Sir Chris Hoy's breathtaking Olympic medal haul, Cav's unbeatable Tour de France sprinting and World Championship success, then Brad's unprecedented domination of the Tour and his Olympic gold all breaking new ground for British cyclists.

For better or worse, we know more about cycling than ever before. When I first went to Europe as a teenager, British cycling fans were more likely to know what the record on the E72 25-mile time-trial course was than who had won Liège–Bastogne–Liège. I went to races like Het Volk and the Tour of Flanders as a first-year professional knowing no more about them than I knew about the Superbowl or the Ryder Cup. I knew they were a big deal, but that was about it.

Now we can study the sport twenty-four hours a day all year round. Satellite television shows us bike racing every week. Dedicated websites keep us up to date with every tiny piece of gossip and every obscure result. Magazines burst at the spines with information about the anaerobic threshold of the latest would-be Eddy Merckx, or what some obscure Australian junior champion likes for breakfast. Twitter tells us where the stars are, what music they're listening to, how that knee injury is coming along. And newsgroups overflow with opinions about who's thinking what, who's doing what and who's taking what.

If you want to read about who stuck what needle in whose arm at what race in the back of whose car in 1983 or whenever, then I'm afraid you're reading the wrong book. This is a book about cycling, not about drugs. There are acres of information about that sort of thing on the internet and in other books, you don't need it from me, and I'm not interested in talking about it. I want to talk about cycling.

I've retired. I've walked away from a life that's the only life I've known as an adult. I'm in my fifties, I've got a dodgy ticker and I want to spend some time with my kids before it's too late instead of driving three times round the world every year. I want to ride my bike. And it just occurred to me that I've got thirty-five years of stories to tell.

I've never really stopped to think about the bigger picture of my life in that time. It's only now that it's done with that you can pause and say . . . 'Well, that was quite a ride.' Going to the Olympics three years after I got my first bike. Being unbeaten for a year in British time trials when I was still a teenager. Riding the Tour de France a dozen times. Wearing the yellow jersey for a day. Rooming with Lance Armstrong. Becoming a *directeur sportif* and winning the Giro d'Italia. Taking over at the biggest British team ever and winning the Tour de France.

And that got me thinking about the other stuff. Living as a virtually feral kid on the Ashdown Forest. Climbing trees to watch telly through the windows of other people's houses. Me and my brother sleeping in the back of Mum and Dad's Minivan as we emigrated to Germany. Going from being a lifelong vegetarian to eating blue steaks in France at four in the morning and putting on two stone in my first season abroad. Riding to races in the pouring rain on my race bike in my race kit. Living in a broom cupboard because I hadn't paid any income tax. Lying on the side of an Italian mountain when my heart stopped working.

I thought there must be some people who'd want to hear about that sort of thing. The tough bit would be re-membering it all. As a result, you'll find over the course of this book that I'll be asking some other voices to help me tell the story and recall the bits that I've forgotten.

I think that in 2013 we ought to be able to talk about cycling with enough knowledge of the background, enough recognition that the sport's awkward relationship with its public is now in a new, more open and healthy phase. It would be nice if we could start talking about the actual business of bike riding again.

So here we are. This is my book about my life.

If I didn't think I would be writing this thing ever, I certainly hadn't planned on writing it now. 2012 was the most glittering year in British cycling history, and I'd had a role to play in the chorus line. I was looking ahead to 2013 and 2014 as the head *directeur sportif* at Sky, but things change.

My second career, the one in cycling management (or my third if you count gardening), started pretty much by accident when I became *directeur sportif* of the Linda McCartney team in 1999, three seasons after I'd finished as a pro rider. It got going in earnest in 2003 when I joined Bjarne Riis's Danish CSC set-up. I found my element as an assistant *directeur*, something I did happily for the rest of the decade, first with Bjarne and then under Johan Bruyneel at his Discovery and Astana organizations. It suited me down to the ground: I would turn up at a race, drive the car, use my experience of racing to help the guys through, and try to meet whatever objectives the team had set.

I joined the brand new Sky team at the launch in 2010 in a similar role, but quickly found myself in charge as head *directeur sportif*. Life changed pretty drastically. The extra salary was gratefully trousered, but with the money and title came greater responsibility, greater pressure, more paperwork, more meetings, more management, more miles, more problems to sort out and more general aggravation. I was working with less experienced people, and while their missionary zeal and enthusiasm were welcome, it was a lot less relaxed than I was used to, and I always had a lot on my plate. Not so much fun for someone like me who's always looking for an easy life, and I've been unwell at times.

I suppose that at this time I ought to give you a brief outline of my health problem: I've got a form of arrhythmia, which means my heartbeat goes out of sync and stays out of sync until something is done to fix it. I've had four cardioversions – where they stop your heart and start it again – one ablation, one stroke, and one heart failure. I've also had a pacemaker fitted. I'll tell you more about it later on, and it'll be easy to skip if you find that stuff as boring as I do.

Not helped by my worsening health, my three years at Sky were exhausting. The pressure to get results and to get stories in the news all the time was greater than at any other time in my career, and as head *directeur sportif* I was closer to the sharp end of that than I had been at previous teams.

I'm often accused of being a bit old school, and I would

probably have to agree with that. Cycling is a results business and I understand that, but in my opinion when I joined Sky there was too much concentration on image, style and newsworthiness. Being a media company, they were a lot more image conscious than my previous teams. For instance, you'd go to a race that was part of your build-up for something else, you'd get a result in an early stage and then, all of a sudden, they'd want you to go flat out for victory, even though that might damage your prospects for the bigger event you were preparing for. I'm acutely aware of the need to keep sponsors happy and to stay in the public eye, but I felt the balance tipped too far in that direction at times, sometimes to the detriment of preparation and performance. It was short-termist: we'd be most likely to please those people by keeping our eyes on the main prize – winning the Tour de France within five years, as was the stated aim of the team – rather than getting diverted looking for daily titbits in every race we entered. We had to establish ourselves as a serious team first.

I had spoken casually to other teams, but nobody would be likely to match Sky's generous salary, and I enjoyed the buzz. The challenge of leading Brad and a British-based squad to the Tour de France was a massive carrot, so I ignored the side turnings, ignored the possibilities, ignored the quiet life and pushed on.

There was a constant battle in my mind between wanting to chill out, take an easier ride, give my ailing body a break and spend more time with my family, and wanting to provide for them. It was like being on a speeding train and watching stations flash by the window. I had to just tell myself not to look at those stations or I might find myself getting off.

After the Sky domination of the 2012 Tour de France, I didn't see too much of Dave Brailsford and the Sky hierarchy. There wasn't much time for celebration as the Olympics were hard on the heels of the Champs-Elysées, and then after London 2012 I was off for some more European races. I was meant to see Dave at the Tour of Lombardy, my last big race of the year, but he was unable to make it, so we rolled on serenely to the end of the season without much discussion.

My period of happy contemplation came to a pretty abrupt end on 10 October. The United States Anti-Doping Agency released their report into their investigation of Lance Armstrong. Though I wasn't named in the damning report, for some people my long friendship and working relationship with Lance meant guilt by association.

My phone began ringing immediately. Newspapers, radio, television, cycling magazines . . . where do these people get your number from? I didn't really want to talk to anyone. I'm not naïve enough to think that everything had been sweetness and light at US Postal and the other guises Lance had won the Tour under, but it wasn't something I knew much about or felt qualified to talk about. My riding career ended the year that Lance got ill, so I hadn't ridden with him in his post-cancer years, and my *directeur sportif* job at Discovery began in Lance's last season before his first retirement. My primary job in that year, 2005, was to run the team for the Giro d'Italia, where we scored a famous win via Paolo Savoldelli. I only ended up going to three races that Lance rode that season. I'd had disappointingly little time working alongside the man who'd been my close friend back in the early nineties at Motorola, so most of the events covered by USADA's investigation were a mystery to me and I would have felt a fraud talking about it.

Eventually, I talked to Dave Brailsford on the phone. There was a general discussion about Lance and the report, and the implications for Sky. Dave had made it clear from day one with Sky that the team would operate a zero tolerance approach to drug use, and nobody with any prior convictions or admissions would be employed.

It seemed to me that Dave had something on his mind, something that was troubling him. After a pause, he told me that he was finding it more and more difficult to protect me from the fallout from the stories about Lance. He said that he was constantly having to justify my presence on the team.

It took a moment for his words to sink in. I was amazed to be told that I needed protecting. As far as I was concerned I could hold my head high. I was not implicated in the USADA report, and had no involvement in the catalogue of Lance's misdemeanours beyond the fact that we were friends and that we'd been teammates before his Tour de France reign had begun. The weight of the last few years suddenly felt very heavy upon my shoulders, the thousands of miles, my kids looking older and different every time I saw them, my heart issues and the general weight of a million types of aggravation, day in, day out.

'You know what, Dave? I've had it. I'm done with it. All this bullshit. If I have to take a walk, I'll walk.'

I felt disgusted that I could be forced out of my job, be deprived of my ability to provide for my family, not by my employers, but by rumours and internet forums. There was nothing from anybody who knew me, nothing about me in this immense investigation, just opinion and conjecture from people with no connection with me whatsoever. It's a reflection on how society works in the twenty-first century. Thanks to the likes of Twitter, everybody's an expert.

Dave seemed taken aback, and asked me if I meant I actually wanted to leave.

'Retire. I'm going to retire.'

As soon as the words were out of my mouth it was like I was ten years younger. Everything rose from me and I realized that I'd been wanting to do this for ages.

I could have seen myself staying on that train I'd been on until I dropped down dead. I would have been happier gardening. Staying at home digging holes would always have been preferable, but you won't be surprised to hear that the pay isn't great.

I should explain that I'm just not passionate about cycling and success in the way that Dave and Shane Sutton are. It's their passion and drive that have dragged the Sky dream into existence, that have ultimately put a British rider on the top step of the Tour de France podium. For me, it's always been a job. Not just Sky: cycling, full stop. In the old days I just wanted to ride my bike and earn a living. Later on, I would turn up, drive the car, swear a bit, and go home again. That didn't mean I didn't give 100 per cent. I loved my job, but I was coming from a different point of view to them.

I knew that I couldn't get a better deal than I was on at Sky. Despite all the grief, it was in many ways the ideal job for me. I knew I'd been good for them too, and had been given the opportunity to reach the highest heights as a *directeur sportif* with them. I had nothing left to prove and this was the perfect time to walk away.

Later, I sat in the kitchen thinking about it all. I was relieved about the fact that I wouldn't be putting up with any more crap. I felt massively pleased that I would be spending more time in Sussex, began daydreaming about taking the kids on holiday, going to the Tour de France as a tourist, maybe getting up to see the Arsenal a bit more often. But I was also overtaken by a growing sense of anger. There were so many insinuations about my involvement in the Armstrong furore on newsgroups and Twitter – Yates must have known about it . . . he was clearly up to his neck in it . . . they were all at it – and I felt that I had been forced to defend myself because of this sort of tittle-tattle, and had ultimately lost my job over it.

Sky's response to the Armstrong news was to announce that they would be interviewing all members of staff to see if they had ever been involved in doping of any kind. Those who admitted to past misdemeanours would be treated with kindness and understanding but have their contracts cancelled. Those who denied complicity but were later discovered to have lied about their involvement would be fired. I was glad I had already made my decision. I felt by then that no matter what I said I would be subject to whispers and innuendo, and was pleased to be looking forward to life on the outside.

The meetings took place in London at the hotel where the management team was gathering to plan Sky's 2013 season. I went into a room with Dave and Steve Peters, the team's psychologist, where I reiterated my intention to retire and we discussed the terms of the split. It was like a divorce, I suppose.

At one point, Peters said that I seemed aggravated.

'Damn fucking right I'm aggravated,' I replied. 'I've given thirty-odd years of my life to this sport and it's come down to this.'

The meetings drew some blood. Bobby Julich and Steven de Jongh both admitted to doping during their riding days and left holding their P45s and bicycle clips. Both were popular members of the management team and guys with a massive amount to offer.

As for me, we reached an agreement that I thought was fair and I thanked the team. We drafted a press announcement that would explain that I was retiring for health and family reasons and that I strongly denied suggestions that I had ever doped or been involved in doping, then I went back to Sussex to draw some deep breaths and ride my bike a bit.

A day went past, then two, then three, without a press release appearing from Sky. You wouldn't think it would be a problem for a team that has such a big PR operation. A full week went past and then we went into the second weekend since we had shaken hands. Still nothing.

The Sunday morning brought an unpleasant surprise. The *Sunday Telegraph* splashed the headline:

SEAN YATES PARTS COMPANY WITH TEAM SKY AS DAVE BRAILSFORD'S DOPING CULL CONTINUES

Sean Yates, one of the men who masterminded Bradley Wiggins's Tour de France victory in July, has left Team Sky after admitting an involvement in doping.

I'm guessing that at the British Cycling annual dinner, which had taken place the previous evening, the *Telegraph*'s man, sniffing for a story, had spoken to a few people, put two-and-two together and come up with five. It was factually incorrect and genuinely hurtful. Sky rushed out the original press release, which appeared to be little more than a whitewash in the circumstances. It was annoying, to say the least.

Now, I understand the argument that says that people who choose to live their life in the public eye don't get to pick and choose whether they have good or bad things written about them. But what about my mum? When she rides her bike down to the shops every day, does she choose to have people asking her about her son being a drug user? And my kids? Is it right that they can go to school and be taunted by other children that their dad is a liar and a cheat?

I hadn't been following the Leveson Inquiry into press standards with any greater interest than most people up to that point, but was suddenly given a view of astounding clarity about how making things up, jumping to disingenuous conclusions, or just plain outright lying in order to sell papers can affect people's lives. Not just the people they're lying about either, but their families.

I hadn't expected my career to finish like this.

So that's where I'm coming from. I want to talk about my life in cycling, to try to tell you what it's been like. It's about the sheer pleasure of riding my bike. It's about the sport, the routine hardship and the fleeting glory. It's about being an idol and living in poverty at the same time. It's about winning, losing and surviving. It's all about the bike.

Chapter Three

'I've got some cheese straws from the baker's in the village, Sean,' calls my mum from the kitchen. 'There's some coffee in the pot, but I suppose you want to make your own like you always do?'

'Yes please, Mum.'

2013 marks the forty-seventh year since my mum, dad, my younger brother Christian and I moved to this cottage in Forest Row, East Sussex. I was six. I thought it would be good to come and chat to Mum and see what she could remember about those days. I see her all the time – my place is only a few miles away and my ex-wife and the kids are higher up the lane – but it's rare to talk about stuff properly, like it is for most people, I suspect. You just chew the fat, catch up and move on.

'We moved here from Worcester Park, in south-west London,' Mum reminds me. 'I'd met your dad at art school in Epsom. We'd spent six months down in Cornwall living in a Romany caravan that your dad had heard about, then we headed back to Worcester Park to that nice little flat, and you and Chris came along.'

My dad, Roger, was always coming up with ideas. Once he'd decided he was going to do something, it filled his thoughts until he did it. Like when he saw an advert for a boat you could build at home. The *Daily Mirror* ran a competition in the late 1960s to design a sailing dinghy that people could buy in kit form and affordably get into sailing. The result was the Mirror, a dinghy still popular today. Despite having no experience of sailing that I knew of, my dad bought a kit and took over our living room for several months of gluing and construction. God knows how he got it out of the door. To call my mum stoical about his various projects would be a massive understatement. She was a saint.

Within months of moving into the two-up-two-down cottage, he'd pulled down a dividing wall and all the downstairs ceiling with some sort of plan to open it all out. He replaced the old ceiling with polythene while he was finishing the job. My younger brother Conall sorted it out in the end and put a new ceiling in. That was in 2010. My poor Mum had been living under a temporary polythene ceiling for more than forty years.

Anyway, it was one of Dad's ideas that brought us to Forest Row in the first place, as I got Mum to recollect:

'Your daddy had read something somewhere about Rudolf Steiner schools, and he wanted you to go to one. There was one in Forest Row, so that's where we ended up.'

Michael Hall was – still is – a school in a big house called Kidbrooke Park located at the end of a long drive leading through landscaped parkland away from the A22 as it heads out of the village towards Eastbourne. It's a beautiful place and is long established now as some-where to get an alternative form of education. Steiner schools, or Waldorf schools as they're also known, after the Waldorf–Astoria cigarette factory in Stuttgart where the first one opened back in the days following the First World War, are supposed to nurture individual thought and personal development, encouraging kids to think for themselves and go their own way. My main memory of school is that I was on permanent detention for playing football, something that wasn't allowed because it was 'unsuitable use of the feet'. I'd sneak a tennis ball in and get caught. Or even kicking a pine cone around the grounds with my pals would be enough to get us some extra hours.

I just wasn't cut out for school. I wasn't academically minded. I wanted to be outdoors all the time, and Michael Hall was better than most for that. I think I would have hated any school that I had to go to; the Steiner system was no different in that respect. At least when the middle of the afternoon came around I would be flying out of the door and into the forest.

We lived on one of the unsurfaced lanes that joined the village of Forest Row to the vast expanse of the Ash-down Forest – five thousand acres of heathland, mixed woodland, lakes, streams, tracks, paths and limitless adventures for kids growing up in the sixties and seventies without a TV or any computer games. Known worldwide as home to Winnie the Pooh, the Ashdown Forest was my home too.

By today's standards, my upbringing was a strange mixture of strictness and *laissez-faire*. On the strict side, we weren't allowed sweets, biscuits or things like that. 'People didn't really eat between meals in those days,' Mum muses, as she offers me another cheese straw. 'I do remember us going over to your Aunty Margaret's in Guildford, though . . . you ate so many cakes you made yourself sick.'

'Yes, it was like she'd bought the whole Mr Kipling factory.'

My mum can't really remember why we weren't allowed a TV, but she doesn't seem to think it was much of a big deal. I, however, remember lying along the branch of the big oak tree across the lane with Chris and watching tiny screens through neighbours' windows.

But we had so much more freedom. As a teenager I used to roam across the forest all day and all night with Chris and our friends, forever coming up with games to play, activities to follow, competitions to take part in. I was always the organizer: charts, reports, tables all had to be compiled and kept up to date, whether it was for football, cycling or our own *Superstars* contests we dreamt up, mirroring the old BBC series that used to pit the sporting heroes of the day against each other. I wanted to be Brian Jacks, destroying the opposition with a million parallel bar dips in a minute, recreated between fence posts or on a low branch somewhere.

It was a change for my mum to be living down here, but it sounds like she took to it pretty quickly. Her dad, Charles Gaskin, started a bronze foundry on the Fulham Road back in the 1920s. When they expanded Chelsea Football Club, the foundry was in the way, so they moved themselves a bit further towards Chelsea itself. My uncle Michael is still the chairman, but he's retired these days. They cast bronze sculptures for the likes of Henry Moore, Jacob Epstein and Claudia Koch, and my dad worked there for a while too. I suppose it was the perfect mixture of craft and graft for him; he always liked making things. For some years when I was a kid, after we'd got interested in sailing, he was a sail-maker at a loft down near Chichester, driving across Sussex to get to work. That was one of many jobs he has had throughout his life. It's fair to say he has an artistic temperament. At one time, he did henna tattoos for tourists in Portugal. Now he lives in Sweden running a concert hall.

After the boatbuilding and alternative education, my dad's next obsession was another Rudolf Steiner concept, a form of expression through dance called eurythmy. It wasn't anything to do with Annie Lennox, it was more like ballet, a performance art that was supposed to make you a more spiritual being in tune with the world around you. Dad thought that was great and decided to start a new career as a eurythmy teacher. When I was eight, he moved Mum, me and Chris again, this time to Stuttgart, to study to become a eurythmy teacher.

We drove all the way there in the family Minivan. That was an Austin Mini made into a van, not the sort of huge people-carrier Americans call minivans. Mum made up a bed on top of all our belongings behind the driver's seat and Chris and I slept there on the interminable journey across Western Europe. It must have been winter; I can remember icicles on the inside of the roof dripping down as I looked up at them while we trundled down the old concrete roads of France, Belgium and Germany.

The eurythmy college was part of the Steiner set-up in Stuttgart that included a school, so I was moved there from Michael Hall. I didn't speak a word of German, so, unsurprisingly for a kid who hated school anyway, it wasn't much fun and pretty isolating. I would sit in class until the morning break, go out to play, and not come back. Every day. I used to go and sit under a tree somewhere, then hang around at the door of the college next door to the school and wait for my dad to come out at the end of the day, then we'd walk home together. My mum stuck it out for six weeks, then said enough was enough and brought us back to Forest Row, where she has remained ever since. Dad hung on in Germany the full four years to qualify, but his career as a eurythmy teacher eventually petered out.

People often seem to think my family is weird, but it doesn't seem weird to me. All families have a bit of strangeness about them when you dig; what's normal for some people is another family's screaming lunacy. I'll admit we were a bit unusual, but what's normal?

There are actually five of us brothers and sisters: me the eldest, and Chris three years behind. After a break of about fifteen years, Mum and Dad went back into the family-making business and produced Ella, Conall and Oriana in quick succession.

You might have thought that the family connection with the foundry would have made me a Chelsea fan, but the team I plumped for was Arsenal. It's been that way for better or for worse ever since. My brother Chris was Chelsea, and my best mate Paul Divall was Leeds – three teams that seemed to always be up against each other at the top in the late sixties and early seventies, when we were football mad. I remember the long build-up to the 1972 FA Cup final with my Arsenal taking on Paul's Leeds. We talked about nothing else for weeks beforehand, and Paul kept talking about it for weeks afterwards too, thanks to Sniffer Clarke's winner in Leeds's 1–0 win. I'm still smarting.

My neighbour Paul was my main partner in crime, and still is in many ways, even though we're both in our fifties now. I used writing this book as an excuse to hook up with him and see what he remembered about those days. Heading up the dirt lane from our childhood homes, we wandered again across the beautiful wild open spaces of East Sussex and deep into the tall trees of Ashdown Forest.

'I remember the first time I met you. Well, talked to you,' he says, as we meet outside his mum and dad's old house, a couple of doors below ours on the lane. '"Hey, come and look at this!" you said to me and my little sister outside the house. We followed you warily across the lane to the foot of the old oak tree over there, and you'd caught and killed an adder somehow. You were, like, "Look, look!" and, as we bent in to see it properly, you went, "Aaaarrgghhhh!" and flicked it up in our faces. I crapped myself, you bastard.'

Paul wasn't encouraged to hang around with 'those hippy Yates kids'. His dad was ex-army and very strict. The Michael Hall pupils were seen as a bit weird and other-worldly to the families who sent their children to the normal village school, and we kept our friendship largely secret. 'I would hear a seagull noise in the lane and say, "I'm going out,"' remembers Paul. That was our signal. 'My dad would say, "OK, but don't go further than the top road," and we'd be off.'

Today, we're walking up the lane and across the top road and away, much further away, just like we did after being expressly forbidden all those years ago.

It was this part of the forest that got me in my first serious bit of trouble, when I built a camp out of old wood and dried bracken here. All well and good, until I made the mistake of thinking that what it really needed was a nice little fire. It went up like a straw Guy Fawkes. I raced down the lane back home to get some water, but by the time I got to the house the flames were lighting up the sky and I could hear the fire engines coming up the main road.

For more than ten years, our gang – me, Paul, Chris and our other friend Richard – roamed across here, forever looking for things to do. We'd build cannibalized bikes out of scrap ones rescued from the village dump at the bottom of the hill, just behind where the offices of Paul's building company now stand. We'd ride them all over the forest, as far as Crowborough, Hartfield or even Tunbridge Wells. We'd ride east to Harrison's Rocks, near Groombridge, to go climbing. Later we'd ride as a quartet down to Cuckmere Haven, or all the way to Brighton with our skateboards on our backs.

There was hardly any traffic on the roads. I shudder to think of my kids riding all over Sussex now. We used to hammer it along like a team trial squad, long before we knew what a team time trial was. Chris had this massive gentleman's roadster with curvy handlebars and rod brakes. He used to get in an aero tuck holding the bars right in the middle, just like I would descend the passes of the Alps years later. Chris was a whippet, younger than me and Paul but with a natural speed. I took after Mum and her iron constitution, never ill or sick, feeling the same every day no matter what. Sadly for Chris, he was more like Dad and seemed to pick up everything going. He contracted glandular fever at 14, which really weakened him for a long time and put paid to any thoughts of professional sport, but he still made a really decent club rider well known and respected on the southern time-trialling scene. He's a tough enough outdoor individual these days, having spent years working on sites for Paul's company and others. He's also a mean guitarist, as anyone who's seen a few pub bands in Sussex will agree. One of my more bizarre trophies is an electric guitar I won at the Tour of Belgium in 1989, and it sits in the living room. Chris can noodle away on it for hours when he comes round.

The four of us rode for miles, but woe betide anyone who got left behind.

'We'd ride everywhere; you always deciding where we were going,' says Paul. 'The trouble was, the rest of us would never know where we were and you wouldn't wait or come back. Richard and me got totally lost out near Oxshott one night just as it was getting dark, and we had to phone our parents from a call box. You weren't very popular that night.'

We probably did most miles of all right here in the trees beyond the top road, in a patch we called the Ups and Downs. There's a series of what everybody knows as bombholes. Are they actually caused by bombs? Who knows, but I'm sure you know what I mean. We had a course that would later be recognized instantly as a BMX track, but this was before BMX bikes. We were on old clunkers, usually without brakes.

'The last thing we used to put on were brakes, right?' says Paul. 'Wheels, frame, pedals, chain, and off we went. I wore out the soles of my Dr Martens a few times; they were the only way we had of stopping.'

We must have covered literally thousands of circuits of those few obstacle-littered yards. It took about a minute or so to go round, I think.

'You should know. Everything had to be recorded. Quantified. There was always a notebook with charts and numbers in. And you had to win everything. We were so competitive all the time. I thought I was useless because you would always win, whatever we were doing. It wasn't until I got to secondary school that I found out I was pretty good at sport.'

It's true, I was obsessed with recording everything, creating competition, finding ways of noting it all down. And then, once the competition was created, I had to win it. I was the oldest, so I ought to, and I was so competitive. It would always be me, then Paul, then Chris, then Richard. I used to try to think of incentives to try to keep them interested. If we rode up the lane from the village, I'd offer Richard tuppence if he could reach the last speed bump before Chris or Paul.

We head out of the trees where the Ups and Downs still lie and on to the football pitch on the plateau before the sports club. We played for hours and hours up here, Paul taking shots and me hurling myself around in goal. He was really good, a county standard central midfielder who could have gone all the way if going to work and a broken leg hadn't interrupted him.

'I thought you were going to be a professional goalkeeper, though,' he says, possibly with the benefit of some rose-tinted spectacles. 'No, seriously, you were that good. I couldn't believe it when you went off to be a cyclist instead. I thought you were going to play for Arsenal. Especially as their goalie was Bob Wilson. Everyone knew he was rubbish.'

There was a thick patch of undergrowth, just in between the Ups and Downs and the football pitch, where I used to hide my boots after games. Don't forget, I wasn't allowed to play football. Mum and Dad trusted the school to make wise decisions, and if the school thought football was bad, then football was bad.

After a while we started organizing teams around the village and setting up proper eleven-a-side games and competitions. There were the Red Devils, the Local Yokels, and our lot: Divvie's Demons, after Paul.

'We used to thrash everyone at everything: football, cycling, *Superstars*, you name it,' remembers Paul, as we cross the pitch and drop down across the golf course. 'Even golf, when we didn't get chased off the course. Except cricket . . . I don't think we had the patience for cricket.'

One of our first forays into competitive cycling was as Divvie's Demons, when the four of us entered the Strawberry Fayre festivities for the Queen's Silver Jubilee just down the road at Ashurstwood. There were all different categories and age groups and a course that raced up the dreaded Wall Hill. Our quartet rode over to a bike shop near Reigate and bought matching caps to turn our plain white t-shirts into a Divvie's Demons team strip. I won my category, Paul won his, Chris won his and Richard would have won his too, but he sat up just before the line and got squeezed down to third. We felt unbeatable.

We drop down across the golf course and cross the cutting that carries the stream along the bottom of the valley with a run and jump that has us laughing about the forty-plus years since we first did that. On rainy days we used to carry an old canoe down to here and paddle it, wade it and drag it down the three miles or so of winding watercourse that leads into the Medway as it flows past Hartfield.

'The other thing we did, when we were really little, was go the other way, up to the source of the stream in the forest somewhere,' says Paul. 'I must have been about seven or eight, you would have been ten. Lorraine would have been there too.' Lorraine was Paul's little sister, and she was part of the gang. Paul was only allowed out if he took her along as well. Their parents would have died with horror if they'd known what we were getting up to.

We curve right and trek up away from the golf course and into the trees, roughly following the route we'd taken all those years ago. Paul reminds me of that day.

'I remember that you wouldn't turn back until we'd found where it rose. We waded up there in our normal clothes for hours, soaking wet. Lorraine was miserable and wet through and I knew we'd be in the shit, but of course we kept on following, just like we always did. We finally got to this sort of puddle where it pooled up from below the ground. You jumped in wearing all your clothes, thinking it was ankle-deep and you'd just make a little splash . . . and disappeared. You were in right over your head. We had to pull you out, drenched, sodden.'

It was to the top of this long drag, somewhere up near Wych Cross, that we used to push abandoned motorbikes to ride them back down to the bottom. It took hours to get them up here and we'd be shattered by the time we got to the start of our run. These old things were long conked-out scooters and mopeds that we would imagine were lean, mean scrambling machines, and we'd fly back down through the trees on flat tyres, rarely making it to the bottom without catapulting over the handlebars at some point. It took so much time and effort to get up there we'd only get about three runs a day in during the summer holidays.

You'd think that we'd be shattered after breaking our-selves into bits all day, but then we'd sneak out at night and make mischief. I used to climb out of my bedroom window, skip across the low roof on the kitchen and shin down into the garden, meet Paul and Richard and go and pull up plants in my teacher's garden. Not some-thing a future gardener should be too proud of, but I'm not here to make myself sound like a better person than I really was. One of our pals said he would come along one night, and jumped out of his bedroom down to the lane without thinking of how he'd get back in. His parents got up the next morning to find him curled up on the doorstep.

'Do you remember Bongo?' asks Paul.

Bongo was, for want of a better description, the village nutter. He was clearly in need of a bit of help, one of those characters who would get care in the community in more enlightened times, but in those days roamed free, chasing kids through the woods, their parents' warnings to 'Watch out for Bongo!' ringing in their ears. We'd be out in the forest making a tree house or a camp, and we'd catch a glimpse of him watching us from the bushes. We'd run screaming for home across the golf course with this madman racing after us, roaring at the top of his voice. Later, as we got older and nastier, we would bait and taunt him if we came across him in the forest somewhere, throwing sticks, and worse, at him.

As we got older, we also became something of a nemesis for the village copper, Mr Rye. He'd chase us through the woods on foot or through the village on his bike. One day, he came up to me and said, 'Yates! You've got a catapult, haven't you?'

'Yes, but it's broken, Mr Rye,' I answered.

'Broken, is it? Well, so are seventy-six panes of glass at the sports club. What have you got to say about that?'

'It wasn't me.'

We became what is now called 'known to the police'. A younger local kid, who was a right tearaway, boasted to us that he'd nicked some money from the petrol station, so we bullied him into going back and getting some more for us. He did, too. We spent it on cider and broke into the scout hut to drink it. Next thing we knew, the police had arrived, and we're all sprinting into the night, scattering. Knowing who it would be, the police called at our houses. One of our friends had waded through the stream to escape and had run home and jumped into bed, soaking wet under the covers. 'Has your boy been at home all night?' asked Mr Rye.

'Yes, all night,' said his mum.

'Tell him to come downstairs, please.'

'Erm . . . he's asleep, I don't want to wake him.'

'Now, please.'

He squelched into the living room shamefaced, fully clothed and soaked through.

Busted.

The police were out again when a load of us from the village gathered at Michael Hall one September evening for a massive plum fight. Much of the school landscape at Michael Hall had previously been orchards, and the trees were heavy with juicy black fruit that we would pick and then hurl at each other until it got dark. Unfortunately a lady had overheard someone excitedly going on about the plum fight and thought they'd said 'gunfight'. Riot vans turned up from East Grinstead (though I'm not sure there's ever been a riot in East Grinstead).

Busted.

'I remember you coming back with your first proper bike,' recalls Paul as we stride out back across the forest towards the houses and the dip where our favourite massive tree still stands.

'The Frejus, the purple one?'

I'd been given £150 in Premium Bonds and had decided to cash them in for a bike. Dad had driven me over to Guildford to buy it after we'd seen an advert in *Cycling*, so I must have started to take an interest by then. We got to this guy's house and agreed a price with him but he wouldn't take a cheque – looking at Dad and me you couldn't blame him – and we had to come all the way back to get some cash.

'We were mucking about over there in the dip in the big tree and you came storming down the hill, screaming, "Look at my bike!" riding this fancy racing bike straight down through the trees and across the roots.'

'Oh. I think I remember what happened next.'

'Yes, you pulled a massive broadside skid, slid it towards where we were watching with maximum noise and spectacle, hit a root side on and totally pretzelled the back wheel. Brilliant.'

My dad was none too pleased.

The massive tree above that dip that was our hangout for many summers and winters is still there. It was obviously coppiced at some point, and where its growth was stilted, a platform formed itself before the tree continued its annual progress, making the ideal camp for teenagers trying to escape their parents and authority. Today, anyone watching will be rewarded with the incongruous sight of two men in their fifties climbing the branches, searching for initials and messages carved with pen knives in the days when they were boys.

Crossing back over the top road as it turns from tarmac

into dirt leads us to start talking about our favourite of all mischief games: 'borrowing' my dad's car every night. I'd slip out of the bedroom window and hop into his Fiat 128, letting the handbrake off and allowing it to roll out into the lane and trundle down past Paul's. 'Lorraine and I would be watching TV with Mum and Dad and we'd hear the old seagull cry from outside. I'd say, "I'm going to pop out," and my Dad would say, "OK, but take your sister with you." We'd jump in, gently pull the doors shut and bump it down the lane, the engine bursting into life at the bottom, then we'd be off, flooring it round the forest tracks.'

One night, we were flying up a little rise and there was a bump and the engine died. We didn't know it, but we'd broken the distributor cap. Fortunately, we weren't far from the A22 to Eastboune, so we rolled it off the forest track on to the main road. I told Paul and Lorraine to get out and push – always the bossy one – but it was too heavy for them to move it, so we put Lorraine in the driver's seat. She was 12, I think.

'Yeah, me and you started to push it down the A22 in the middle of the night,' says Paul, 'then we got on to the downhill and the engine burst into life. I went arse over tit as the back of the car lurched away from me. Lorraine was kneeling up on the driver's seat screaming.'

I just managed to get an arm in the window and pull myself through it into the front seat. That was probably our closest shave of the lot.

'The best thing was that your dad didn't fix it for

months. He just thought he had a dodgy battery or something. He used to roll it out of the drive every morning and we'd hear him trying to bump start it as he went past our house.'

You might wonder how Dad didn't realize somebody was driving his car round the forest every night. Surely he would notice the dirt for one thing? The thing was that my dad, being my dad, had decided to clean the Fiat one day. He'd done a lovely job, it was glistening and shining . . . at least until it dried out. He'd used Ajax kitchen cleaner and scoured the paintwork to a mottled dull mess. It always looked dirty after that, no matter where it had been or who'd been driving it.

Being the eldest in the gang, I left school first and went to work as a gardener. I just knocked on some doors round the village and built up a little round of houses that I would visit, one or two a morning every weekday. I'd cut lawns and trim hedges until lunchtime, go home for a glass of squash then go out on my bike for the afternoon. I timed my rides to be passing the school in East Grinstead just after chucking-out time and chase the school bus back down the A22 to Forest Row.

'Yeah, we'd be pulling faces at you from the back seat,' says Paul. 'You'd have your front wheel about six inches from the bumper, battering yourself to stay in the slipstream as it accelerated up the hill. Then you'd blast past us on the drop down into the village and be sitting at home like you'd been there all day when we got back.'

The gang survived me going abroad when I was 20, and I would still be making plans and organizing everybody as soon as I got home. Brigadier Yates, as Pippa, my ex-wife, used to call me, with a roll of the eyes and a sigh. Instead of bossing everybody around in bike races, *Superstars*, climbing, skating, golfing, canoeing and God knows what, I'd decide what pub we were going to. I'd ride my bike all day, come home, drink a litre and a half of cheap cider, then head out. We'd meet at the Swan, have a beer, then I'd say, 'Come on, we're going to the Brambletye,' or one of the other pubs, and everybody would funnel out behind me. I don't know what made me such a psychopathic individual, but that was how it went. Let's go left, let's go right, and everyone else just followed.

By the time I could drive legally, we would hack it up the A22 to London in the middle of the night. We could make it to the underground car park in Park Lane in an hour, then spend the night doing doughnuts or reversing the length of the deserted space with the accelerator pressed to the floor. Pretty standard country kid fare, really.

We got ourselves in a spot of bother at a disco over near Sharpthorne one night. They used to put these nights on for local kids at a big old hotel out in the woods, and there would invariably be a bit of a row between rival gangs from different villages.

'Yeah, I started that one, I think,' says Paul ruefully. 'I tried to nick this bloke's hat and got myself thrown out, so we all piled outside. I was pissing on his scooter to get my own back when they saw me and jumped me. From Crawley Down, they were. Next minute, we were all fighting in the dark in the trees, weren't we?'

'The bouncers started steaming in and I shouted, "Leg it!" and we ran to the car and zoomed off.'

'Richard was in the back seat, saying, "One of them hit me in the stomach; it really hurts." He pulled his shirt up and there was a load of blood and a slit in his gut. "Bloody hell, Rich, you've been stabbed!" We couldn't believe it.'

I span it round and floored it to the hospital. Poor old Richard. He always got a rough deal. Richard was the youngest of our gang all the way through from when we were little kids right up to grown men, and he suffered a bit, always last. At the time I thought I was helping, pushing him, but looking back you could call it bully-ing, if you wanted to take that point of view. Even when he didn't want to come out, we would make him. We always needed him to make up the quartet, or to make up a team, or to just be there; it wasn't the same without him.

As we stroll back down the hill towards our childhood homes, we pass the fields we used to cross to play another one of our favourite games. We used to call it 'spying', but there wasn't much spying involved. We would cut across the fields into the gardens of the big houses on the far side of them and sneak through them, trying not to get spotted.

'That was one time where Richard didn't come last, when that bloke set his dogs on us.'

I was probably about 12. The four of us ran for our lives across the field back towards Paul's house with these raging Staffordshire terriers chasing us.

'Chris was always the fastest runner,' says Paul, 'then me and you, then Richard. On that day, Richard came past all three of us like we were standing still, then cleared that six-foot hedge and ditch as if he had rocket boots on.'

Chris and Richard both worked for Paul's building company for many years. Our childhood antics have long been a source of amusement over a pint over the years, but things took a surprising turn at the firm's Christmas party a couple of years ago.

'I was chatting to Richard at the end of the evening; we were both well sozzled,' Paul tells me. 'I was saying about what a brilliant upbringing we'd had together, how much fun it had been for all of us, when he said, "Well, it was fun for you, maybe." I was like, "Come on, Rich, they were great days," giving him a drunk hug, like you do. Next thing I know he was in tears, pushing me away, sobbing, "You and Yates, you bastards, you ruined my life! My mum and dad hated you! You left me in Oxshott in the middle of the night!'

Richard has moved to Bulgaria in search of a new life, crofting on a small farmstead. I hope it's working out for him and he's happy. I had no idea that not all of our quartet had enjoyed being a part of it as much as me. It makes me feel a bit rotten and reminds me that I'm not the easiest person to get along with at times, as I'm sure my ex-wife will agree.

As we get back to Mum's, I look up to my old bedroom window in the roof and have a sudden memory of lowering my little sister Ella out of it in a climbing harness when she was a toddler. I dangled her down until she was level with the front door and got her to bang on it until my mum answered it. Not for the first time, she nearly passed out when she opened it and was nose to nose with a giggling three-year-old.

My mum just shakes her head when I remind her and pours us a cup of tea with a weary smile. It's funny how we take on our parents' characteristics. People have told me I talk like my mum: slowly, with a swallow between sentences. But Paul also tells me that I sit like my dad, too:

'Slouched on the side of a chair, not in it, legs stretched out. Both of you drive like that as well. The main difference is that he would always have a roll-up hanging from the corner of his mouth.'

My mum and dad could never do enough for me: my mum putting up with my constant antics with a shrug; Dad putting his whole life on hold to support what I wanted to do. First it was sailing, towing our dinghy all around the country to regattas and races, then it was cycling. He would spend hours in his shed working on my bikes, filing bits off them, routing the cables, cleaning chains, oiling bearings, then drive me to races wherever they may have been.

Paul's dad was stricter than mine – in fact, they couldn't have been more different – and Paul wasn't even allowed in the shed, certainly not allowed to touch his tools. He spent more time with my dad in our shed than he did with his own.

'We went to do a time trial up on the A2 near Bluewater, didn't we?' I ask him.

'Yeah . . . that was the final nail in the coffin of my cycling career, even before it started,' he recalls, smiling. 'Roger helped me take my mudguards off my bike, as it wasn't cool to race with them on. I thought I could sneak it out to the race the next morning, but my dad discovered what we'd done and went mad. He was up into the middle of the night putting them back on. I still raced, but my head wasn't in it: I was hopeless. That was that.'

These days, Paul's son Jordan is a promising motocross rider, and Paul will do anything to help him, just like my dad was with me back in the day. I try to help my kids too, buying bikes for my eldest son Liam and racing with him, but Paul and I agree it's a fine line to tread between being a helpful dad and a pushy parent.

I set Jordan his training plans now, and I'm helping other people with coaching and training through my friend John Sharples's coaching business. One thing I wish I could get younger riders to do is spend their entire childhoods outdoors racing round the countryside like nutters. By the time I became a full-time cyclist, I had such strength and an appetite for training that has never left me – and I put it down entirely to my childhood. We were really powerful kids. I wasn't a big lad, I only really grew when I was 17 or 18. By then I was already blessed with all this fitness and strength from all the antics we got up to; then suddenly I was big too. It defined my career, really.

Back at Mum's, over another pot of coffee, Paul and I find ourselves remembering more indulgent nonsense that we used to get up to.

'No wonder we ended up so strong,' he says. 'Do you remember when we wanted to build a skate ramp? We nicked all those bags of cement from right up the other side of Michael Hall and carried them all the way back to the Ups and Downs.'

My mum closes her eyes and shakes her head. 'I don't think I want to hear this.' It's not the first time.

'There's something else I need, Mum. All these things that I'm going to have to talk about in the book . . . well, they're a long time ago now. I'm not sure if I can remember any of it.'

'Ah, I know what you're getting at. Your cuttings.'

I clamber up into the loft and haul a huge grey and yellow Delsey holdall bearing the badge of the Linda McCartney Pro Cycling Team. It's been up here a while, but it's stuffed to the brim with old magazines, newspapers, scrapbooks and black and white photographs. I'd like to say it's full of memories, but the initial rummage just brings up things that I'd forgotten completely . . . pictures of me in Australia on a mountain bike with panniers . . . my training columns in *Cycling Plus* . . . a scrapbook completely full of pictures of horses (no idea; don't ask) . . . the athletes' handbook from the Moscow Olympics. It looks like it's time to start remembering a few things.

Chapter Four

So I might have called time on my involvement in professional cycling, but I can't stop riding my bike. I reapplied for a racing licence and got reinstated at the grass-roots level of the sport in Britain, a '4th cat'. I've been riding a few local races lately with my eldest son, Liam. On my fifty-second birthday, we entered a race together on the Dunsfold circuit and I led him out to win the race in a bunch sprint. He's got potential; could be a decent rider, and has been picked up by the Catford CC development team being sponsored by Jeff Banks. However, when I suggested going up to the Hillingdon Circuit to do a race together a couple of weeks ago, he said: 'No. I don't want to go.'

'Why not?'

'Because last time I raced, all you did was shout at me!'

'That's because you need to man up, boy!' I replied, but I couldn't help laughing, as it was virtually word for word the same conversation I'd had with my own dad about sailing when I was 16.

Dad and I used to go all over the country sailing that Mirror he'd built. In the winter we'd put her in at Weir Wood Reservoir, a big stretch of water just over the hill from Forest Row, and in the summer we'd go down to Eastbourne; but we'd also travel as far afield as Cornwall, Wales and even Scotland for competitions, with the dinghy rattling around on the trolley behind the Fiat. I loved it, but what I really wanted was a boat of my own: a Moth. I had a scrapbook and got busy with the Copydex and Pritt Stick, pasting pictures of Moths taken out of my dad's old sailing magazines. The only problem was that the minimum weight for someone who wanted to sail a Moth single-handedly was eight stone, and as the scrawniest 16-year-old in Sussex it just wasn't happening.

Dad was pretty volatile and stroppy, always cursing, swearing and losing his temper when things didn't work out as he expected – with the wind, the weather, the boat and his junior sailing partner often appearing to combine to ruin his day. One day, as he was preparing to take us to another competition somewhere, I said, 'No. I don't want to go.'

'Why not?'

'Because last time we raced, all you did was shout at me!'

From then on, it was Chris who went sailing with Dad, handily getting to be old enough to go at just the right time.

One thing I'd become interested in on the way to these

events was cycling. Driving down to Eastbourne we would pass these guys on the A22 doing Sunday morning time trials and I would be amazed by the speeds they were doing, wondering if me, Chris, Paul and Rich could get out there and do it. We'd cut our teeth with these long rides all over Sussex, now I wanted to actually race against the real sportsmen.

I was a fan. My pals and I would ride into East Grinstead on a Saturday morning and spend the day looking at trick bits in the skate shop, flicking through LPs in the old record shop, Grays, and leafing through magazines in WH Smith. I started to head straight to the sport section and pull out *Cycling*, which was a weekly newspaper then, rather than the magazine it is now. I would read the stories about the time-trialling heroes – Alf Engers, Eddie Adkins, Dave Lloyd and Phil Griffiths – the personal duels between them every weekend, up and down dual carriageways all over the country. Alf was my favourite. *Cycling* was full of stories about how he would turn up in his Jag, get out in his full-length sheepskin coat and start putting his bike together. Alf was the bad boy; he'd been expelled from school, was always in trouble with the cycling authorities, and he used to just hammer right down the middle of the road. If cars wanted to pass him, they'd just have to pull out and go round. I've always liked the rebels in sport, the Ronnie O'Sullivans, the Mike Tysons, the Charlie Georges, they just appeal to my contrary nature, I suppose. They're the ones we like to talk about, aren't they? The ones that keep sport buzzing. Alf held the 25-mile record pretty much continually from 1969 to 1990. The only time he lost it was in his most famous head-to-head with the supercool Eddie Adkins. It was on the E72 in Essex, and Adkins took ten seconds off Alf's old record of 51 minutes dead to take the record. It turned out that Alf would only be without the best time for a few minutes of those twenty-one years, though, as he came in about ten riders behind Adkins with the stellar time of 49 minutes and 24 seconds. That time stood right up to 1990 and the modern era. Not for nothing was Alf Engers known as The King.

Out on the bikes, we would organize our own little time trials and make up stories about Alf, Eddie, Lloydy, Griffo and the like. We rode over to this bike show that was on in Eridge. It might have been the long hot summer of 1976, or possibly the following spring. The Capital Radio Fun Bus was there, so we knew it was a big deal. There were stalls with the latest bikes on, including one at the stunning price of £430 that had the four of us drooling. There was bike polo which we watched avidly, then a road race, where the bunch stormed around before being outsprinted by none other than Alf Engers himself.

Dad and I went down to Handcross on the old A23 to see Phil Griffiths breaking the London-to-Brighton-and-back record. It actually started and finished there, near Crawley. There were about ten blokes watching, plus me and Dad, when Griffo finished, covered in sweat but victorious. I won't ever forget his first words at the finish when somebody asked if there was anything he needed: 'A good strong woman.'

The very first copy of *Cycling* I bought had a pull-out colour picture of Alf Engers sitting on his orange Jack Hearne time-trial bike, with every conceivable piece of it drilled out to save weight. I had that picture on my bedroom wall and would dream about racing against The King. I didn't actually meet the man himself until 2006 when I turned up at a race and found that his son was riding. Alf, in his sixties then, had come along to watch. I just had to go up to him: 'I had a picture of you on my wall, Alf.'

I wrote a letter to Val Baxendine who was president of the East Grinstead Cycling Club, the local racing club. Val wrote back and invited me to come out on their club run. One of the few school subjects I was any good at was needlework, and I sat up in my room cutting out the letters EGCC from an old sheet and stitching them on to the back of my tracksuit top. I rocked up for the start of the ride outside East Grinstead cinema on my purple Frejus wearing my leather school shoes.

I was beginning to grow at last, and the seatpost was too short for me. I took it off and replaced it with an old broom handle, bolting the saddle to the top of it using a clamp from a kids' bike that we'd pulled off a skip. Then I dropped the broom handle into the frame of the bike and drilled a hole through the whole lot so I could put a bolt in and hold it all together. Perfect.

The first time I had a puncture on the Frejus, I was

well prepared. I knew the top boys used to carry spare tubulars with them – old ones still tacky with the glue that had once held them fast to a rim – so I had one of those with me. I wrestled with my flat tyre at the side of the road, unable to understand why I couldn't roll the airless rubber off the wheel. Eventually, thumbs battered and bruised, I prised it off. No wonder it had been so tough: it wasn't a tubular, it was a 'clincher' with a flat inner tube inside. I didn't have one of them, so I put the sticky old tub on it anyway and pumped it up. I rode it like that for weeks.

I was 16 when I started going out with the East Grinstead. Paul wasn't allowed to join – his dad wasn't keen on it – and the others were too young at that stage, so I struck up a friendship with another teenager there, a bloke called Brian Phillips. We would be friends for the rest of our lives. I drilled holes in my brake levers, my handlebars and my cranks, just like Alf. The handlebars were the best. You just used to have a little bit of tape on the very bottom of the 'hooks', all in the name of weight saving. When you got up to speed, the wind would start whistling through the holes. You could run your fingers up and down the bars and play a tune like a recorder.

My first time trial was the East Grinstead Cycling Club Wednesday evening time trial at Godstone, a ten-mile race over a course that would never be considered for an event now. You went out, did a left, another left, then just turned around in the middle of the road and came back the same way, turning the two left-handers into right. You would never turn across the flow of traffic in any time trial now, let alone three times. Traffic just wasn't something you had to worry about in the seventies like you do now. OK, a fair few people had cars, but the roads were empty compared to 2013.

Anyway, I did 26 minutes 22 seconds in my first '10'. One of the local hotshots won it with a 24-something, and from the reaction of the people at my club it was clear that they thought I had something. I didn't have a lot of skill – Chris was always better at hockey and football than I was – but I was strong, and skill doesn't count for much in cycling.

I stopped going to school. It wasn't for me. I thought that I might like to be an outdoor education instructor, having lived pretty much wild on the Ashdown Forest for so much of my childhood, and with the sailing and climbing I'd done behind me. I got the train up to Fort William to do a three-month trial at the Loch Eil Outward Bound Centre. It was an amazing place, the mountains towering over the loch on all sides. I was a general dogsbody, which involved all sorts of hard manual graft, dragging kayaks and boats about, cleaning things, digging things up, but also getting out on the water, walking up Ben Nevis, clambering up rock faces and trekking off into the wilderness. It was an incredible experience and perfect for me. Just as I started to think that this could be the ideal career, somebody pointed out that becoming a full-time instructor there would involve going to college and studying for a qualification. Well, that was that. No chance. I headed back south happy with my stay, feeling tough, fit and a bit more independent, but certain that I would never be doing that for a living if it meant going back to school.

Back home, Mum and Dad had some news. Chris and I were getting a little brother or sister, who turned out to be Ella. That was a bit of a turn-up, and I thought I'd better start paying my way around the place. Just turned 17, I started that gardening round. A family friend knew I was looking for something to do and asked me if I wanted to have a crack at his garden once a week. He recommended me to somebody else, then a couple of others got in touch, and suddenly I had a proper round of five houses around Forest Row, one a day.

I tried to enter a race on the Q10 course on the Tonbridge Bypass because it was renowned as a fast course, but I couldn't get in as I didn't have a fast enough time yet. I went down there anyway and rode around the course in the misty early morning half-light to see what it was like. I was so keen to ride that I waited until the event had finished and rode the course again after the last man had gone, my dad timing me. The mist had cleared by then and it turned out to be a lot harder than it had looked earlier. I think I did 22 minutes and something, which would have been a fairly decent time.

Once Dad realized that I had the opportunity to be useful, he turned his attention to doing everything he could for me, his obsessive nature working in my favour this time. The first major impact he had on my cycling career was taking it upon himself to organize me some sponsorship. He used his gift of the gab to sweet-talk Tony Mills and Mick Coward, who had a shop up in Sutton, into supplying me with some kit. The shop was called Emperor Sport, after the great Belgian rider of the 1960s, Rik Van Looy, 'The Emperor'. They were proper riders, Tony and Mick, they'd been professionals and ridden top races, so I was a bit in awe of them with my new-found love of *Cycling* and all the stories I was reading. Tony was the man at the front of the shop; Mick was the frame builder, turning out lovely pieces of steel for many of the top riders in the south.

I'm not sure exactly what deal was cut. Tony and Mick supplied bikes and kit, my dad organized it all, and my uncle Michael stumped up some cash. What I am sure about is that I had absolutely the best of everything. The frames were simply beautiful, handcrafted and smooth-finished works of art. My dad used to spend hours in the shed filing and drilling so that my cables could run internally, a new trick we were seeing in the pages of *Cycling*. I would go out and beat myself to pieces around the lanes of Sussex on my battered old Frejus, then turn up at a time trial on my Emperor Sport with 24-spoke wheels, a monstrous 56-tooth front chainring, tiny 3-speed block and Clement No.1 silk tubular tyres. It felt like I was flying.

I think that the first race I actually won was the Southborough and District Cycling Club New Year's Day 1978 Ten-Mile Time Trial. The time I recorded is lost now, but it must have been a 24-minute ride, I guess.

By the start of the 1978 season, my first of really being a bike rider, I wasn't taking it seriously, I was riding for fun – something to do as a bit of a skive between a few hours of work. I was 17 and I'd started seriously growing, one of those famous spurts that surprises parents – neither Mum nor Dad are tall people – and infuriatingly forces them to buy new clothes for their kids at an age they wish they'd be clothing themselves. I was filling out too. Not fat – I was doing too much bike riding and gardening on an empty stomach for that – but my frame was growing. I could have sailed that Moth now, but I had other things on my mind.

I'd joined the Archer Road Club, based up in west London, on a recommendation as it was thought to be a better set-up for an aspiring racer than East Grinstead. That was a path that Bradley Wiggins would take twenty-odd years later, also under the watchful eye of Stuart Benstead, a club stalwart right across all that time. The first road race I went to was a junior event at Frant near Royal Tunbridge Wells. I was riding in the same field as Steve Sefton and Dave Akam, classy riders who would go on to have decent careers. I didn't really know what I was doing, but my strength made up for my lack of craft, and I broke away with Dave Akam and outsprinted him. I threw up a big two-handed salute on the line and found myself in deep trouble with the chief *commissaire*, Eddie Wingrave. Taking both hands off the bars was a dangerous thing to do and was heavily frowned upon in amateur racing, giving the powers that be every reason to disqualify me. However, I think he took pity on a young boy managing to win the first race he'd entered and let me off with a warning.

After Frant, I went to do one of the circuit races around Crystal Palace Park that have been a fixture of the summer cycling calendar for so long that the Palace itself was probably standing when they started. Steve Sefton was there again, as was his '34 Nomads teammate Tim Stevens, but I managed to slip both of them and get another win.

Graham Watson, later to become a cycling photographer and a good friend, says that we met around this time. He was doing a bit of racing himself, though he was a little older than me:

'I recall it was a 2/3 cat race in Lingfield or Ashdown Forest, and that they agreed to let juniors ride, as Sean was amongst them,' remembers Graham. 'I quit after a few laps; he won. I realized then I was useless and that he was going to be very good. A significant step in hindsight, amongst many that pushed me to be a cycling photographer as opposed to being a cyclist.'

I ended up with about twenty wins in 1978, mostly in time trials, but a fair few road races as well. I used to ride everything the same way: blast it round and hopefully end up covering the course quicker than everyone else, whether it was against the clock or in a bunch. I'd come back from Scotland really strong from all the outdoor labouring and yomping and it didn't take long to quicken up on the bike. I won a few junior events, like the Sussex Divisional Road Race Championship, and then I rode a 55-minute 25-mile time trial down at Arundel, two and a half minutes quicker than the guy in second. That got me my first *Cycling* headline and they even spelt my name right. You wouldn't think there would be too many opportunities to mess up a two-syllable name, but the various errors and mistakes that cropped up had my family in stitches when *Cycling* came out on Thursdays, or the *East Grinstead Courier* dropped on to the mat. Looking back through the scrapbooks now, I can see a few Shauns and the odd Steven, plus Yeats here and there too. Maybe they just thought I was poetry in motion.

When I stepped up to become a senior – I turned 18 in May 1978 – I realized that I was going to have to up the mileage. My first senior road races were way too hard for me, the distances were so much longer. The turning point for me was the Folkestone–London, a Classic race that attracted a decent field, and I got an absolute belting thanks to the extra distance that seniors rode. This just wouldn't do. If I was going to do this properly things would have to change. I thought to myself, 'It's easy to be good, all I have to do is train.'

It was around this time that I discovered that I had an enormous appetite for training – I still have. I loved riding, and just wanted to push myself as far as I could, as hard as I could; seeing how deep I could dig, how much hurting I could take. I wouldn't necessarily recommend it – a more scientific approach works for most people –

but my lifestyle didn't really change for the next four years. I would pitch up at a house at nine in the morning, cut lawns, trim hedges and pull up weeds until midday, then back to Mum's for a glass of water and a bun. At 1 p.m. I'd be out on my bike, hours and hours over the roads round the forest, every day without fail.

'Jenny and I sat Sean down and said we didn't mind him not working if he wanted to commit himself to cycling,' says my dad now. 'We had one stipulation: he had to train. I never had to say that again.'

I liked riding on my own – everybody else had work or school in the afternoons – and I liked to go long distances without food or water, something all sports scientists will tell you is a bad idea. Listen to them, not me. I can remember riding past village shops and longingly look-ing at orange juice cartons and cans of Coke stacked up inside. Sometimes I would get home absolutely belted and just sit in an armchair with my head down and my hand out until my mum put a glass of water in it.

Dad and I talked about track racing and how I might be suited to the endurance events like the pursuit. Chris and I had bodged a fixed-wheel bike together from the dump at some point, and it was still in the shed. In fact, I can remember Chris riding it out to watch me at a time trial over near Tunbridge Wells then trying to ride it back over the hills into a massive headwind with its huge 99˝ gear, his legs buckling and his face contorted with the effort of trying to get uphill. I used to time myself on a training circuit over towards Crawley, finishing at the Duke's Head near Felbridge. One day, I went on the old fixed monstrosity and caned it round, my knees nearly popping out of my legs. At the finish, checking my watch, I forgot I was riding a fixed-wheel bike and stopped pedalling. Going from 25 mph to 0 mph in one yard can only have one result and I catapulted myself straight over the handlebars into the middle of the road. No helmets then, naturally, but I was more concerned with somebody seeing me than smashing my face in.

So I'd had a tiny bit of experience on a fixed-wheel, but never ridden any events they were intended for. I'd never been to a cycling track of any description, let alone a velodrome like the swanky new one that had recently opened in Leicester. However, my good time-trial results persuaded my dad that it would be worth going up there for the National Track Championships and a tilt at the Individual Pursuit. Dad, Chris and I drove up there with a tent and a borrowed track bike for the week. I didn't really know what I was doing, but from what I could make out there wasn't much finesse about it, you just went as hard as you could for five minutes. I think I ended up sixth, which seemed pretty good for a lad who'd only been riding a bike a year and had never been on a track.

On the way back down the M1, towing a trailer full of all our camping stuff and a big old canvas scouting tent, the trailer got a puncture. We couldn't tow it with the flat and there was no spare. In despair, Dad unhitched the trailer and left it on the hard shoulder somewhere near Watford Gap and drove all the way back to Forest Row. Dropping me and Chris off, he found a spare wheel from somewhere and drove all the way back to find the trailer patiently waiting for him. Imagine leaving something on the hard shoulder for hours these days!

I started 1979 with a bit of a bang when I won the first big time trial of the year, the North Road Hardriders event, but the one that got me noticed was a win at the Perfs Pedal in Hampshire, the traditional season-opening road race. I broke away over the hilly downland course with another 'tester', Nick Frewin from Bournemouth, and then outsprinted him a couple of minutes before the bunch arrived. That was one of the last races I rode in the Archer jersey. I wasn't really interested in the social side of the club and they were so far away that there was never anybody else from the Archer in the races I was riding, so I hooked up with the '34 Nomads, who I thought were a pretty cool bunch. They were based out of South Wimbledon, but were scattered all over our part of the world. Maybe that's what the 'Nomads' thing was all about. Steve Sefton and Tim Stevens rode for them and they were guys who were always strong in the races in my area. They lent me a track bike to do the roadman's pursuit event at the Herne Hill Good Friday track meeting, which I won. I liked the idea of being in a team occasionally rather than a total lone ranger when I rode road races. I could get my fill of being an individual in the races against the clock.

The real joy of 1979 was that time trialling. Ten miles

was my best distance, but I really wanted to get up there in the 25s too. I'd read about how Alf trained specially for big events, building the mileage, then some intense speed work, then 'tapering' in the week before the race to arrive in absolutely peak condition. I'd been 19 for a couple of weeks when I went to the National 25-Mile Championship Time Trial in Suffolk, having followed King Alf's recipe to the letter. I lost by a minute to one of my heroes, Eddie Adkins, who broke the championship record, and finished in third spot behind Phil Griffiths, another of the men whose performances had been inspiring me since I'd got that first bike. I did 54 minutes 26 seconds, which was my fastest time over the distance to date, so I was happy enough.

That proved to be my breakthrough performance. From being a prodigious curiosity on the local scene in Sussex and Kent, I was catapulted into being a nationally recognized time-trial specialist.

A week later, we were back in East Anglia riding another 25 on the A12. At the finish, the timekeeper called me over and said, 'Listen, son, are you sure you went the right way?' As the course involved going out down one side of the dual carriageway, leaving it at a sliproad then coming back down the other side, I couldn't really see how somebody could go wrong and didn't know what he was getting at. 'Yes, I've done it before, I know the course,' I said, mystified. 'Why do you ask?'

'Because the watch says you've done 51 minutes 56 seconds,' came the reply.

'I did come third in the National 25 last week,' I laughed. He looked at me as if I was one of those 14-year-old Chinese golfers winning PGA tour events. The next day I won the Clarencourt Road Race in Surrey too.

My dad was amazing. I'd started riding with a guy called Ray Palin, who was a fireman. His shifts often meant he could train in the day. Ray and I would meet in the afternoon after I'd done my gardens and do four hours over the downs to Hastings and Eastbourne. On the way back I'd meet Dad at Wych Cross on the A22 and ride behind the car for forty-five minutes. He'd be driving at 35 mph with me tucked in behind the boot spinning 53 x 16 like crazy to keep up. He'd be slouched in the driver's seat and smoking his roll-ups as usual, puffing the smoke out of the open window. The thing I can instantly remember from those rides is the smell of the tobacco; it used to drive me mad and I'd be swearing at him the whole way.

He ripped the front passenger seat out of the Fiat and put a bed in instead. I remember going off to Essex to do a time trial on the A12 near Colchester where, as no. 61 in a race that began at 6 a.m., my start time was 7.01 a.m. Mum woke me at 3 a.m. and handed me a bowl of cereal, which I wolfed down then got into the car virtually comatose. I lay down in the bed and went straight back to sleep while Dad headed off into the gradually breaking dawn with my bike stowed behind the driver's seat. We repeated this pattern a lot. Before I turned senior, we'd been to some Peter Buckley races, which was the national series for juniors. We left Forest Row for one in Sunderland at 1 a.m. I have a vague recollection that the race had a daft name like the Chubby Chicken Road Race or something equally unimpressive, but I got a top-ten finish so we thought it had been worth it.

That 1979 season went like a dream. I wish they'd had power meters then: I reckon I could give the likes of Brad and Froomey a hard time about the numbers I must have been putting out.

I would finish every training ride by riding up the steep hill of Chapel Lane from the centre of the village and sprinting flat out for the 100 metres or so between the two speedbumps. The second one was right on the flat at the top and I would see how far I could freewheel past it to measure how well I was going. As a result, I felt like I would win pretty much every road race I entered, because I would be able to use my time-trialling strength to get the numbers down in the lead group, then have my Chapel Lane kick to finish it off. I used to read about Freddy Maertens in *Cycling*, this awesome Belgian guy who had won seven stages in the Tour de France one year, both sprints and time trialling. It was said that he used to set out from his home in Belgium and ride as hard as he could with a tailwind until he was absolutely knackered, then turn around and force himself to ride home. That sort of thing appealed to me.

The road racing was fun and I loved winning. I developed my own victory salute: holding one hand aloft in a

V–for–Victory. The secret meaning for me was that it was two–fingers–up to everyone behind.

Looking back at the scrapbook now, it's clear I was enjoying a bit of a golden period. *Cycling* had an article that read:

> If some yardstick were needed to gauge the impact of Sean Yates on the racing scene, a study of the *RTTC* handbook reveals some fascinating statistics. In 1978 just two 10-mile time-trial rides inside 21 minutes were recorded. It was the same story in 1977 and in 1976 – only two riders managing sub-21 minute rides each year. Then, in 1979, along comes Sean Yates, just 19 years old, and knocks out six consecutive 20-minute rides, culminating in the unique feat of getting inside the existing competition record twice on the same day.

That was a pretty good day. I beat the old record (20 minutes 26 seconds) by 19 seconds in the morning on the A3 at Ripley, then went to another event in the afternoon on the Tonbridge Bypass and did 20-18. I could have probably gone a little bit quicker in the afternoon, but I'd made some sort of stupid deal with myself to ride the whole thing in 56 x 12 just to say that I had done it. As a result of churning the massive gear round, I blew up a bit over the last couple of miles. I think the National 25 was the only time trial I lost that year – I certainly didn't get beaten over 10 anyway.

Dad wanted to get me involved in the GB set-up, and it looked like the best bet would be the national team time-trial squad. The four-man team race was a World Championship and Olympic event back then and taken very seriously. We went up to the Black Cat Roundabout on the A1 in Bedfordshire for a trial. On one team were the first-choice guys – I think they were Bob Downs, Joe Waugh, Des Fretwell and Steve Lawrence – up against the new talent of Ian Cammish, Pete Longbottom, Ian Leckenby and me. I think there was also a third team – plenty of competition. Once again, I didn't really have a clue what I was doing, but I was very keen. I felt like I could rip the road up and every time I came through to the front of the quartet, the pace went up. It meant we were going pretty fast, but it disrupted the rhythm of the team. I was pulling so hard that after five miles I'd dropped Ian Cammish, who went on to dominate domestic time trialling in the eighties. Pete Longbottom and Ian Leckenby were really good but smaller guys, and I ended up having to make most of the effort as we trailed the more experienced quartet by a margin by the finish.

The national coach at the time was Jim Hendry. He called me over at the finish and said, 'You were probably the strongest rider out there, but you don't have any technique.' And that was it. At the time, I felt that a teenager coming along and upsetting the cosy arrangement for the guys that were already on the team wouldn't be popular, and it certainly seemed to be the case when they sent me home without so much as a 'We'll call you.' Looking back, it's incredible that they could discard somebody for lack of technique when he'd never done the event before. What is coaching for?

Dad was furious. He immediately started scheming to find another way to get me involved at national level and began talking about the track instead of the road. He got me a trip to Stoke-on-Trent to try out with the national team pursuit squad. The coach, Eddie Soens, took one look at me on the borrowed bike, and hollered, 'Boy! You look like a bloody postman!' My position was that bad. By the end of the session, thanks to Eddie mucking around with my position and me getting used to the track, I was beginning to get the hang of it.

The track was promising enough for Tony and Mick to sort me out a nice Emperor Sport track bike. I was second to Tony Doyle in the Individual Pursuit at the National Track Championships in Leicester and as a result found myself firmly in the national squad. In those days, the World Championships for road and track were combined in one country; the Netherlands for 1979. After Jan Raas won the road race on the iconic course at Valkenburg, just like Philippe Gilbert thirty-three years later, the cycling world decamped to Amsterdam. Tony was racing in France on the road and was our number-one pursuiter, but he chose to do the points race instead in Amsterdam, meaning that the national silver medallist got the nod. That was me. Just over a year after I'd done my first circuit of the track, I found myself at the Worlds.

Travelling abroad with the national squad for the first

time was quite an experience. I've realized over the years that there is a very different atmosphere around track teams to road teams. I think it's to do with the events themselves: Chris Hoy can spend four years preparing for one 30-second race, whereas the continual circus of road racing rolls around the world from one place to another clocking up race after race. As a result, the track squads can be nervous, excitable and edgy compared to well-established road teams. In addition, as there were separate amateur and professional events in those days, the amateur team tended to be loaded with young guys looking for some entertainment. The Amsterdam Worlds certainly felt a bit like a school trip. There was quite a bit of tomfoolery, waterbombs out of hotel windows, running up and down hotel corridors banging on doors, that sort of thing. I remember the Swiss team complaining about us, which was a great achievement as far as we were concerned. I didn't set the world alight with my result, but for somebody who'd arrived so recently on the scene it was well received and it helped cement my place in the organization's thoughts.

I got to ride my first international time trial at the end of the season when I was invited to start at the Grand Prix de France in Versailles thanks to some judicious lobbying by Tony Mills. This was the top *contre-la-montre* for amateurs in France, and I was part of a strong British presence. Tony Doyle, Steve Jones and Robert Millar were all a little bit older than me and had been racing in France for a while.

Dad and I drove down there like we would to any other race, except there was a ferry trip in the middle. When we got to France, we drove straight through a *péage*, the alarms going off all around us. We didn't know what was going on.

The race itself was a proper event: closed roads, a start ramp, lots of people watching, press coverage, etc. I flew down the ramp and hammered out on to the course, which was about 50 kilometres and quite hilly. The course was actually used again as part of the prologue of Paris–Nice in 2012 at the start of Brad's golden year, and I drove the car behind him remembering the roads from thirty-three years earlier. After a while I caught my minute man, a French guy, and cruised by him. He proceeded to stick like glue to my back wheel, an act of cheating which I'd never seen in British racing. I told him to fuck off a couple of times, but it wasn't working, either because he didn't understand me or didn't care, so I let go a massive gob of spit right in his face. That seemed to do the trick. Years later I was at a race with Paul Sherwen and he introduced me to a French bloke, saying, 'Hey, Sean, this is the bloke whose face you spat in!'

This was embarrassing.

'Oh. Hello. Sorry about that.'

In the end, the race was won by the Danish rider Hans-Henrik Ørsted. He became the holder of the amateur World Hour Record shortly afterwards. All four of the British riders placed in the top ten, with me in sixth. I finished ahead of Phil Anderson and Robert Millar, whom I'd been reading about in *Cycling* as they gobbled up seemingly every French race they entered. It was a good feeling and I wanted to come back for more.

Anybody taking an interest in my French racing career would have come to the conclusion that I was a right stroppy git, and they would have had a point. On my other trip to France that year, as part of the national squad's track programme, I raced an international pursuit at the Montargis track. I got to the final, where I was up against Alain Bondue. I didn't know who he was, but he would go on to have a really decent career, including an Olympic silver and a two-year stint as Individual Pursuit World Champion. I was on my best track wheels with my white strips, but they were better suited to wooden-boarded tracks, and Montargis was concrete. We started the race, and BANG! I punctured. It was like a gun going off in the stadium, there was a big startled shout from the crowd, then they let me get a spare and we started again. A few seconds in, BANG! Another flat! I lost my temper, chucked the bike down, tore off the 'piss-pot' lid we used to wear then and drop-kicked it high into the air over the centre of the track. That caused quite a commotion, mainly along the lines of, 'Send the lairy English kid home,' I think.

Being involved in the national squad meant I got to go to some good races. I went up to Scotland in the spring of the following year as part of a GB team to do the Girvan 3-Day and won it. I won the first stage in a sprint from a small group, then kept the jersey through the other stages. There was some really good team riding; we were a powerful squad with my clubmate Glen Mitchell also part of it. He won a stage too and we all worked hard to protect my lead. It would be a useful lesson if I ever ended up riding on the road for a professional team. Glen, Tim Stevens and I also formed a '34 Nomads trio that finished first, third and fourth at that year's Folkestone–London. I nearly messed up the sprint, getting manœuvred into the front around the last bend as I didn't realize we were approaching the finish line. Forced to lead it out, I just stuck it in the big gear and whacked on the pedals as hard as I could and nobody came round. Winning there felt really good – this had been the scene of my wake-up call to get my finger out a year previously.

Dave Akam, Glen Mitchell and I were driving up to Leicester regularly for track training. The Olympics were only months away now, and we thought we might be in with a shout of a medal. We would tailgate each other up the M1: Glen in his Capri, me and Dad in the Fiat; or sometimes I'd be with Dave and his dad in their big old Rover V8. When I raced time trials, I used 177.5-mm cranks, a great big 56-tooth chainring, which was pretty much standard then, and either a three-speed block or four-speed if it was hilly. That had 12-, 13-, 14- and 15-tooth sprockets on it, which meant I was using up to a 126″ gear. On the track, the coach Willi Moore had us riding an 88″ gear on 165-mm cranks to increase our pedal speed and suppleness. All that meant was when I got home from these sessions and got back on the time-trial bike I was munching up the road. It was brilliant. I'd also got the idea from somewhere of wearing a sort of hairnet to increase my aerodynamics. Looking at a picture now, it looks like I was wearing a bald wig from a joke shop. My other innovation from that season was a pair of clipless pedals. Though they didn't really make their entrance on the professional stage until 1985, when Bernard Hinault rode the Tour de France on them, there was a pedal made by Cinelli that you used to slide your foot in along grooves and then put in a pin so it fixed solid. It was great for time trialling, but too dangerous for road racing; you'd never get your foot out.

At time trials, Alf Engers was always the man of mystery, turning up suddenly at the start. I wanted to be like that, so me and Dad would pick up my number from the HQ then whisk off somewhere else to get ready. One day we were in a layby on the Tonbridge Bypass getting ready for an event on the Q10 course. I was standing by the back of the car and my dad was pinning my number on as Mick Ballard rode past, warming up on the course. He was known as the King of the Q10 to me and didn't take kindly to this teenager coming along and beating him, let alone becoming the competition record holder. He shouted, 'Why don't you wipe his arse as well while you're at it?'

In training for the 1980 National 25, Dad took me up to the Tonbridge Bypass again to time me over the 10 course to see what my speed was like. He clocked me at 19-12, nearly a minute faster than my competition record, on my normal road bike. Quite a rivalry developed between Dave Akam and myself. We were both on the national squad for the team pursuit but he didn't make the cut for the Olympics, which was a shame as we'd been to a lot of races together. He really wanted that ten-mile crown, and he broke my competition record while I was away in Moscow with the national squad, but I came back and managed to shave a couple of seconds off his time. The 19-44 I did on the Q10 stuck until the following season. George Clarey, Dave's coach, told me years later that he'd followed me round the course to make sure I didn't cheat by drafting other riders or lorries! With the advent of tri-bars and disc wheels, the event has changed beyond all recognition now, and both Michael Hutchinson and Brad have taken the record under 18 minutes.

We went up to Boroughbridge in North Yorkshire for the National 25 Championship and I managed to win it this time. For me it was the blue riband of time trialling and I was really chuffed. In fact, finding the old *Cycling* report shows I used that same word then. Chuffed. It was a championship record time of 51-30, nearly two minutes faster than the previous figure, and the best time I'd ever ridden in a 25 by about half a minute. Beating the reigning champion and hero of mine Eddie Adkins to win it made it even more special.

A few years ago, my mate Brian Phillips went up to a RTTC dinner and came back with a DVD of that

1980 National 25. Unbelievable. When I saw the shots of me riding by in a '34 Nomads–C P Hart skinsuit, I had a flashback to seeing a guy filming me with a cinecamera from the pillion seat of a motorbike. The most astonishing thing is the complete and utter absence of traffic. At one point, a Ford Cortina goes by. This was on the A1! In those golden days, Brian and I would leave Forest Row of a weekday afternoon, ride down the A22 to Polegate, go left down through Hastings to Rye, left again, Hawkhurst, Wadhurst, Frant, Groombridge and back over the forest, and be two-abreast the whole way. In 2013 you'd be lucky to make it out of the village before somebody mowed you down in a fit of road rage.

When people ask me now about my career wins, I'm sure they're expecting to hear about something in a Motorola or Fagor jersey, but I often think of that day. Looking back, that 1980 National 25-Mile title gave me as much pleasure as anything.

I had so much energy in those days. The biggest risk to my progress was bashing myself up doing something else. I used to go skateboarding every night, and had loads of scrapes and grazes that everybody thought were bike injuries. I didn't really train on Mondays as it was my recovery day after a weekend of racing, but I used to strap my board on my back and ride down to Brighton Cave to skate. It was a three-hour round trip. I used to have a little transistor radio strapped to the bars for the ride and would be forever tuning it as I rode along. I didn't care what it was – music, news, phone-ins – just as long as I could get some sort of reception. The local hotshot at the Cave was a kid called Mad Mark Baker, who was unbelievable. I would skate a bit then watch him, then try to copy him and bash myself up. They had a fibreglass bowl called the Blue Bowl, which people came from all over to ride. You won't be surprised to hear that my board was homemade, with Laser trucks and Alva conical wheels. Tony Alva was the main man everybody used to talk about; his legendary tricks riding empty swimming pools in Los Angeles would be the main topic of conversation. I read recently that he does gardening now, which made my day.

Then I started playing in goal for Forest Row FC on Saturday afternoons. That's where my dad drew the line. 'I don't like to stop you doing things, son,' he told me, 'but you could mess everything up. You could end up missing the Olympics because you've twisted an ankle playing football. How stupid would that be?'

A case in point was the National Track Championship that year. I was in a '34 Nomads 'B' quartet in the team pursuit and came third, which we were pretty pleased with. The Nomads 'A' team won the thing, led by Ron Keeble. He was the club legend, having ridden the team pursuit at the Munich Olympics, amongst other things. As the time came to roll on to the track for the third-place ride-off, Ron started looking round. 'Where's Sean?' he was saying. 'Has anyone seen Sean?' There was an athletics track next to the velodrome, and I was practising my high jump. He went mental. Fortunately, he hadn't seen me a minute before, when I'd been timing myself over 400 metres, trying to be David Hemery.

David Hemery had won the 400-metre hurdles at the Mexico Olympics in 1968, but I knew him better from *Superstars*. I was hoping to have a go at the Olympics myself.

Chapter Five

Me and Tony Doyle. Tony Doyle and me. That was the story of 1980. Who would be going to the Olympics?

We were both in the likely starting line-up for the team pursuit quartet, but only one of us could do the individual pursuit. Doyley had been undisputed GB number one for some time and was clearly head and shoulders above everybody else. He looked like a shoo-in for Moscow, but then this big 19-year-old from Sussex started showing up and running him close.

It probably began in the summer of 1979, a year before the Olympics. I turned up at my second National Track Championships for the 4000-metre Individual Pursuit a bit more clued up than the boy-on-a-borrowed-bike Disney story of the previous year. I had a lovely new custom-built Emperor Sport track bike and an aero hat, and my technique had been improved by riding with the team pursuit squad. I was full of confidence after winning race after race that spring, and wanted to take my time-trialling form on to the track.

The first round at the Nationals was a bit weird, as Doyley's opponent didn't show up and he had to ride on his own. I qualified with the best time, but he was down in eighth place after his enforced solo ride. We both went through our rounds as scheduled, with Doyley seeing off Dave Akam in the semi-final to set up our head-to-head for the gold medal. I sped out of the traps into an early lead, but Doyley quickly pulled me back and we stayed neck and neck for a few laps. His experience and competitive edge really told in the second half of the race and he ground out a three-second margin on me by the finish, but we'd both gone under five minutes, really good international standard timings.

Things swung my way a little bit when we headed to those World Championships in Amsterdam. I think Tony was so confident of being selected for the Individual Pursuit at the Olympics that he decided to opt out of doing that event at the Worlds to concentrate on the points race, so I got the nod. I didn't set the world alight in Holland, but had shown enough to leave the impression that I was improving fast and could be the coming man.

By the time Olympic year came around, there was little to choose between us. In the spring, we were both part of an England team that rode the Sealink International, a peculiar little stage race that used to begin in Holland and finish in England. In the 6.3-kilometre prologue time trial in Rotterdam I was first and Doyley was second, with only two seconds between us.

The clock was ticking towards July and Moscow, and no decision had been made. Willi Moore, our GB team coach, and Jim Hendry, the GB team manager, decided that the European Cup event in Munich at the end of June would be the showdown. All the main Western nations were going and it would be a great pointer for Olympic success. I was fastest in the qualifying round, then lost by .25 of a second to the Norwegian rider Jan Iversen in the final. I had ridden 4-42, which I think was a new British record. Unfortunately, Willi and Jim's intended ride-off hadn't materialized, as Tony hadn't appeared at the track, complaining of a cold. I felt I was in the box seat now. Though I might have lost to Tony the year before, I was manifestly improving and had clocked the fastest ever British time at an event he should have been at.

A private ride-off at the Leicester track was organized, and we headed up the M1 once again. This time Doyley never really got going, having some sort of bike problem, and the race was called off. We were both in the squad for the team pursuit, so neither of us would be staying behind in England, but a decision still hadn't been made. All of which meant that we boarded the plane to Moscow still not knowing who would be riding the Olympic Individual Pursuit for Great Britain.

There is no doubt that in recent times cycling at the Olympics has lost some of its cachet. When the Olympics went 'open' at Atlanta in 1996, dismantling the lines between professional and amateur, it ushered in a new era, where the world's top pros could compete for the first time. On the one hand, this would seem only to improve standards. But on the other, for amateurs, the Olympics were everything, the unobtainable shimmering Holy Grail at the very pinnacle of our sport. For the professionals, while the Olympics are far from being just another event, there are many other races jostling for importance in the calendar. Despite their class as riders, neither Sammy Sánchez nor Alexandre Vinokourov would claim to be the best cyclists in the world, despite them being Olympic Road Champions in the open era. Even Jan Ullrich, the one modern Olympic Road Champion who could justifiably lay claim to being the best rider in the world at some point, would put his Olympic title well behind his Tour de France success. In 1980 it was different. Yes, many cyclists could go on to have professional careers after the Games, but for an amateur, it was a glittering prize above all others.

In addition, many of the Russians and East Germans you encountered at the Olympics could waltz into any professional team, but were barred by the restraints of Soviet policy from doing so. The Olympics was their pinnacle whichever way you looked at it.

International politics and the Cold War nearly stopped us all going. Potential competitors from all over the Western world held their breath as President Jimmy Carter announced an ultimatum that would lead to the USA boycotting the Games if the USSR didn't remove its troops from Afghanistan. The Soviets did no such thing, and the Americans led a boycott that was sixty-five countries strong.

Back in Britain, the government was in an unenviable position. Margaret Thatcher's Tories hadn't been in power long and were sitting on a precarious majority. While they wanted to support the US, they were also acutely aware of the backlash a public in the grip of recession could deliver if their Olympics were taken away. They only had to look at the negative effect England's failure to qualify for the World Cup in Argentina had on the previous regime. So they fudged it. They said they disapproved of the Olympics in Moscow, but it was up to the individual national sporting bodies to decide. Since very few turkeys have ever been discovered voting for Christmas, we were going.

People often come back with stories from the Olympics of the glorious opening ceremonies, of marching around the stadium waving their national flags and waving to the vast crowds, of being stopped and congratulated in the street. Moscow wasn't like that. For starters, we didn't go to the opening ceremony because of the boycott. We were billeted in a grim block of flats that were straight out of a Cold War spy drama. I was rooming with a scouser called Terry Tinsley, a fast young sprinter and a really great bloke. Like me, he was new to the set-up; we were outsiders to some extent, a lot of the team having been together for a few years by that stage.

'We were both outsiders, not part of the clique,' explains Terry. 'That's not unusual in teams when you go away, that sort of thing, a bunch of guys from different backgrounds spending a lot of time together – people tend to split into groups. I guess it's different now, there's a more professional approach from when you're very young. We just used to fit our training in around work. I remember getting the letter telling me I'd been picked for the Games, handing it to my dad and just sitting on the floor in the kitchen in shock.'

To train, we either had to book a session on the Olympic track, which was as congested as you might imagine, or be bussed out to the road time-trial course, which was on the Moscow-to-Minsk highway in a forest about 50 kilometres out of the city. As we rode along the long, straight roads through the thick woodland, armed guards were posted every fifty yards. God knows what they thought might happen.

Tony asked for a ride-off in the velodrome. I was happy to have the decision made on what had already gone before, as my recent results had been great and I felt he had been avoiding competing with me, but I would go along with whatever they decided. Jim Hendry agreed to Tony's request, but told us that he wouldn't necessarily choose the winner to race in the real event. That sounded a bit barmy to me – why have it if it wasn't going to be the deciding factor? – but he said it would be useful practice for us anyway.

'The tension was unbelievable, it had been building and building for weeks,' remembers Terry Tinsley. 'It was a bigger event for us than the Olympic final itself.

Because the pursuit was the first event of the Games, there was a lot of suspense anyway, years of waiting coming to a climax, I suppose. Somehow we'd ended up out there still not knowing who was going to ride, which was unbelievable really. Even then, there was time to ramp it up a bit more, as the first track session was cancelled and it had to be rearranged again.'

We lined up across the Olympic track from each other and started off. It was a weird atmosphere – tense – with the whole team there, and a load of other people just going about their business in the background. The guy calling my lap times couldn't make himself heard and I didn't know what was going on. I felt my concentration begin to waver and started to lose my mind. My head fell off, as they say. All of a sudden, my nose burst open and I could feel the blood filling my nostrils. I'd had nosebleeds before, often in times of great pressure, but never actually in an event. Riding my bike was when I felt free of pressure. I swung up the track and out of the race. Doyley pushed on and clocked an awesome 4-42 to show he was in good form. I just slowly rode back down the banking and in to the track centre, my Olympic dream in tatters.

'Doyley was one of the most experienced guys out there, despite not being that much older than Sean,' says Terry. 'He'd been at the top for a while and was living and racing on the Continent. There was plenty of pressure on both of them, but his experience probably meant he handled it a little bit better than Sean. As soon as

Sean's nose went, you could see something was wrong. There was nothing between them at the time, but he filled up with blood immediately and sat up abruptly. That was that.'

You could say that it came as something of a surprise when we got back to our barracks and Jim Hendry announced that I would be Great Britain's representative in the Olympic Individual Pursuit, due to start in a couple of days' time. Tony was absolutely furious and I couldn't blame him. While my performances had been good, he had been given the chance of a ride-off and had taken it with both hands.

According to my tattered old cutting from *Cycling*, Jim Hendry said at the time, 'It was a difficult decision, and it was sad having to make it. Both men had identical times, the fastest for years, but Yates had been faster at Munich. You could say that I used my eye for a bike rider.' That last bit would have been certain to wind Tony up, as he had real class on the bike. In the same paper, Tony admitted that it had caused 'a bit of aggravation' between us. I guess in hindsight that Jim and Willi's plan was to allow Tony his ride-off, I would win and everything would be right with the world. It didn't work out that way.

Tony had been a stalwart of the national squad for a while and he had a lot of friends and supporters in the team. Nights back in our digs were tricky: people would bang on the door to my room all through the night; I'd go to lie down and find my pillow covered with toothpaste.

Terry was absolutely brilliant, very supportive, and between us we laughed about it and it didn't affect me too much.

The Individual Pursuit was the first event on the track. I wanted to reach the quarter-finals – I thought that a medal was unrealistic considering the opposition and my lack of experience at that level. The noise was immense in the velodrome, unlike anything I'd come across in the short time I'd been racing. It was hard to keep calm and measure my effort, but the qualifying round went well and I fought my way through to the quarter-finals, which were a straight knockout.

My opponent was to be Hans-Henrik Ørsted, the Dane who had put three minutes into me over 50 kilometres at the Grand Prix de France, and was also the amateur World Hour Record holder. Once again, I flew out of the blocks and had an advantage over him for the first 1000 metres. Gradually, though, he began to pull away. I clocked 4-41, a British record, and finished sixth, making my mum very proud. She has my number – 100 – framed on the wall in Forest Row to this day. I can't say whether that would have been enough to beat Tony Doyle, but I can say with some certainty that he wouldn't have got near Robert Dill-Bundi, who won the gold for Switzerland in 4-35. In the qualifying round he'd set a new world record of 4-32. This was all on normal road-bike-shaped machines: no low-profiles, no tri-bars, no disc wheels, no carbon fibre. Due to the luck of the draw in the pursuit, Ørsted's 4-36 was only good enough for a bronze.

Tony's response was to immediately turn professional, but first we had to put aside our differences and ride the team pursuit along with Malcolm Elliott and Glen Mitchell. We went all right. In fact, we went more than all right, as for ten minutes we held the world record with a 4-19. But then we had to sit and watch as a string of other teams rolled out and beat our time. Eastern European teams filled the medals; USSR, East Germany and Czechoslovakia pushing us out of the running. We also finished behind the Australians, who included in their number one Gary Sutton. Fortunately for me his brother Shane, who'd been in their Commonwealth Games winning quartet two years earlier, wasn't in the team. I'd never have heard the last of it.

Tony became professional World Pursuit Champion in Besançon later that year, which was a pretty good two-fingered salute. I came home and won the National Pursuit Title at Leicester to go with my National 25 crown. Tony wasn't in the competition, of course, having turned pro, but Dave Akam was, and I beat him in the final.

Terry Tinsley turned pro too. He won the sprinters' triple crown at the 1983 National Track Championships, the clean sweep of the Sprint, the Omnium and the Keirin. Not so the next year. 'The other pros didn't like somebody winning everything; they wanted to see the cake shared out a bit more and combined to squeeze me out, but I'll always have those titles.'

Terry is a contract manager now. 'They were great

days and I loved rooming with Sean, but he was a better cyclist than a gardener. I still wouldn't let him cut my grass.'

The cheek.

Tony Mills had been busy again. This time he got me a ride at the Grand Prix des Nations in Cannes. In those days there were two races – one for amateurs and one for professionals – the amateurs doing one lap of the circuit and the pros two. I flew down there and was met at the airport by the organizer, Albert Bouvet. He put me in a hotel with a young, blond, bespectacled French amateur called Laurent Fignon. He and I went out for a ride round the circuit the day before the event and he half-wheeled me the whole way round. I was getting a bit pissed off with his macho antics, and I couldn't believe the way he was smashing himself up the hills, absolutely eyeballs-out. I loved training hard, but the afternoon before the race seemed a bit crazy even to me. I put two minutes into him the next day and felt very pleased with myself. I doubt he gave it too much thought when he was winning his first Tour de France less than three years later.

Julián Gorospe, a climber who would give many years of service to the likes of Pedro Delgado and Miguel Indurain, won our race, just in front of Stephen Roche, who was about to leave his apprenticeship at the Parisian ACBB club to turn professional with Peugeot. His teammates from the previous season, Phil Anderson and Robert Millar, had already made the step. I put my National 25 winner's cap on back to front, raced around the Riviera and came sixth, which seemed OK.

A chap I knew vaguely from the UK scene, Stuart Hallam, happened to be in Cannes on his honeymoon. He had his bike with him and put it in the back of his car and drove round the course behind me in the race as support. I didn't have need to call upon his services, which was probably fortunate for both of us, but it was great to have somebody I knew in my corner.

Roche was a really nice chap and made me feel welcome in those circles, recognizing me from the race we'd done together at Versailles the previous season. He introduced me to Mickey Wiegand, the manager of ACBB, the Athlétic Club de Boulogne-Billancourt. Even an English *arriviste* like me knew about the ACBB. It was the best-known and most established route to becoming a professional cyclist for English-speaking riders. Roche, Millar, Anderson, Graham Jones and Paul Sherwen had all spent their big-time race apprenticeships there. Mickey congratulated me on my ride and suggested I send him a CV. I flew back to England full of the future.

I was to see Stephen Roche again a few weeks later when I went for a second tilt at the Grand Prix de France. This year it was at Saint-Priest, down near Lyon, and was over a course due to be used in the following Tour de France. This time I was only five seconds off winning, beaten by the same man who had so recently pulled back the curtains on a prospective European career for me, one Stephen Roche.

Mickey Wiegand came up to me at the finish. '*Yattez,*' he said, a pronunciation I would get used to over the years in France, 'don't worry about the CV. You're in.'

Chapter Six

It was late evening as I rested my forehead against the coach window and saw the signs telling me we had arrived at the Gare du Nord, Paris. I was 20, it was January 1981, and I was off to seek fame and fortune in the bright lights. Woo-hoo.

It didn't seem awfully fame-and-fortuney as I got off the coach. My body was all twisted up by the interminable journey from Victoria Coach Station; sitting slouched like my dad the whole way probably hadn't helped. I had an old suitcase full of all the clothes I would need for the next nine months, an Emperor Sport racing bike, and £50 that Mum had given me just as I'd left. The official letter I'd received from the Athlétic Club de Boulogne-Billancourt had told me to get this coach and there would be somebody from the club at the Gare du Nord to meet me. At this hour the station was pretty much deserted, and there was no sign of any tracksuited official.

Fortunately, I was not completely alone. When I'd arrived at Victoria to get on the coach, there had been another lad on the same journey. John Parker was another cyclist who had been out before and was headed back to Paris for reasons that have been lost in the mists of time. Crucially, he knew that the lack of a reception party was par for the course.

'It's a test,' he said. 'Have you got the address?'

I fished in my pocket and found the details I needed. Then me, the bike and the suitcase set about getting ourselves to the western suburbs on the Metro. I'd been on the Tube once or twice – a bit of a thrill for a country boy – but at least they spoke English in London. Finally I walked along the quiet street and found my destination. First obstacle surmounted.

I'd trained pretty hard that winter. I did a quick 25 in the rain a week before Christmas, then I'd had a screamer in the Southborough and District New Year's Day Ten-Mile Time Trial round all the little lanes, taking a couple of minutes off my course record. Chris was second, marking the end to a really great festive period, my last Christmas with us all living at home.

The day after I arrived in Paris, I got my '34 Nomads kit out and went for a training ride with some of the ACBB boys. Boulogne-Billancourt is wedged into the big western bend of the Seine as it heads out of the capital by the Bois de Boulogne. It didn't take us long to get beyond the ring road and out past Versailles into the Vallée de Chevreuse, rolling countryside I was familiar with from my first Grand Prix de France. Then it was back to the *service course,* as I was to learn to call all team HQs from now on, for a fitting for my new Peugeot team bike. To all intents and purposes, ACBB was a full professional set-up, funded and equipped by Peugeot with the aim of providing a flow of riders to their professional road squad and Tour de France team. Riders like Eddy Merckx, Tom Simpson and Bernard Thévenet had worn the famous white Peugeot jersey, ringed with a chequered flag. Now my predecessors, Stephen Roche, Robert Millar and Phil Anderson, were doing the same. A poster on the wall of the *service course* depicted another ACBB old boy, Régis Ovion, who had become the 1971 World Amateur Road Race Champion while at the club. My new ACBB jersey had chequered sleeves echoing the pro team, and the name of the sponsors across the chest, but was a classy grey and orange. My bike, as all collectors will guess, was pure white, like all the old Peugeots.

The only trouble with being a famed production line – as ACBB was – is that you have to keep producing the goods. Mickey Wiegand drove me and a couple of others down to the training camp in his old Peugeot 504 without getting out of third gear. He was a pensioner and drove like one. When we got down to the Côte d'Azur (I know!), the team were put into a little hotel near Mickey's home in Les Issambres, just across the bay from Saint-Tropez (I know!). Everyone except me, that is, because as the chosen one of the new litter, I was to stay at the boss's house, along with the *directeur sportif*, Claude Escalon.

I wasn't the only English boy there; we also had John

Herety, a savvy sprinter from Cheshire who was great company. After a couple of weeks enjoying riding in the winter sunshine alongside the Med, we entered our first race, the Grand Prix de Saint-Tropez. The start line was quite an experience: the maximum number of riders in an amateur road race in Britain at that time was forty, here there were two hundred and forty guys on the line! The race was a number of circuits of the town, crossing the finish line in front of *la Mairie*. Perhaps because of the fear of being rammed in amongst so many others, or more likely because I just used to ride like that, I rode off the front and found myself throwing up a two-armed salute in my very first race for ACBB.

Next, we headed to Toulon for a similar race, except this time there were 350-odd starters. Carnage. The decent teams went flat out from the start to thin it out, which suited me. There was to be no lone breakaway this time; instead we came into the finish in a decent-sized bunch and I led John Herety out to take his first win for the club. Two races, two wins for the English boys.

ACBB provided us with a little apartment back in Boulogne-Billancourt. As well as me and John there was Jeff Williams, a Mancunian who was the best English climber for many years, and a talented guy from Southport called Kevin Reilly. We got our bikes, our kit, our travel and accommodation at races, all that. The only thing we didn't get was money. My mum's £50 wasn't going to go very far, and I needed to eat. As a result, prize money was very important to us, and we set out to win as many spot prizes, or *primes,* as we could. John and I were well suited to that sort of racing – circuits, sprinting on each lap for a prize, getting involved at the finish – but it was much harder for Jeff. As a climber made for the high mountains, Jeff would have been an asset to any big stage-race team, but these races around small towns just didn't suit him and he had very few opportunities to show his skills. He and Kevin found the going a bit tough out there.

The apartment in Boulogne-Billancourt was great. It was on the third floor of a typically tidy Parisian block. I can't remember Kevin being there much; he may have moved out sooner than the rest of us or gone back to England. John liked cooking and I liked cleaning up – I have OCD according to my kids – and Jeff liked to watch us doing both. I wasn't homesick at all, but keeping in touch with home wasn't that easy. You forget what an immense impact emails and texting have had on our lives until you look back. I had a girlfriend back home in East Grinstead, Katie, and I used to write to her all the time. I used to write to Mum and Dad too, as they didn't have a phone. If I needed to speak to them I would call Paul's house and his mother would walk up the lane and get Mum or Dad.

John Herety has got a better memory than me: 'It was a tiny little apartment in a block of flats, with a kitchen table that you could just squeeze four guys around, if you didn't mind moving to get the fridge open,' he recalls. 'Fortunately, we never had to squeeze four round it, because Sean used to sit on the draining board by the sink. I can picture him now, legs dangling down, shovelling in jam sandwiches like they were on special offer in Tesco.'

John was the boss in the flat. He'd got there first and the neighbours and landlord seemed to see him as our representative. He got it in the neck one day from a committee of residents complaining about me.

'The thing with Sean was this: if he said he was going to train for four hours, it had to be four hours,' he says. 'If we were due back at half past five and we got back at quarter past, he'd carry on for fifteen minutes. That in itself isn't so weird, but instead of heading back out, he would do laps of the underground car park at absolutely maximum speed. He loved the squealing the tyres made on the corners, like he was in *The Professionals* or something. Some old dear would come down to get in her 2CV and this mental *rosbif* would nearly run over her toes on his bike, going faster round the car park than she drove on the *autoroute*. I got a right bollocking.'

It was about this time that I started eating. Eating seriously.

I'd been a vegetarian my whole life up to that point. All the Yateses were, not really because of high principles, but Mum and Dad (it sounds like a Dad idea in retrospect) thought it was healthier. It had certainly been good for me. I'd got big, strong and lean on a diet of vegetables and heavy training, and had no complaints.

One of my first races when we got back to Paris was

a big amateur event called Paris–Evreux, finishing up in Normandy. Graham Jones had won it for ACBB a couple of years previously and he was now making waves at Peugeot, so it was a good target for me and John, especially as John was from Cheadle like Graham. We were woken at 4.30 a.m. and taken like sleepwalkers to a restaurant where we were given huge plates of pasta and *steak haché* to eat. Imagine making a pot of spaghetti bolognese for a family of six, taking all the nice rich tomatoes, onions, basil and garlic out, then eating the lot yourself. At five o'clock in the morning. I didn't figure at Paris–Evreux.

I started to chunk up in a big way. There were lots of factors. Firstly, I'd never eaten meat. The French ate a lot of it, and a lot of heavy red meat at that. The injection of protein would probably be great for somebody trying to build some bulk, but I had plenty of that to start with. It was probably akin to suddenly downing great tubs of bodybuilding protein powder. Allied to that, my late two- or three-year growth spurt had ended. I would be 6 feet 2 inches from 1980 until I started shrinking, like I am now. As a result, a lot of the extra energy that my body had been burning in order to grow was now surplus to requirements.

It was the first time I had been a full-time athlete. I was used to working hard in the morning, training all afternoon, having dinner, getting up and doing it all over again. Not only was I burning it off then, there simply wasn't time to sit around eating cakes.

In Paris, we'd go for a ride in the morning then laze around. My favourite trick was to go to the patisserie along the road and buy a huge family butter cake. It's a sort of white cake, made of absolute pure fat. I'd mush it all up, dump the lot into a salad bowl and sit there eating it with a spoon like it was a bowl of muesli.

'Preparing [the cake] was a total ritual for him, like a heroin addict cooking up,' says John. 'The cake would be divided into squares, then the lot would go into the sort of bowl reserved for family fruit salads. Then a large pot of *fromage blanc* would go over the lot. That gave him the excuse to call it "yogurt cake" like it was some kind of health food.'

There was a supermarket just across the street, Eddie Le Clerc's, as we used to call it. I had an absolute love of Lion Bars – I don't remember them being around in England when I was a kid; they may have arrived here a bit later – and I used to buy a five-pack of them. On one memorable occasion I contrived to eat all five of them between exiting the supermarket and opening our front door.

Another thing that I used to do makes me cringe to think of it now. As I've explained, I'd always been keen on training and pushing myself, and I used to do press-ups and sit-ups in the evenings back in Sussex. Now, with time on my hands, I got my press-ups up to five hundred a day. I had arms like Geoff Capes. Great for chucking a shot-put or pulling trains on *World's Strongest Man*, not much use to a 20-year-old would-be professional cyclist.

Tim Kerrison and the coaches at Sky would despair if any of the young guys started doing that, but I didn't have a coach. Nobody did. You'd get the programme of races you were meant to be riding, turn up, ride, and go home. I didn't have a coach in the modern sense of the word for my entire career. Now, a guy in his forties who works in a bank gets a coach to tell him how to ride two sportives a year.

When I arrived in France, I was 79 kilograms. That wasn't bad; it felt close to my natural weight. Plus, it was January, so you'd expect to slim down as the racing miles began to have an impact. Instead, by May I was 88 kilograms. Hmm.

I sucked as a bike rider, but survived on strength alone. In a lot of the races we were doing, that was enough. The power that had seen me stomping round all those amateur road races and time trials in England sustained me through the spring in France, and enabled me to win enough *primes* to survive.

As well as the *prime* money, I found a nice little sideline fixing tubulars. All the racing bikes had 'tubs' on them then, and they were expensive to replace. I became known as the guy to go to if you needed a tub mending. I'd rip the old tyre open, take the inner out, find the hole and patch it, then sew it all back up again. Once again, my Michael Hall needlework skills served me well. I charged ten francs a tyre; about a pound. It was enough for some more cakes, anyway.

By July, I realized that if I was going to make a life

out of this I was going to have to get serious. 'Serious' is a word you hear a lot in professional cycling. 'He's not serious' is often used as a dismissive term for riders who aren't prepared to dedicate themselves to being the best they can. Well, for the first half of my opening season in Europe, I wasn't serious. I had to learn.

I started to train properly. We were very close to the Longchamp racecourse, and a huge chaingang used to turn up to ride on the road that followed the racetrack every evening. I used to head out of the city for four hours in the Vallée de Chevreuse, then join the Longchamp bunch on the way back in and do another couple of hours. It was incredible riding, a massive bunch absolutely tearing round the course, trying to rip each other's legs off. I loved it, and I felt myself getting back in the groove. In style, the training was very similar to those long rides I'd done with Ray Palin a couple of years previously, where we would ride over the Downs then spend the last hour flat out behind my dad's car.

'I didn't go to Longchamp that often,' says John, 'but I decided to go down there with him one night. I couldn't believe it. Everybody knew Sean. This big shy English bloke who hardly spoke a word of French was a legend. '*Voilà Yattez! Yattez arrive! Ici Yattez!*' they were all saying as we rolled up. I couldn't figure it out until we started riding. Within five minutes he was churning 53 x 13 and flying round this little circuit at about 30 mph with about sixty French guys trying to keep up with him. He loved it. *Le Roi de Longchamp*.'

France goes mad for cycling for one month a year. It's a bit like Britain with Wimbledon: for a couple of weeks, everybody is a tennis expert. The Tour de France is the French Wimbledon in that respect, and for July, cycling rules. Before the final stage of the 1981 Tour de France headed up the Champs-Elysées, myself and John would be wearing our ACBB colours in a supporting motor-paced race.

If you've never seen motor-paced racing, it's a bit of a hoot. It's still popular in Belgium and northern France, and often forms part of towns' carnival programmes or *kermesses* as they're known in Belgium. Each rider has his own assistant to ride ahead of him on a moped, or 'derny'. The derny rider goes as fast as he can without dropping his man. You end up with an event that's a similar effort to a time trial, but very, very fast and much more exciting to watch. Most northern European pros grow up on a diet of motor-paced training, and the garages of the parents of aspiring cyclists will invariably have a moped parked in them. Many long nights are spent by mothers, fathers or older brothers and sisters traversing the long straight lanes of Flanders and northern France on a moped with a young rider busting a gut to stay in their slipstream.

So my first experience of the crowds on the Champs-Elysées at the end of the Tour was riding round six inches behind the mudguard of a derny. My dad had driven over to watch, so I was very keen to make him proud and give him something to tell them about in Forest Row. I was going pretty well; I may not have been experienced at the derny, but the skillset required was right up my street. On the day I was beaten into second place by that guy with the glasses, Laurent Fignon. At the time, I suspected that it might have been a fix, as I kept shouting at my bloke to go faster, but he wouldn't. I still had something in the tank. Later on in my career, when I found out just how many of these carnival races are pre-arranged so that a local favourite wins to keep the crowd entertained, I was sure that my derny race in Paris in '81 had been organized to make sure the Parisian rider won. But like my first encounter with Fignon the year before in Cannes, I doubt he was bothering about it too much when he won his first Tour de France in 1983 at the age of 22.

Along the street from us in Boulogne-Billancourt was a butcher's shop. At the end of the weekend, after our racing, Monsieur Boucher (as we used to call him) would take ten francs off us in return for a package of meat. Unless one of us had won, that was, in which case it was free. We'd take it back, unwrap it to see what delights we had been given, and John would cook it up beautifully. When we finished that derny race on the Champs-Elysées, we were back at the cars enjoying a little bottle of cold beer in the celebratory atmosphere when Monsieur Boucher showed up with a freshly prepared baguette that he had brought over from Boulogne-Billancourt for us. From then on, whenever I finished the Tour de France, Monsieur Boucher would be there, right up until the mid-nineties.

In 2010, I was leaning on the bonnet of the Sky Jaguar after completing my first Tour as Sky *directeur sportif*, when a middle-aged French lady pushed through the crowd and called to me. She explained that she was Monsieur Boucher's daughter. Sadly, he had passed away, but she thought he would be very pleased to see me there. Then she handed me the baguette she had made.

'Really? I didn't know that,' says John. 'Monsieur Boucher was a superstar. I think he was president of the ACBB. You couldn't get a more typical Frenchman; if he'd have come riding up the street in a stripy jersey with a string of onions round his neck you wouldn't bat an eyelid. Madame Boucher was a tough cookie, though. I used to ride past first and look through the window to see if she was in there minding the till. If she was, I'd come back later. If she wasn't there, we'd get a lot more for our ten francs. He loved the fact that I liked cooking and would talk me through all the different cuts. Sometimes, he'd get two stewing steaks and hide veal between them and wrap it up so his wife wouldn't know he was giving us the good stuff. I didn't even know what veal was. I'd get home, peel back the stewing steak and say, "What the hell is this pink stuff?"'

There isn't a lot of proper racing in France after the Tour finishes, so I came back home to see everybody and to try to see if I could get selected for the World Championship Road Race, which was going to be in Prague that August. There was a race called the Benedictine Grand

Prix around Market Harborough that cleverly preceded the Worlds by a couple of weeks and was designed to be over exactly the same distance, 187 kilometres. It was a horrible day, raining continuously, and there were dozens of punctures due to all the crap being washed out on to the road after a dry spell. I got away early on with a guy called Steve Wakefield and we rode together for over eighty miles. It was much longer than a normal British road race, and we were both tired, but he really hit the wall in the last twenty miles and told me he would have to sit on. Just as we got inside the final ten miles, I had a puncture. Despite a quick change, I thought that was my chance gone, but Steve realized that to attack when I'd been towing him would be a bit underhand and he sportingly just carried on riding. I managed to bridge back up to him with about three miles left, then got away in the last few minutes.

The GB team for the World Championships went to Switzerland to ride the William Tell Grand Prix as a final warm-up. Phil Thomas kept us amused. He was known as 'The Maggot' on the UK scene, a street-smart sort of character who was always ducking and diving. Every morning at the William Tell GP he would look at the route for that day's stage and say, 'If I can just haul myself over that climb, I reckon I could win this.' Needless to say it never panned out that way for him, but we admired his optimism, and it made us smile every day. I think I won the sprints jersey in Switzerland. It was a week I remember with a lot of fondness. Let me rephrase that: I remember hardly anything about it, but what I do remember, I remember with fondness.

The distance and pace of the Worlds was excruciating. Out of a six-man GB team, myself, John and Bob Downs finished in the bunch, but we hadn't been able to have any effect on the outcome, which was a win for a Russian guy in a two-man break. We were all talking about the next year's race which, unbelievably, was going to be in Sussex, wondering whether we'd get selected and if we'd be riding the amateurs' event or the pros' race. There's a picture in an old *Cycling* of John and me rolling over the line looking absolutely wasted. The caption reads, '"I was wrecked, and I mean wrecked," said Sean Yates.'

Heading back to Cannes towards the back end of the season for the Grand Prix des Nations, I knew I would be seeing Mickey Wiegand again as he lived down there, but also I was due to meet Maurice de Muer, boss of the Peugeot team. He had masterminded Luis Ocaña and Bernard Thévenet's Tour de France wins and was a big cheese, so I was on best behaviour. My 'sponsor', as they saw him, Stephen Roche, was having a stellar first professional season with Peugeot, winning the Paris–Nice stage race, and they were keen for me to join him. They offered me a two-year contract and I said yes.

My best result of the year came at the Grand Prix de France. After my sixth and second places over the last two years, I finally got the win I'd been pushing for. In 1981 it ran around the coastal town of Royan on the Gironde, north of Bordeaux. It seemed that for the whole back half of the year I was scrapping with Martial Gayant. He's now a *directeur sportif* at Française des Jeux, but in 1981 he was even younger than me and a really decent bike rider and time triallist. He beat me at Cannes in that year's Grand Prix des Nations, then I chased him down when he tried a lone break in the Paris–Connerre Classic and beat him in the sprint. The Grand Prix de France was the last big time-trial rendezvous of the season, so putting a minute into him there felt good. All in all I got sixteen victories during my year at ACBB, which I was very pleased with, and they seemed satisfied that they'd got some value out of me.

Peugeot started to ramp up a bit of publicity for my signing. I'd had some experience of being 'the next big thing' at ACBB, and it looked as though it was happening again. I went out to Munich for a medical and some tests after signing. It was the first time I'd done a ramp test, though far from the last, and I have to say I do them virtually for fun these days, especially as people take more notice of them. Anyway, if you don't know the concept of a ramp test, essentially you do it on a static bike with everything wired up to record your power output, heart rate, etc.; and you ramp up your effort step by step until you collapse. Right up my street. On this first occasion in Cologne, I got through the final two and a half flat-out minutes at a steady 550 watts, which they said were the best figures they'd seen since the heyday of Eddy Merckx. I felt pretty good, but then you find yourself looking at *l'Equipe* headlines like PEUGEOT SIGN NEW EDDY MERCKX and you start to feel a little bit queasy with the anticipation and pressure.

So our little apartment in Boulogne-Billancourt began to wind down. One legacy that I wasn't particularly proud of was the semi-circle of bleached dead grass at the bottom of the building below our third-floor balcony. For some obscure reason, but clearly related to my OCD tendencies and contrary nature, I had taken to having a wee off the balcony before going to bed every night instead of using the little bathroom. So much for the consummate gardener.

Jeff Williams was heading back to England, where he could make his willowy presence more acutely felt. It paid off: the following season he became National Road Race Champion and won one of his perennial National Hill Climb titles. John Herety had also landed a pro contract in France, but to be a sprinter with the Coop–Mercier squad rather than Peugeot, with the veteran Dutchman Joop Zoetemelk.

'I wouldn't have got my deal without Sean,' says John, kindly. 'No, it's true. I had strong interest in me specifically because of the amateur Classics I won that season, especially Paris–Rouen. I wouldn't have won any of them if Sean hadn't been riding for me. He would beast it on the front to keep it all together, then lead me out for the sprint.'

I'd assumed that if we were going to turn pro, we'd

both end up at Peugeot. That was what was meant to happen at ACBB.

'I wasn't keen on going to Peugeot as they had a few useful sprinters there already, and I wasn't sure I'd get a ride in any decent races,' explains John. 'Then I realized that Mickey Wiegand, who was a great wheeler-dealer, didn't want me to go to Peugeot either as he'd done a deal with Wolber that they could have a rider, so that sounded like a good idea. We went up to this big bike show in Paris, Le Salon du Cycle, to sign, but they tried to stitch me up with a lower figure than we'd agreed. New pros got a pittance anyway, so you didn't want to give any of it away. Claude Escalon marched off the Wolber stand, straight on to the Mercier stand and struck a deal with them on the spot. I didn't have anywhere to live, but the *directeur sportif* said that I could live in a flat above his family's bike shop in Tours. For free. "OK, I said, but can I bring Sean?" They liked that: it was a Cycles Peugeot dealership and they'd have a Peugeot professional living upstairs.'

John told me about the deal with Coop–Mercier and the flat in Tours. There was supposedly better training down there, decent weather and nice countryside around, so I decided to go with him. I couldn't let his cooking skills get away from me that easily.

Chapter Seven

Every time I had tried something new in cycling – every time I'd moved up a level – I'd won. My first junior road race, my first season time trialling, my first season road racing, my first go at the track, my first race with a French club . . . cycling seemed pretty simple.

Turning professional was not like that.

When I'd moved up from the UK scene to the French scene, I'd expected it to be a big step, but it wasn't. The racing was bigger in every way – bigger fields, bigger crowds, bigger prizes – but it wasn't any harder. I expected turning professional to be much the same. After all, the guys I'd be racing with and against had all been riding at the level I'd been at within the last few years.

I couldn't have been more wrong. I got an absolute hiding. Until that point, I'd been able to survive on my natural ability and strength. Within a few weeks at Peugeot, it became clear that would not be enough. The past few years of joyful constant overtraining began to catch up with me, and my health crumbled. I was constantly sick with something or other, lurching from race to race as an also-ran, overweight and out of my depth. There was no guidance; you got your race programme, turned up, got belted, went home. John and I had moved into this little place in Tours, which I liked, but we were far from the Peugeot *service course*, which was back up in Paris. The only guy on the team who lived anywhere near me was Roger Legeay, who was in Le Mans, whom I saw a couple of times, but he was still the best part of 100 kilometres away, and my French was still hopeless. That said, I doubt there would have been any more support if I'd been nearer; things just didn't work that way in those days.

It started badly when I showed up at the training camp feeling run down and spent five days in bed with flu. I'd gone to Paris and back for the team presentation from Victoria on the overnight bus, then we drove all the way down to the Med for our training camp, which left me drained, and I picked up a virus somewhere along the way. I'm sure I must have been ill at some point in my twenty-one years before that, but I can't remember it. I thought I was dying. A bit of a contrast to the year before, when I'd strutted around Saint-Tropez as a winner in my first race.

When I was a kid, I used to ride everywhere in the big ring, smashing around Sussex in 53 x 17, knowing no better. When I joined ACBB, I discovered that everybody trained on the small ring, spinning the gear round quicker to improve their pedalling suppleness and powers of recovery. Mickey Wiegand, on that first Côte d'Azur camp, had said to me, '*Yattez*, if you don't take the chain off that big ring, I will take the big ring off your bike.' Now, in the pro ranks, they were all on the big ring all the time, but spinning it as fast as the amateurs had spun the small one. Peugeot had these macho guys like Gilbert Duclos-Lasalle and Jacques Bossis laying it down all the time; every training session turned into a massive burn-up that invariably ended with me getting my head kicked in. I went to Het Volk and the Tour of Flanders and was totally out of my depth. It came down to a fairly unavoidable fact: I couldn't keep up.

The main reason I got in the team for those Belgian Classics was that the French guys hated racing outside of France. 'We hate Belgium. The food's shit, the roads are shit, the hotels are shit, the TV's shit,' was the general attitude. So much so that whenever we raced up in the north, we used to stay in a Novotel at Neuville-en-Ferrain, just across the border from Flanders in France. When it got to the actual race itself, the French riders would often climb off at the first feed station and hide behind the *soigneur*'s car as the *directeur sportif* drove past. At the end, they'd say, 'Damn it, somebody let a wheel go on that last climb; I was right in there until then, didn't you see me?' when they'd been sat in the *soigneur*'s car with the heater on listening to the radio for the last three hours. In the days before blanket TV coverage and race radios, you could get away with that.

It worked both ways. There would be absolutely no

plan, and very little teamwork. During a race, you might go back to the car to get something for somebody, or be asked to go on the front and chase a break down, but that would be as far as it went. It was every man for himself. At that first Het Volk in February, for instance, Graham Jones did a storming ride and got second. I had no idea: there was no plan for him to go for it, no plan for us to support him and nobody asked. I got to the finish absolutely out of my box and miles down expecting everybody else to be the same, and there was my teammate coming off the podium.

Up until then, I hadn't really thought much about riding in the wind. I'd been strong enough to ride up the outside of the bunch when I felt like it. Now I was in a bunch controlled by monsters like Hinault, Francesco Moser, Maertens and Kelly, and when the hammer went down, you were just clinging to the wheel in front. I'd be riding along with an experienced little guy on my left, sheltered from the wind by my size. We'd swing round a bend and the wind would be coming from the other side and, as if by magic, he'd be tucked in on my right, sheltered again. The further towards the back of the line you were, the longer the elastic when they accelerated out of a corner or over the top of a rise. You'd have to chase like crazy to stay on, then ram the brakes on as it concertinaed at the next corner. Repeat to fade.

The French v Belgian thing hasn't really changed that much today. The French riders go to the Belgian races because they have to if their team is on the World Tour, but they couldn't really give a shit; whereas it's everything to the Belgian guys. For the French riders, the Tour rules. Everything is geared to getting an entry to that and making a good showing there, and that hasn't changed.

Sean Kelly remembers those times: 'I spent the first couple of years of my pro career living in France too,' he says. 'I was in Besançon with the French half of the Flandria team, but then I moved to Belgium when I joined Splendor. It was just like that, the French moaning constantly about the Belgians. There weren't that many English speakers in the peloton at that time, so Yates and I used to chat quite a lot, especially in stage races. The first couple of hours used to be quite relaxed in those days and you'd have time to catch up. Not like now.'

The other thing that came as a bit of surprise was how ordinary the kit was. My Peugeot team bike was a bit of a clunker compared to Mick Coward's beautifully finished Emperor Sport frames, and my dad would have cried when he saw the prosaic cabling arrangements after he'd spent hours and hours in the shed filing and smoothing every entry point on my bikes. He even took my seatposts and cranks and milled them down until they were as thin as could be and as smooth as a baby's bum. For time trials, they didn't have special wheels, just normal road wheels. I used to take the fantastic 24-spoke hoops that Tony and Mick had given me that had served me so well on the Q10 and E72. The clothing was pretty nasty too.

We had thick jerseys and woollen shorts with a rock-hard lump of leather in them. At '34 Nomads we had Assos kit, which was absolutely cutting edge and would still be lovely to wear today. As the Peugeot shorts were plain black with their logo down the side, my girlfriend back in East Grinstead embroidered Peugeot on a couple of pairs of my Nomads shorts and I raced in them instead.

After my health picked up and I started training properly, I turned a bit of a corner. I was still too heavy – 84, or 85 kilograms – and I wasn't the star I'd been at the lower levels, but I put a couple of decent rides together. I even used the Emperor Sport wheels to win a couple of time trials, one in the Circuit de la Sarthe, and another one in the Tour d'Indre-et-Loire, regional French races that got good coverage over there. The team were pleased, but I was relieved that I'd signed a two-year contract, or my professional career might have been a much shorter affair.

I'd begun to find my niche in the team. While I wasn't winning races, I was able to get up there and make a difference. I was able to lead out our sprinter, Francis Castaing, a few times, and I got along well with Stephen Roche and Robert Millar. Our paths didn't cross as often as you might think, as they were in the A-Team and I was more often than not in the second string, but I seemed to fit in OK when I was called up. What looked like being a disastrous début season actually panned out into being a solid introduction to the professional ranks.

The deal that John Herety had signed with Coop–

Mercier included lodgings with the family of the *directeur sportif*, a very well-respected former star rider called Jean-Pierre Danguillaume. We lived over the family bike shop run by Jean-Pierre's parents, and his brother lived out the back. We had a room each and our own little kitchen, and shared a bathroom with the family. Peugeot were paying me £500 a month, which was plenty enough to live off, and certainly better than the previous year's scramble for *primes* to let us eat. I'd passed my test back in Sussex that winter and Uncle Michael bought me a car, a German Ford Taunus that we called 'The Charger', which was like a sort of souped-up Cortina, and I proceeded to smash it round Europe at a rate of knots. It was a V6 with sidepipes and it made a fearful roar. It sounded like a Spitfire. Everyone in Forest Row knew when I was home. It was even worse after I crashed it: coming home from France once I spun it on the Tonbridge Bypass and ripped a sidepipe off, so I was basically driving it with no exhaust after that. I put it back on with some toestraps, but it wasn't doing anything.

John has just reminded me that the first time the rest of the team had come into contact with The Charger was at the very start of the year. The older guys at Peugeot had this thing going on that the younger ones would have to drive down to Le Sud for the camp. As a result, Roger Legeay and Hubert Linard rocked up at the Danguillaume Cycles Peugeot dealership for a lift to the Côte d'Azur feeling all pleased with themselves. They soon changed their tune when they saw – or more than likely heard before they saw – The Charger rumbling up the street. But they couldn't back out as they'd be stranded in Tours. We shared the driving, but I'd wedged the driver's seat back as far as it could go and fixed it there. Not only was I a bit leggier than them, I had adopted my dad's driving style of being virtually horizontal. There are cars with back seats nearer to the steering wheel than The Charger's driver's seat was. Linard, a little guy in any walk of life, was driving when we came up to a *péage* station somewhere in Le Midi and he realized with horror at the last moment that he couldn't reach the clutch properly. His foot slipped off it and we shot past the astonished assistant who was leaning out of his little window with his hand out for the few francs we owed. 'Go, go, go!' I shouted and we sped off, never to be seen again.

In 1982, the World Championships were in England. The Worlds were still held in August then, and the track champs at the road races were staged in the same country. I was keen to become World Pursuit Champion, and set that as my target for the summer. John and I came home in June, while our respective A-teams prepared for the Tour de France, and I realized that my form wasn't so bad, after all. I won some local TTs in decent times and found out that there was indeed a gulf between being an amateur and a pro in France, as my condition was about the same as it had been the year before on home roads. It was the races that were harder. We both went off to do the Professional National Road Race Championships for the first time and ended up coming first and second, John pipping me in the sprint, which was probably lucky or he wouldn't have cooked dinner for me ever again.

'There was a massive rivalry between home riders and "foreigners" at all the races we did in Britain,' remembers John. 'It would be me, Sean, Graham Jones and Paul Sherwen against Keith Lambert, Sid Barras, Bill Nickson and the like. There would be loads of different jerseys but essentially only two teams.'

Peugeot had no real interest in me riding the World Pursuit for my country, but said they would pay for my bike, as a track bike wasn't part of our team-issue kit. I got a super-duper new low-profile track machine built by Cliff Shrubb, the legendary south London frame-builder. I've still got it in my loft. Even that small amount of Peugeot interest petered out, though, and I ended up paying for it myself. I set myself a massive workload for June and July to build the strength and speed I would need for the pursuit. I would ride a two-hour interval session in the morning, spend three hours on my old gardening round, do five hundred press-ups, then do another two hours of intervals. Brian Phillips was home from university and came with me on the interval rides. I bet he wished he hadn't. I was in that familiar full-on training mode, trying to crush everything in my path, and probably myself too. We'd come back over the forest with Brian crying. I remember the next year he told himself that he wouldn't go through that again and, when he got home from Cambridge for the summer, he decided to ride to Hastings and back flat-out every day to be ready for my return. He did it for a week before completely collapsing in exhaustion. By the time I arrived he looked like a ghost.

Halfway through the programme I went to Leicester for the National Championships, on the same track where the Worlds would be, and breezed through the Individual Pursuit to a gold medal, beating Tony Doyle in the final on my new 'funny bike' to please the intrigue-hungry cycling press. To be honest, although Tony and I would never be mates, all that Moscow stuff was well in the past as far as I was concerned. I just wanted to win, whoever I was up against, and I'm sure Tony felt the same.

I'd never felt so good. So, of course, I headed back to Forest Row and ramped it up a bit more. Slowly but surely I absolutely rode myself into the ground. By the time the Worlds arrived I might as well have been hitting myself in the face with a shovel. They were a complete disaster and I was furious with myself – not for over-training, which is what I should have been thinking, but for going so shit. I went out in the quarter-finals, absolutely running on empty. Doyley made it to the semis, but all the talk of an all-GB showdown in the final went up in smoke.

The World Championship Road Race was a week or so later, over really hard roads around Goodwood on the South Downs. It wasn't ideal for me as a course, but it's not every day you get to ride the Worlds in your own county and I knew there would be plenty of people there rooting for me.

During the week before the race I did three eight-hour training rides. Eight hours! Absolute grade-A insanity. The atmosphere at Goodwood was electric, as if everybody in the country who had ever ridden a bike was there on the roadside. It was muggy and hot, but the support was deafening, and I hauled myself up and down the Downs all day, seven hours of chasing and suffering, ignoring the beckoning delights of the pits on each lap. I finished too, down in 44th spot, as Beppe Saronni blasted past Greg LeMond on the last ascent by the racecourse to take the rainbow jersey back to Italy. That meant I had got through 1000 miles that week; a week that had started with me already exhausted after Leicester.

The next day I drove to Paris and flew to the start of the Tour de l'Avenir (the Tour of the Future), the under-23 Tour de France. Peugeot had a strong team supporting Robert Millar, and I'd been looking forward to it, but I was dead. Robert came second to Greg LeMond, but I wasn't there to help. I'd abandoned after a week in total exhaustion.

I flew back to Paris, where The Charger was waiting at Charles de Gaulle airport, forgetting to let the air out of my tyres before putting my bike on the plane. Needless to say, when I picked my bike up from the outsized luggage counter, both tyres had exploded in the unpressurized cargo hold. Miserable and too tired to even lift my arms up, I trudged to long-term parking and dumped it in the boot. The car was boiling, but the mechanism for winding the driver's window up and down was broken, so I pushed it down by hand and set out on the road to Tours, wishing I had a pair of matchsticks to force my eyes open.

On the *périphérique* I ran out of petrol. What a cock.

I got my pliers out of the pocket in the driver's door and set about hauling the glass back up to a closed position, as I'd been doing for months since the mechanism had bust. The glass chose that moment to shatter.

Leaving The Charger with the driver's window open to the world at large, I got the Peugeot out of the back with its flat tyres and rode on down the hard shoulder five kilometres to a bridge and clambered up to the road above. I found a garage and bought five litres of petrol and headed back to The Charger. When I got there, a carload of gendarmes were poking around it.

'*Ah, bonjour,*' I stammered, in the worst possible French accent I could muster, '*Pardonnez-moi, Anglais; non parlez français, monsieur.*' After putting my best blank look on to all the subsequent questions, they rolled their eyes and headed off with many references to English idiots that I understood only too well.

When I got back to Tours, after 250 kilometres with the window open, I collapsed into bed and slept for fifteen hours. I did the same the next day, and the day after that. I'd like to say that I learned my lesson about overtraining. I'd like to say it, but I can't, really.

John and I liked living in Tours and both of us were staying with our teams for the next year, so we decided to stay on with the Danguillaumes. They were fantastic to us, like so many families supporting cyclists across the years in France, Belgium and Holland. Truly wonderful people who would be pleased for you when you won, keep out of your way when you didn't, but always be there for you; a proper home from home. They took me to a scrapyard, for instance, and searched through all the wrecks until they found a new window for The Charger. Coming from such a stable and loving home environment I didn't really fully appreciate their support at the time, but I would have plenty of cause to miss them in years to come.

We would go to the phone box across the street to phone home. Once in a while the phone would go wrong and you could make calls for free. There would be a queue a mile long of locals banging on the glass while we took advantage for hours on end. Phil Anderson showed us a trick involving a coin and a bit of fishing line, like Top Cat, dropping the coin into the slot of the payphone then whisking it back out again. He phoned Australia about five times a week like that.

My tiny salary was enough to buy me a new car at the end of the year, which proves how cheap it was to live in those days and how little money I actually needed to survive in Tours. I upgraded to a French Renault 18 Turbo, which was the envy of Paul and Richard when I took it back to England.

I arrived back in France for my second year with Peugeot, confident that I had served my apprenticeship and was ready to make a real impact. It didn't go to plan. I was shit all year.

I limped back to England in the spring to try to find some form in domestic races and got a place in a strong Great Britain combined team for the Milk Race, the old Pro-Am Tour of Britain. Races like the Milk Race and the Peace Race tour of countries either side of the old Iron Curtain were unique to the Cold War period, as they were the best races that the nominally amateur Eastern Bloc riders could enter. Just as East Germans and Russians could dominate athletics championships off the back of secretive and dubious training methods, they could pitch up at the Milk Race with suspiciously bulging muscles and rip everybody apart. I did five hundred press-ups a day, but I didn't look like that. There was a muscle that stuck out behind their knees that we used to call the 'East German muscle'. It just didn't appear on other people's legs.

There was a British 1–2–3 in the prologue time trial. A prologue is as close as you can get in road cycling to a pursuit, so I guess it was more of a quirk than a surprise that the three fastest men were three survivors of that Moscow team pursuit quartet: Malcolm Elliott, me and Tony Doyle. On the next day I rode on the front into Bristol to try to keep it together for the dependable Sid Barras, who duly won the stage with a really hot sprint. As a result of my prologue the day before, I found myself in the yellow jersey drinking bottles of milk on the podium, which was a bit of a surprise. I contrived to lose it the next day with the combination of a crash and a puncture near the end, but kept pressing the whole race, and got some fun back into my racing.

Actually, the fun had started shortly before the Milk Race, with a time trial round the Isle of Wight. That was the sort of ride I used to do for fun, so to do it in a race was mouth-watering for me. I clocked two and a half hours for the circumnavigation and lopped 12 minutes off the course record. How many people had done it before then I don't know. If I lived on the Isle of Wight (I've had worse ideas) I'd probably do it once a week: no flat roads, few cars, open downland countryside . . . it was like those first days of bike riding. I remembered it two years after I retired, when I was in Mallorca. I rode round the island one day: 330 kilometres in 10 hours 45 minutes. I like that sort of thing.

The other standout event of 1983 was Allan Peiper joining the team. Allan was an Aussie who'd had a similar dislike of school to me; he too would rather be riding his bike than working out logarithms, and had paid his way to Belgium to race when he was 16. He'd been the year behind me at ACBB and was now making the same step up. We got on like a house on fire, and still do. He's on the management team at BMC now, which has given us plenty of time together over the last couple of years.

'Allan was a health fanatic,' John reminds us. 'He would say, "You've got to eat this," or "You should drink that." After he told us that garlic was good for us, Sean went out and bought a massive bulb of fresh garlic, cut it all up and ate it. Not a clove, a bulb. He reeked for days. His breath, his clothes . . . Christ, probably even his bike. When he opened the door to his room it was like somebody had let Clifford the Listerine Dragon out of his cave. Before he had discovered the mouthwash, obviously.'

Graham Watson was appearing around the scene then; he'd started taking pictures at European events around the same time as I'd begun riding them.

'At the 1983 Worlds in Switzerland I ran out of cash,' remembers Graham. It was a hand-to-mouth existence for both of us then. 'In those days there were no ATMs and I probably didn't have a credit card either. I grovelled over to the GB team hotel, found Sean, managed to get him alone and ask the humiliating question: "Can I borrow £200 to get home?" I paid him back the very next week, despite what he might tell you . . . That was a sign of what a genuinely nice lad he was. We were friends but not that close; he wasn't well off, and he trusted me enough to lend me what was quite a bit of money back then.'

That was after I'd given him the contents of my *musette* at Milan–San Remo.

'That's right, you did,' remembers Graham. 'Sean grabbed his feed-bag at the first feed, decided he wasn't hungry enough, and handed most of the contents to me on the *moto*, which I ate, as I was starving. The problem was, he blew up with hunger knock after the Turchino pass.'

Near the end of a long, hard year, I was slated to ride Paris–Brussels. The September Classic was still over 300 kilometres long back then. I packed my race kit into a rucksack, rolled my race bike out of Danguillaume Cycles, and rode into Tours to get on a train. By the time it finally pulled into the Gare Montparnasse it was getting dark and the rain was coming down in sheets. This was a bit of a miscalculation. The race began in Senlis . . . about 40 kilometres out the other side of Paris. Before I could even begin to head up the A1 in the dark and rain with no lights, I'd have to negotiate traversing the capital from one side to the other on a Saturday night. When I finally got to the hotel, dinner was long finished, the team talk complete and the guys readying themselves for bed before the following morning's start. When a drowned English rat arrived in their midst, there was a mixture of reactions: laughter, obviously; relief that I was OK; a certain amount of astonishment, as it had long been assumed that I wasn't coming; but most of all the sort of joyful surprise reserved for people dug out of the rubble of a tall building a week after an earthquake. And no, of course I didn't hear the end of it. I didn't figure on the podium of Paris–Brussels either.

Little else went right that year. I was certain that there would be no chance of a ride the following season, so much so that I'd been phoning round some of the UK-based teams to try to set something up at home. I suppose

I should have been panicking, but that wasn't really my style. I just kept bumbling along, not too bothered. *Que sera, sera* and all that.

It even got as far as me receiving the registered letter thanking me for my services, but that I wouldn't be required to rejoin the team for the following year.

I'm not sure what happened next, exactly. Stephen Roche must have put in a good word again; he was a star by then and Peugeot were trying to ward off other teams sniffing round him, and trying to keep him sweet. In the evenings at races, Roche and Pascal Simon always made a point of telling the management how much work I'd got through that day, which was useful because, as I said earlier, a *directeur sportif* in the eighties would often have no clue what was going on further up the road; he would just look at the result sheet at the end of the stage to find out who had finished where. One thing that worked out for me was that Maurice de Muer retired and his assistant Roland Berland took over, with Roger Legeay as his right-hand man. As newcomers to team management, I think they were worried about the older guard's 'player power', and wanted to bulk the squad with newer faces like Roche, Peiper, Millar and me to give themselves a bit more weight. Whatever the reason, and it certainly wasn't my results, they kept me on.

Chapter Eight

The 1984 season at Peugeot was all about Robert Millar, as he became the first British rider to ever win a classification at the Tour de France – the polka-dotted King of the Mountains jersey – and finished fourth, the best British placing until it was equalled by Brad in 2009 (and bettered by his historic win in 2012).

He also inadvertently made a big personal contribution to my career.

We were rooming together at the Midi Libre stage race, a Tour warm-up event, and he came back into the room one night and said, 'Fuck, that was hard today.'

It had been a flat stage, lots of headwinds and people driving hard on the front – the sort of day I liked. Robert had hung in and hung in, scrawny little so-and-so, 9 stone, wringing wet, and finished alongside me in the bunch. It dawned on me that if it had been a mountainous day and it had been me coming into our room in the evening saying, 'Fuck, that was hard today,' I would have finished an hour behind him. I'd always taken pride in my fitness and strength, but it wasn't until then that the penny dropped. It's good to have power, yes, but you can survive on the flat without quite as much power. In the mountains, it's all about weight or, to be more precise, lack of it. I needed to change.

It wasn't an easy thing to do. I'd taken up doing weights, press-ups and other gym work in 1979 when I got on the national track squad, looking to build my power for the pursuit at the Olympics. I started going to the King Centre in East Grinstead, getting free membership because I was on the team for Moscow. I worked with a guy called Tony York, who showed me all the different exercises and disciplines. Typically for me, I couldn't just do it by halves: I got obsessed with it. I cringe now to picture my 19-year-old self pulling bodybuilding poses in front of the mirror, checking out my biceps and thighs. I was a follower of Tom Platz, the chiselled and oiled Mr Universe, and used to marvel at how far he could push his body to get that ludicrous definition.

'There were never any porn mags in Sean's room in Boulogne-Billancourt,' says John Herety. 'Just body-building publications. I'll leave you to make your own mind up. To be fair, though, he was immensely strong. He would never miss the press-ups, no matter what. In four years of living together, I can't remember him ever missing a day, even if he'd just got back from a big race, or was sick, or whatever. In those first few months at ACBB, he became the archetypal gentle giant. Kevin

Reilly, who was with us then, was good company but did love to wind Sean up. I remember we had a wooden slatted table in the kitchen and he'd sit at it, stabbing at the gaps in the slats with a knife as hard as he could, the knife handle stopping the blade from piercing his legs by an inch. He would push Sean as far as he could, winding him up with comments, pushing and shoving until Sean would finally crack and go, 'Right, that's it,' and hold Kevin down on the floor with his immense arms, kneeling on him. Kevin would be going crazy, but Sean used to say, "Kevin, I am going to hold you down. Until. You. Calm. Down."'

I carried on right the way through until Robert's words, ironically complaining about how hard riding on the flat was, finally sunk in. He was paying a small price for having a little less power on the flat, but I was saddled with the equivalent of a crippling mortgage as soon as the road went upwards.

Robert was unique. I really admired him and always looked forward to the races I'd be doing with him, but he was a difficult bastard at times. I've just realized that I'm talking about him in the past tense, as if he's no longer with us. In a way, he isn't: he never enjoyed the attention of being in the public eye. He liked riding his bike, he liked winning bike races and he liked earning money through doing that, but he found the attention excruciating. He's reinvented himself and is living a new life somewhere today, beyond the gaze he hated so much, and I admire him for that, but I miss seeing him.

He was funny, not in a clowning-around-to-entertain-your-mates sort of way, but he always had a wry way of looking at things. He writes an occasional blog these days, which always makes me smile. I was reading a piece the other day that described an Italian rider as trying to find a bit of style but ending up with a pair of petrol-station sunglasses. That's pure Robert.

He could be incredibly tight, and astonishingly inventive when it came to ways of avoiding shelling out for things. On the *autoroute* he would know all the *péage* stations with dodges and cut-throughs, going so far as to find a gateway off the highway, nip through a field or two and come back out on to the blacktop on the far side of the pay booth. At Charles de Gaulle, if he was flying to a race, he'd leave his car in short-term parking for the duration. When he got back, he'd take a trolley from the rack, take it out into the street and push it up to the car-park entry barrier. The system would be fooled into thinking the trolley was a car and issue a ticket. As the first twenty minutes were free for dropping people off, he'd be in and out like a flash and not a centime down.

We had an expense system at Peugeot that paid you the equivalent of the appropriate train fare to get to races, then you sorted yourself out. Most of us chose to fly in order to arrive and return as fresh as possible. The exception was for team staff – it's easy to forget that the bikes, cars and trucks have to get to races too – who would always have to drive no matter where the race was in Europe. Robert lived near one of the team mechanics

Left: Me at the age of five in Epsom before the family moved down to Sussex.

Below: The Michael Hall school in Forest Row was an interesting place, but I just wanted to be outside all the time. I'm third from the left in the back row.

Bottom: Mum and Dad with the Yates clan: (left to right) my brother Chris, sisters Oriana and Ella, me and Conall.

Above: An early time trial with the Archer Road Club based in west London, where Bradley Wiggins would also later race.

Right: Dad spent hours in the shed filing and drilling my Emperor bike so that the cables could run internally. Not sure about the aerodynamic headgear.

Winning the East Grinstead road race on the Ashdown Forest in front of my watching mum, who is holding baby Ella. Note the trademark salute – V for Victory; F Off to anyone behind me.

Left and above: The individual pursuit in the 1979 Nationals at the Leicester track was when people started to sit up and take notice of me. I came second to Tony Doyle with Dave Akam (right) getting bronze.

Below: My mum has my race number from the Moscow Olympics on her wall at home. As the Official Handbook points out, I was both cyclist and gardener.

Official Handbook
of Great Britain's
Olympic Team

XXII Olympic Games
Moscow 1980

YATES Sean
Forest Row, Sussex
Born 18 May 1960. Gardener.
Height 6ft 1½in (187cm). Weight 12st 7lb (79kg)
Best performances: European Cup Pursuit 1979—2nd
National Pursuit Championship 1979—2nd

Left: Dad and me in the famous Peugeot gear after I turned pro.

Above: He took this photo of me in Paris in 1981 after I came second to Laurent Fignon in the Derny race that took place on the Champs-Elysées before the final stage of the Tour de France.

Celebrating in the traditional way on Blackpool promenade during the 1983 Milk Race. I won the sprint classification.

Left: I was leaner and lighter in 1984 than during my first two years at Peugeot. Here I am ascending the Muur at Het Volk.

Above: I also put in a good ride at Milan–San Remo that year. It must have been cold if I was wearing gloves.

Below: Riding the team time trial, with Allan Peiper on the front, during my first Tour de France in 1984. Robert Millar (hidden in fifth place here) won King of the Mountains for us, but those Peugeot headbands are best forgotten.

Left: More cycling fashion from the 1980s: Ray Ban Aviators. Bernard Hinault once told me that if I took them off, I might be able to see where I was going.

Above: I got a late call-up to the 1986 Tour, but still managed 12th in the prologue around the familiar streets of Boulogne-Billancourt.

It was a terrific race, and my last Tour in the Peugeot colours. Graham Watson took this shot on the Alpe d'Huez.

Above and left: Descending with the late Gerrie Knetemann during the 1987 Tour. I didn't crash many times, but when I did, I made a proper job of it, and frustratingly didn't make it to the end of the 27-stage race.

One of my best wins as a pro came after a 116-mile, five-hour solo break in the 1987 Nissan Classic Tour of Ireland, around the Ring of Kerry.

Above: Things got even better in 1988, with the race leader's *maillot blanc* in Paris–Nice after I disappeared up the road again ahead of Sean Kelly.

Above: That win in Saint-Etienne was followed by one in Jaca during the Vuelta a España, when I outsprinted my breakaway partner Deno Davie for my first Grand Tour stage.

Then came the Tour de France, and a stage win in the individual time trial from Liévin to Wasquehal. I covered the 52 kilometres at an average speed of 49.237 kph, which is still a record for the Tour without tri-bars.

and would bung him a few francs to get picked up, then sleep in the back seat all the way there and all the way back, trousering the expenses.

It was not a malicious meanness, though. After that Tour de France in '84, he was massively in demand on the lucrative *kermesse* circuit around France, Belgium and the Netherlands, and could command a decent fee to turn up and race in the King of the Mountains jersey he'd won. However, he insisted on bringing Allan and myself to all those races and negotiated an appearance fee for his sidekicks that far outweighed our solo value to the promoters. I doubled my annual salary in the four weeks after the Tour thanks to Robert's thoughtfulness.

His humour was cutting and often spilled into rudeness. Once in a hotel in Spain, after a horrible long transfer in the cars in grubby race kit following a stage, we were treated to one of the poorest meals you could imagine. It was stewed pasta with no suggestion of sauce or any other discernible addition, a surprisingly common hurdle in the 1980s. After the waiter had plonked the sorry-looking plates in front of us, Robert raised his hand to attract his attention and said, 'Excuse me, could you please bring some taste?'

People in service jobs would rarely get more than a mumble, and eye contact was to be avoided at all costs. Allan once launched into him after he was rude to one of the check-in staff at Gatwick airport, promising him a thump if he ever spoke to somebody like that again, which caused a bit of a scene.

The Tour in 1984 was my first. I had begun the year a lot better and the team had forgotten all about dropping me the autumn before. Ironically, after it had been his cajoling that had brought me back in, Stephen Roche had left and gone on to La Redoute, where he would be Paul Sherwen's leader for the Tour. Our leader at Peugeot was Pascal Simon, with Robert our wildcard. Pascal had crashed out of the race in 1983 while wearing the yellow jersey, so his leadership was well earned, but we knew Robert's climbing ability spread genuine fear amongst the favourites. He'd won the stage to Luchon the previous year that had put Pascal into yellow, so he was no débutante.

I had started 1984 leaner and lighter than the first two years at Peugeot and had turned in good rides at a freezing and wet 294 kilometres Milan–San Remo and the Tour de Vendée. I'd got my biggest win on the Continent so far by winning the prologue at the Four Days of Dunkirk, beating Eric Vanderaerden and Bernard Hinault and taking the leader's jersey. Sean Kelly was the dominant rider in the Northern Classics back then by a country mile, and the French papers started calling me '*L'autre Sean*'.

I also won again on my favourite old stamping ground of the Isle of Wight. This time, it was a road race, a couple of laps of the whole island then a hard finishing circuit. Allan was on a lone break for most of the day – I remember the weather being gorgeous, and massive holiday crowds in June – but got caught when we got on to the smaller finishing circuits. I got away with Bill Nickson, and we bickered a bit about attacking each other, meaning we nearly got caught. I beat him in a photo-finish, close enough that neither of us knew who had won.

Allan won the Tour of Sweden with a storming ride in the closing time trial, and I was third overall, which clinched both of our places for what would be the first Tour de France either of us had ridden. We were similar riders: strong testers who could pull a bunch along if necessary, making us useful in the big stage races. Those time-trialling skills came out of the bag early in that Tour when I finished fifth in the prologue. I was one spot behind Phil Anderson, who was at Panasonic by then, but two behind Allan, making it a great start for the 'Anglos', as the French used to call the English-speakers, who were starting to make more and more of an impact on their race.

Bernard Hinault won, setting up a duel with my old half-wheeling buddy Laurent Fignon. Hinault was on the comeback trail and trying to win a fifth Tour. Fignon had won it the year before at the age of 22. He hadn't even been meant to ride, having helped his master Hinault win the Tour of Spain already, which was in May in those days. When it was clear Hinault wasn't going to be able to start, Renault drafted Fignon in for the experience and he ended up running off with the yellow jersey. Shunned in the aftermath by Renault in favour of his upstart teammate, Hinault was back with his own team, La Vie Claire, and bent on revenge.

It wasn't to be. It turned into one of the most one-sided Tours in modern history as Fignon put ten minutes into his former leader over the next three weeks, and more into the third-placed Greg LeMond who, like me, was riding his first Tour.

I had another top-ten on the first stage into Saint-Denis, but after that it was largely a story of survival, with a bit of trying to look after Robert and Pascal Simon. There was one unbelievably long stage from Nantes to Bordeaux, all the way down the west coast. Those who have driven down to the Landes or the Dordogne for family camping holidays will know that it is a hell of a long way – a real are-we-there-yet-Dad? day in the car. But on a bike, in a 35° July furnace, it was ridiculous: 333 kilometres was the official distance, and it was run off, or rather strolled off, at the leisurely pace of 33 kph. Any slower and we'd still be out there. The peloton treated it as something of a day off, looking to save themselves for the hard mountain days ahead, and there were all sorts of high jinks and tomfoolery. People were taking drinks off people at the side of the road, starting with water and Coke, then beer and wine, then they were pinching spectators' hats to wear. Somebody even took a camera off a guy and started taking snaps and passing it round.

The only proper Pyrenean stage was in Ariège, a truly beautiful part of France and not overrun with tourists and neon signs like a lot of the Alpine roads. We went over the Col de Portet d'Aspet, the Col de la Core, the Col de Latrape and, finally, the steep finish up to the ski-station at Guzet-Neige. The *autobus* of non-climbers formed after the first climb was out of the way as the big names fought for position ahead of us. It was the first mountain stage, so there was a nervous atmosphere. I just knuckled down and made sure that I was going to finish inside the time limit and survive to fight another day. Up the road, Robert was attacking the small group he'd driven clear at the front of the race and holding off chases by Lucho Herrera and Pedro Delgado to claim a fantastic stage victory. He'd keep Delgado at bay all the way through the Alps too, wearing that King of the Mountains jersey for Britain, or for Scotland, as he would rather have it. Only Fignon, Hinault and LeMond were ahead of him on the general classification when we reached the Champs-Elysées.

I was 91st in Paris, and pretty pleased with the way things had gone. We'd finished with two riders in the top ten – Pascal Simon was seventh – won a stage and a jersey through Robert, and I'd made it round. What's more, I had bragging rights over Allan, who'd ended up five places below me. The three of us headed off on our month-long odyssey of criteriums and *kermesses* in good spirits.

We ended up doing thirty races after that Tour, driving somewhere every day – wherever the race was – then back to Allan's in Belgium. Including the Tour, we had raced for fifty days in a row. Ridiculous. I expected the hardest part to be the travel between the races, and that wasn't easy, but the races themselves were much faster than I had imagined. While it was true that a lot of post-Tour crits and *kermesses* had their results fixed to favour a local hero or a star rider, there were also a whole bunch of hungry local riders eager to make a name for themselves by giving the pro cyclists a really hard time. In this never-ending purgatory of racing, the three of us would be in the dressing room of some little provincial sports stadium, with our heads between our knees, having driven hundreds of kilometres to be there, and there would be forty wild-eyed blokes bouncing off the walls all around us. You had to finish to get your appearance money, otherwise the whole exercise would be wasted, so we had no choice other than to suck up the pain and just keep going.

Jan Raas was the king of the criteriums in Holland. As a former world champion and serial winner of sprints in the biggest races, he held maximum respect and nobody moved without his say-so. His legs were notched, veiny, bulging and leaner than anything else I'd seen, and he was a figure of great admiration for me. I remember a young rider called Teun van Vliet, who would become a friend later, going up to Jan in the changing room before a *kermesse* with his hand up like a schoolkid.

'Please, Jan, can I win today? Please?'

'*Flikker op.*'

I'll let you make your own translation.

Our odyssey took us back to Britain for a few events,

as there was a good August series of city-centre races sponsored by Kellogg's that attracted some decent riders and some good racing. I won the Bristol round, giving me my third victory of the season – it also took the pressure off for the rest of the year as Peugeot renewed my contract for the following year.

That didn't turn out to be Peugeot's most inspired decision, as I was hopeless in 1985. I didn't win a single race. In retrospect, it wasn't dissimilar to 1983: I'd finished the previous season absolutely destroyed and never really recovered. The whole team was beginning to crumble, with Roland Berland carrying the can for the squad's poor performance. It wasn't all his fault, but he didn't cover himself in glory as a *directeur sportif*.

We went to Spain to do the Vuelta a España (my first), and Robert was inspired. He forced himself into the leader's jersey with some sublime climbing and astute thinking. We protected his narrow lead over the last ten days of the race by burying ourselves on the front every day to keep things together while Spanish teams did all they could to wrest back control from the French and the little Scottish guy with the earring. The only riders within striking distance of him as we reached the penultimate stage, in the mountains above Madrid, were Pacho Rodriguez and Pello Ruiz Cabestany. There were three climbs that day and Robert sensibly glued himself to Rodriguez's wheel. As the climbers shot away I was stranded in the *autobus*. With the day gone up the road in front of me and only the ceremonial circuits of Madrid to come tomorrow, I climbed off, exhausted, ten days on the front, job done.

Robert punctured at the bottom of the last climb, but chased his way back on over the top. As a result, Cabestany shook his hand and congratulated him on his forthcoming victory.

What none of the other riders in that sizeable group told him was that Pedro Delgado and José Recio had attacked. Delgado, good as he was, had begun the day over six minutes behind Robert and as such wasn't a serious threat. However, the covert cooperation of the Spanish teams at the front of the field and the race organization, who withheld the usual time-gap information and announcements on the race radio, allowed the two compatriots to build up a seven-minute lead.

By the time Robert realized what had happened, he was isolated and without help. Berland tried to muster support for a chase from other teams, but there were only 20 kilometres to go. Nobody wanted to assist: Berland had not only been sloppy in not paying attention on the day, he'd made the cardinal sin of riling many of the other teams earlier in the race with what they perceived to be French arrogance, declaring that Peugeot needed help from nobody and would win the race in any eventuality. That was the main reason we'd had to reel in attack after attack unassisted for the previous week and a half.

It went down in history as 'The Stolen Vuelta'. Robert finished second in Madrid, leaving few in any doubt that most of the blame was to be laid squarely at Berland's door. That pretty much set the tone for the rest of the year.

The Tour was horrible. Morale was really low. I didn't feel able to contribute anything, which was very disappointing. Robert had great legs, but wasn't really over the mess of Spain, and the team just wasn't in the right frame of mind. After not doing anything of note in the Alps, which came first that year, Phil Liggett asked him about his chances in the Pyrenees and whether he would get more support from his Peugeot team than he had received in the Alps.

'What team?' asked Robert. 'I can only rely on Sean Yates and Allan Peiper; the rest don't even think about me.'

It was kind of him to single us out, and of course we helped him whenever we could, but, frankly, when he needed us most, in the mountains, we were nowhere.

I made it to Paris without troubling the judges at any of the stage finishes, and you could have measured the gap between me and Bernard Hinault, the winner, with a calendar instead of a stopwatch.

1985 was my first year in France without John Herety. He'd headed back to the UK after his three years at Coop–Mercier and would ride as one of the most feared domestic riders for the rest of his career. Of course, that also meant saying goodbye to the Danguillaumes and Tours as well, which was just as hard. Graham Jones was also beginning to relocate his career in the UK, so there was a space at the Lille apartment he shared with Paul Sherwen. I headed north.

Lille was, if I'm being honest, a bit of a shithole. I woke up one day to find my pride and joy, the Renault 18 Turbo, sitting neatly on four piles of bricks in the street, the wheels removed by some local low-life types. The flat with Paul was fun, though; he was the consummate pro, knew all the ducks and dives to make life sweet. I also started to spend a lot more time with a guy called Dag Otto Lauritzen. He had a place in Lille too, and I flitted between the two homes.

Despite being a few years older than me, Dag Otto had only just turned professional. He arrived off the back of a bronze medal in the Los Angeles Olympic Road Race. He'd come to cycling late after an incident-packed early life in Norway, where, as a member of the Norwegian army's crack Hærens Jegerkommando unit, he'd broken his leg in a parachuting accident. Going stir-crazy during his rehabilitation, he'd walked 50 kilometres from his home in Grimstad along the coast to Kristiansand on crutches, just for something to do. He transferred from the army to the police to continue his recovery and took up cycling to regain his fitness. Typically of him, he became Scandinavian Amateur Road Race Champion a year or two later.

I first met Dag Otto at our pre-season medical. We hit it off immediately as part of the non-French clique, with Robert and Allan. He confided in me that he had a problem and it was to do with his age.

'Hey, Sean, I've got a dilemma,' he said, grimacing. 'I told the team when I signed my contract that I was twenty-four.'

That was my age at that time. I was fairly sure Dag Otto was older than me; I couldn't work out how he'd had time to be jumping out of aeroplanes, arresting criminals or riding the Olympics otherwise. 'How old are you really?' I asked.

'Twenty-eight.'

I don't know how he sorted it out, but he managed it.

'Sean took care of me, even though I was older than him,' says Dag Otto now. 'It was all new to me. I was a good bike rider, but I was a Norwegian policeman; I knew nothing about how cycling worked, you know? He was about the only guy I knew in the peloton when I turned pro, because I'd been at ACBB and shared with his brother Chris.

'Sean, Allan and I used to train together. Allan had a car that he'd won at a race, I think, and he'd left it in Lille with us then gone off racing with the team. Sean and I set out in the car with our bikes in our cycling kit to drive to Allan's place in Belgium, where we were going to drop it off then ride back for training. Chatting away on one of the speed-restricted bits of the Lille *périphérique,* I wasn't concentrating and we got pulled over for speeding. The gendarme asked for my licence. Of course, in cycling kit, I didn't have it, nor my passport, nor any other ID. Neither did Sean. He was asked for the car documents and we said we didn't have them as it belonged to somebody else. Then he wanted to know the address it was registered to, but we said we didn't know, as it had French plates and Allan lived in Belgium. What a mess. It took hours of pleading. In the end I got a summons for doing 116 kph in a 60-kph zone, but not even that was simple, as I was in Norway and missed the court date. I think I'm still paying the fines off.'

My forgettable year came to a close at Paris–Brussels in September. I made my way to the team hotel for the start of the autumn Classic the day before the race, getting there a bit earlier than I had two years before, and not quite as wet. I was met by a confused-looking Roger Legeay, who was now running the team after Berland's unceremonious fall from grace.

'What the hell are you doing here?' he asked me.

'What am I doing here? Paris–Brussels, aren't I?'

'No, Sean, you're not meant to be here. You're not on the list.'

In those days, before emails and mobile phones, the team used to communicate mainly through the post. What with being on the road all the time, dividing my time between Paul Sherwen's place, Dag Otto's flat and Forest Row, not to mention the vagaries of the *poste*, I'd had nothing to tell me any different since my original programme had been set months earlier. I was pissed off, but more with the situation and the general tone of such a shitty season than anyone in particular. Roger was an old friend by then and he had always looked out for me. I could tell he really felt for me as I stood there crestfallen on the hotel steps. I took a deep breath and seized the moment.

'So what about next year, then?' I asked him.

'What about next year?'

'Well, have I got a deal? Can I have a ride?'

If ever anybody was going to take pity on me it was Roger right there and then. He gave me a long look, a sigh, and a proper Gallic shrug. 'Go on, then. Why not. Now go home.'

Saved by the bell again.

The 1986 Peugeot line-up was a sorry shadow of former years. The famous Foreign Legion was well and truly dismantled by then: Phil Anderson was leading Panasonic; Stephen Roche had taken his La Redoute jersey on to the Tour de France podium on the Champs-Elysées; Graham Jones was back in England after a couple of years at other French teams; and Robert and Allan were off to join Anderson at Panasonic. It was just me left from the ACBB Anglo production line.

I didn't have a bad year in terms of form and showing, my health was good, but not often having a leader to work for took the sting out of my usefulness. My only win of the year was a stage of the Milk Race in Newton Aycliffe up in County Durham. I took a bit of stick around that time from British cycling fans for saying something silly about wins in UK races 'not counting'. Actually, I always enjoyed racing here; it was just that the team tended to not be bothered about results in British events. What I remember most about that Milk Race was that it was sponsored by Ambrosia creamed rice and they were giving tubs of it away at every stage. I loved it and started grabbing as many as I could every day. By the time I got back to France my suitcase was absolutely bulging with the stuff.

I had been going all right through the spring without setting the world alight, but the team had been a bit rudderless: Francis Castaing wasn't there for the sprints any more, and Pascal was past his best. Roger was struggling manfully with a crotchety, ageing team, and results were few and far between. As part of our Tour warm-up, I did the Tour d'Armorique, and rode into a bit of form, taking the sprints jersey. Of more importance for the team, though, was a crash for Jérôme Simon, Pascal's younger brother, who was lined up to be in the team for the Tour. He banged his wrist, but it looked like it wasn't serious and he would be fine for the big one.

With a few days to go before the start of the Tour, we headed straight to the Le Mans motor-racing circuit to train for the Tour's team time trial. This was a piece of progressive thinking by Roger. Recce'ing individual stages and practising for specific events was virtually unheard of in the 1980s, in stark contrast to today's approach of leaving no stone unturned in pursuit of marginal gains. Iffy form meant I wasn't in the team for the Tour, but I was first reserve, so was part of the training group. This meant a pretty boring and hard day's work for me, as I had to sit on the back of the line while the team lapped the circuit getting their changes right and judging their speed. After a few laps I pulled off into the pits and got changed. Our veteran *soigneur*, Michel de Coq, gave me a lift to Paris, and I flew back to Forest Row.

It was beautiful end-of-June weather and it was great to see the forest in full bloom after being away for months. I took a stroll down the lane from Mum and Dad's, across the main road into Michael Hall, and walked through the lovely grounds remembering all the fun and games I'd had there as a boy. I walked all the way up to the top lake. There was nobody about. I stripped off for a swim. Fantastic. I'd done a few laps when I heard somebody come panting up the hill. I stopped to see who it was. Not the first person I'd expected to see, it turned out. It was Mum.

'Sean, you have to come back, you've had a phone call.'

We must have had a phone line put in by then.

'What is it, Mum?' I asked, fearing the worst.

'It was a man from Peugeot. They need you to come and ride the Tour de France.'

Jérôme Simon's wrist was worse than originally thought and he wouldn't be able to ride. I ran back down the hill, packed, and flew straight back to Paris.

The prologue in 1986 was actually around the streets of Boulogne-Billancourt. Knowing people in the area was handy and we were able to warm up on the rollers at the house of an ACBB guy who lived near the start. Dag Otto was really up for it and had got hold of some oxygen from somewhere, and was training in this guy's garage with an oxygen mask on, while the rest of us took the piss out of him. A fat lot of good it did him: he finished 130th. Even in training, it had a total reverse effect: ten minutes after the event he was flat on his back in the garden hyperventilating, with the rest of us killing ourselves laughing. 'I thought I was going to die,' remembers Dag Otto.

With no pressure and no expectation I rode to a tidy 12th spot behind Thierry Marie, who was flying the modernity flag with an aero lid and a saddle shaped into a fairing on his lo-pro time-trial bike.

I think this was the last Tour before they restricted the number of entrants. There were twenty-one teams of ten men apiece. The early hours of the race weren't as frantic as they are now and there was less road furniture – sleeping policemen, central bollards, chicanes – but there were also no radios for your *directeur sportif* to tell you to look out for corners, obstacles and dangers either. I remember the first bonification sprint at Saint-Quentin on the opening stage: 210 guys all trying to win it on a narrow street. Needless to say, the first week was littered with crashes. *Plus ça change*. After that, they limited the field to two hundred and cut teams to nine members. There's talk now about cutting it to eight, with the desired effect being to make it harder for any one team to control the race. I wouldn't have a problem with that, as it ought to make it less congested too, but the powers that be will probably use the extra space generated in the field to invite another team or two to ride.

Away from Peugeot, it was a terrific race, one of the great Tours de France. Bernard Hinault, after promising to help Greg LeMond, his young American teammate who had worked tirelessly for him as he took his fifth Tour in the previous edition, instead attacked his protégé and claimed the yellow jersey early in the race.

Hinault was an incredibly imposing character, the last true *patron* of the peloton; the boss. Since 'The Badger' retired there have been plenty of strong riders who've commanded the respect of their fellow professionals, but nobody so clearly in charge. Sean Kelly was a huge leader, but in a quieter way – and he didn't impose himself on the other riders, more on the race. Greg LeMond was too much of an outsider to wield true influence. Miguel Indurain was very easy-going and let events take care of themselves. Lance would have liked to take charge and often did, but he wasn't well liked enough to have more than grudging obedience. Mario Cipollini always asked – and received – a lot from his teammates. Marco Pantani was an enigma. Johan Museeuw was probably the most popular amongst the other riders by the time I retired and was something of a *patron* for the northern races, but he either chose not to ride or carried less influence in the big tours. It's in those three-week races that this influence comes into play, as the race develops day by day and the characters in the soap opera develop.

Bernard Hinault used to ride in the front line all day in 53 x 13, a massive gear, just staring at everybody around him, daring them to attack. He would make it clear that it was to the benefit of everybody to take it easy, unless it was him that wanted to attack, of course. In those days before energy gels, riders used to carry *la topette*, a little pot in their jersey with a double shot of sugary espresso for a boost in the finale. I remember Hinault taking his out of his jersey pocket and holding it up in the air, saying, 'If anybody attacks this morning, I'll take this, and then you'll see what happens!'

In a massive mountain stage the year before, 270 kilometres from Morzine to Lans-en-Vercors, across many Alpine passes that would be a hellish day of survival for most of us, Joël Pelier attacked on the first climb. Hinault was furious, bridged straight across the gap and told him in no uncertain terms to get back where he belonged.

In that same race, I think, I had taken to wearing Ray Ban sunglasses. Oakleys were yet to become *de rigueur* in the bunch, and the Ray Ban Aviators were popular because you could bend the wire hook behind your ear to hold them on down a bumpy descent. As we came into a stage finish, I think it was Nancy, I found myself shoulder to shoulder with Hinault and there was a slight coming together. 'Take your glasses off, Yates, you might be able to see where you're going!'

During that Tour in 1986, Hinault attacked on the Tourmalet while wearing the yellow jersey. It was pure madness. LeMond couldn't attack him; Hinault was his leader, and five minutes already separated them on general classification. Nobody else carried too much of a threat and La Vie Claire were strong enough to see off any surprise challengers. That stage was a monster: after the Tourmalet, we went over the Col d'Aspin, the Col de Peyresourde and then up the steep climb to the ski-station at Superbagnères. At one point on the Aspin, Hinault was nearly ten minutes ahead of LeMond over-all, but he was tiring after attacking so early, and a group of chasers, including the American, caught him on the Peyresourde.

Superbagnères is one of my least favourite climbs in cycling – steep, relentless, long, straight sections rather than hairpins interspersed with respite – and it always seems to come at the end of a long hard day. I remember going up it on another occasion, a long way behind Robert Millar in 1989 when he was winning his last Tour de France stage. On that day in '86, Hinault blew a gasket and LeMond took back nearly all the time he'd lost to the champion in the preceding days without ever actually attacking him. He just followed the moves of others. Considering Hinault's renown for being one step ahead of the opposition, in my opinion that day saw one of the daftest pieces of riding in history by a man who won five Tours de France. He had the sixth in the bag, the reputation of the greatest rider of all time sealed in perpetuity, his already-announced retirement from the sport set to be marked with a glorious bookend. But no. In his overarching desire to show the young upstart who was boss, Hinault revealed his feet of clay. If you look up hubris in the encyclopedia, you'll find a picture of Bernard Hinault in 1986.

The talk of the race was the split in the La Vie Claire team. Hinault and his French foot-soldiers would sit on one table at dinner, LeMond, Steve Bauer and Andy Hampsten on another. No words were exchanged.

LeMond took the yellow jersey decisively in the Alps and kept it. By the time we reached the crowning stage on Alpe d'Huez it was pretty much done and dusted and the two outstanding riders of that year's race rode clear together, Hinault all friendly with LeMond and making out it had all been part of his grand plan all along. My uncle Michael had come out to see me and cheer me on. He told me later that when the duo rode past, minutes clear of everybody else, they were laughing and joking, somewhat in contrast to me an hour or so later, fighting the bike like it was made of pig iron, tongue hanging out, desperate for the line.

Three days later, after completing a hilly stage that finished on the Puy de Dôme, I snuck out of the Peugeot hotel after dinner and found my way to the hotel that the Fagor team were staying in that night. There I had a clandestine meeting arranged with the *directeur sportif*, Pierre Bazzo. My old friend Jean-René Bernedeau was one of the established riders there and had been pleading with Bazzo to sign me. He told me that he'd cornered Bazzo and said, 'Boss, we have to sign Yates. He's unhappy at Peugeot, he's going nowhere there, they're no good for him. He can pull the whole peloton along on his own.'

'*Yattez? Il ne passe pas un pont!*' replied Bazzo

dismissively. That translates as 'he can't climb a bridge!'

Bazzo must have relented, because I found myself creeping back into the Peugeot hotel with a scrap of paper bearing Bazzo's signature indicating that we had a deal for 1987. Literally, a scrap of paper; a napkin or something. It was going to be more money, more responsibility, and Fagor had convinced me that they were the French team on the rise, while Peugeot disappeared towards the plughole.

On the Champs-Elysées a couple of days later, Peugeot had hired a ballroom in one of the large old hotels lining the boulevard for a reception to celebrate the team's completion of the Tour. All the suits from Peugeot were there, as well as the team hierarchy, assorted helpers, staff and hangers-on, and some skinny, exhausted, sun-browned cyclists. The boss of Peugeot got up to make a speech to the assembled motley crew and picked that precise moment to drop the bombshell that the team would not be continuing beyond that current season. Nobody could remember a time when there hadn't been cyclists in the peloton wearing that distinctive white chequered jersey. There was a massive sense of disappointment in the room, and disbelief that they would choose this of all moments to make such a crushing announcement.

'It was probably my worst moment in cycling,' remembers Dag Otto. 'We hadn't won any stages, but we had worked hard and slogged all round the Tour representing the team – we were proud to finish. And then

that. Jesus. Couldn't they have at least given us a week
or something?'

I kept very quiet and checked my pocket to make sure
I still had the napkin with Pierre Bazzo's signature on it.

Chapter Nine

Though I'd been a professional cyclist for five years, it had always been with one team, a slowly evolving unit of riders, management and staff. Moving to Fagor demonstrated that not every team works in the same way. In fact, it demonstrated that not every team works, full stop.

Lille hadn't been ideal. I didn't really like the city and the surrounding areas were more bracelets of factories and villages straggling along main roads than genuine countryside. There was also the ridiculous France v Belgium situation, where people from either side of the border would refuse to cross over unless absolutely necessary, whereas to an English visitor the countries were interchangeable in practical terms. It was just silly.

Getting to races was tricky, as it was a two-and-a-half-hour drive to Charles de Gaulle on a good day. In rush hour, you could forget it.

I decided to go back to England and commute from there. Having a little bit more cash in my pocket helped, and it was great to spend more time with my friends and family. Conall and Oriana had come along to join me, Chris, Ella and Mum and Dad, so there was loads to do around the place and I was very happy. I could get dropped off at Gatwick within half an hour of Forest Row and head anywhere I was needed.

Fagor was a peculiar set-up. The sponsors were – still are – washing-machine manufacturers. They were based in the industrial heartlands of the Basque Country, near San Sebastián, but their market was mainly France, and the team reflected that. Pierre Bazzo didn't seem to have much of a clue, not remembering where we were sometimes, not knowing what races were coming up, and his team talks were either baffling or non-existent. Fagor had plenty of cash but no obvious direction, and the absence of a leader for the biggest races was glaringly obvious.

At Peugeot there had always been a real sense of pro-fessionalism – at the *service course* and out on the road – that came of being such a longstanding proud team. The mechanics at Fagor were gleefully free of that kind of responsibility. There were never enough wheels and the ones we had were shocking: I could break a spoke just by sitting on my bike. I ended up bringing my own wheels from home.

One day I was discussing gears with one of the mechanics, asking for a 23-tooth sprocket to be fitted for the next day's stage. 'You don't need a 23 tomorrow, you'll be fine on a 21,' he said.

'OK . . . Have you actually been up these roads before, then?'

'Er . . . no.'

'Let me ask you a different question, then: have you got enough 23-sprockets to go round?'

'Ah. No.'

That'll be the reason, then.

I liked the riders there, though. Jean-René was there, of course, plus another Frenchman called Eric Caritoux, who was a really nice guy. Johnny Weltz, whom I would run into again later in our careers, had just arrived from Denmark as a new pro, and the Irishman Martin Earley was with us.

My happiness at the new lifestyle and a feeling of freedom at the new team had an early effect: I had my best road-race victory as a professional to date at the Grand Prix de Cannes. It was a decent race that looped the low mountains behind the Riviera before a finish in the middle of the town. Kelly and Fignon had both won it in recent editions, so it was worth winning. It's defunct now, which is a shame, a victim of the globalization of the early season races as teams go further afield in search of good weather and richer start money. I knew I was going well, as I'd managed to get third behind Eddy Planckaert and Kelly in a bunch sprint during Paris–Nice, and I'd ridden well without getting anything. I got in a break at Cannes, with a few guys including Yvon Madiot and Kim Andersen, who'd both won it before. I drove up the last big climb at my own pace rather than trying to match the changes of speed, and Madiot jumped me near the top. He should have gone sooner, for there was enough time for me to catch him on the descent, pass him and time trial to the finish alone. My first continental road win in six years of professional cycling.

Throughout 1987 I continued to drop weight. I just thought a bit more about what I was eating, especially at races. I'd always eaten what I wanted during stage races, finishing off race food after stages, during transfers, and at the hotel before dinner. Now I began to wait until the evening and ate properly at dinner. I rode my first Giro d'Italia and the pounds dropped off through the race. It was a crazy race, though. Stephen Roche was locked in battle with his teammate Roberto Visentini in a war that ripped their Italian Carrera team apart in a similar way to Hinault and LeMond at La Vie Claire the year before.

At the Giro, though, it was open hostility rather than the phoney war of Bernard v Greg. Visentini was the defending champion and had the lead at the start, then Stephen took it off him, then Visentini put time into him in the San Marino time trial to regain the lead.

Fagor didn't have a leader as such – we were just hanging in, looking for breaks and opportunities. We had a right result in the first week when Jean-Claude Bagot won the first mountain stage, taking the pressure off us. All hell broke loose on a mountain stage that finished up on the Austrian border when Stephen bridged across to a break and refused to obey team orders instructing him to wait for Visentini. Virtually the whole Carrera squad got on the front to chase down their own man. Back down the line we were breathing through our arses to try to stay on, and people were blowing left, right and centre. Total carnage. Unfortunately for Visentini, he was one of those blowing and he lost the jersey to my old team leader's open rebellion.

Visentini was the defending champion, looked like a filmstar and carried a corresponding popularity with the Italian fans. They went berserk at Roche, trying to punch him on the climbs, swearing and spitting at him whenever they could.

Robert Millar, leading Panasonic and still full of memories of that 'Stolen Vuelta', rode next to him in an act of friendship and solidarity on those climbs while the *tifosi* bayed for the Irishman's blood. On Roche's other shoulder was his last loyal Carrera teammate, Eddy Schepers, the others all in Visentini's corner.

Millar's boss, Peter Post, was livid. Robert was second overall in the race, but instead of trying to take advantage of the Carrera split, he planted his flag squarely in Stephen's camp. They finished first and second in Milan to a chorus of boos, Stephen in the *maglia rosa* of winner and Robert in the green jersey denoting the race's best climber. Little did I know it when I was hanging on the back of the train in those frantic final days in Italy, but the seeds of my near future were being planted during that race.

Sean Kelly reminded me about one day in the Dauphiné Libéré. We think it was that year because we can remember the Colombian teams being there, Café de Colombia and Postobón. It was a really hard day in the lower Alps: lots of nasty climbs and tricky descents, and it didn't stop pissing with rain.

'I'd been trying to ride into form for the Tour de France,' says Kelly, 'and when I lost contact with a group of Colombians on a climb I rode within myself. There was a break gone anyway so I wasn't threatening the stage or the GC. I was pretty good at descending, so I left the group I was with as we started to make the descent and was catching the next group as quickly as I dared. All of a sudden this thing came past me and I thought, "Feck! What the hell was that?" I assumed it was a motorbike, but of course it was Yates. I remember there was a straight bit then a chicane, all of it awash with water, and I thought, "Jaysus, he'll never make that." He did, though.'

He rode up to me the next day laughing, and said, 'What were you doing down there, you lunatic? There was no way you could have won the stage, the break was long gone.'

I just shrugged my shoulders. 'I like riding downhill, I suppose.'

The 1987 Tour de France was exciting for Anglo fans. For the first time in the modern era, there was a British team on the start line: ANC–Halfords. There were two genuine Irish challengers: Stephen Roche, fresh from his Giro success, and Sean Kelly, by now long established as the World number one, and at last a serious competitor in the Grand Tours as well as the Classics. The race looked wide open: for the home fans there was no Hinault, and Laurent Fignon had come back from his injury problems but was yet to find his best form. Most startlingly, Greg LeMond wasn't there to defend his title as he had somehow got himself shot while hunting with his brother-in-law a couple of months previously and had been lucky not to be killed.

In one of the first instances of the Tour de France's desire for a global audience, the start was in West Berlin, which was a bit freaky, a couple of years before the wall came down. We were there for about a week in all, from the team presentation to the end of the first weekend. The first week was crazily fast – a peloton free of the control of Hinault eager to express itself, I suppose. Those of us who had been around for a while were missing him immediately. The race had come a bit early for ANC, who weren't blessed with great organization but showed massive guts under my old time-trial hero Phil Griffiths as *directeur sportif* to battle through the race.

The highlights for me were seeing Stephen Roche win, obviously, and Dag Otto scoring a famous solo win in the Pyrenees at Luz Ardiden. He was at the American squad, 7-Eleven, who were making their début at the Tour and were a breath of fresh air on the stuffy European scene, a great benchmark for ANC–Halfords.

I came out of the Tour de France at 73 kilograms, the lightest I'd been since I'd left school. I would ultimately decide that my ideal race weight was somewhere around

75 or 76 kilos, that 73 was a little bit too light for my frame, as I found out later that summer when I pitched up at the National Track Championships for the professional pursuit and was seen off a bit too easily by Tony Doyle. Being a proper Tour de France rider and winning on the track weren't going to sit easily next to each other for me. The extra power I wanted on the track had literally been weighing down my professional road career and one would have to go. Looking at the old cuttings now, grimacing at the memory of Doyley catching me in the final, I said to *Cycling*, 'It has been three years since I last rode the track. I saw the championship in *Cycling* and I thought it would be a bit of fun. I had forgotten how hard it is, I will never ride it again.'

When my strength came back after the illness, I felt all right. I was selected for the World Championship Road Race in Villach, Austria. Sean Kelly was flying and I thought he would win a race he'd been trying to win for a long time, especially with Stephen Roche as a foil for him in the Irish team. It nearly worked out like that: Roche launched a late attack as a stalking horse for Kelly but the other members of the lead group, worried about towing Kelly to the finish, failed to close Stephen down and he scored a solo victory to put a rainbow jersey on the living-room wall next to the pink and yellow ones he'd already brought home to Dublin that year.

I owed much of my early career to Stephen Roche. Not only had he recommended me to ACBB and Peugeot, he'd dug me out with a word in the right ear when my job was in the balance. In my first winter with Peugeot in 1982 he had invited me to stay for a week at his home in Paris when we'd got back from that first training camp. Over our rides that week he filled me with the sort of information you need to survive; not just who the good riders were and what to look out for in the races, but where I should open a bank account, what I needed to sign at *la Mairie,* the useful stuff that anyone landing in a foreign country needs to know. Now, this friendly, caring Irishman had won a scarcely believable triple crown: the Tours of France and Italy and the Worlds, all in the same year. I was delighted for him.

I was alongside Roche and Kelly again a few weeks later for the Nissan Classic Tour of Ireland. I was going well, having finished in the top ten at the pro Grand Prix des Nations the week before, and was looking forward to a good end to the season instead of my usual exhaustion. Knowing I was in good shape, I was pissed off when a break with all the key players went away on the second stage and I missed it. Johnny Weltz was in there representing Fagor, and all the other main teams had somebody there, so there was no real chase. The break finished 26 minutes ahead of the rest of us, making the rest of the race a private battle between them. I was still smarting the following morning when I decided to attack not long after the start at Killarney, in the scenic west of Ireland. The stage was a circuit of the famously beautiful and mountainous Ring of Kerry. The bunch weren't so keen on aggressive racing after the previous day's hard riding, and Paul Sherwen told me that they chased hard for about ten miles, but I felt good and kept pressing on and eventually they relented and let me get on with it.

The scenery was amazing. I just kept rolling a big gear round and enjoying riding, telling myself that it was like one of my old training rides over the forest. As the day went on, the roads got narrower and the hills steeper. My lead over the bunch reached 22 minutes, which was great, but also finally stirred them into a chase, as I had begun the day 26 minutes off the lead. The last climb was a monster, the sort of road I'd want to ride on a holiday, not in a race, and certainly not when I was trying to hold off a chasing bunch. It was 18% and a couple of miles long, a tiny little bumpy bit of tarmac set into heather and peat bog. I had a 23-sprocket on, but wished I had a 25. I wove from side to side, just trying to keep going. I'd been out in front in the wind for 100 miles by then. The knowledge that if I made it over the top I would be OK kept the pedals just about turning over, although I can't pretend the thought of walking didn't cross my mind.

I rode into Tralee with a smile on my face, nine minutes in front of the race leader Sean Kelly, who won the sprint for second. I had been in front for five hours and knocked off 116 miles on my own. My best win as a pro.

'It was one of those days where a guy rides off and you think, "Ah, don't worry about it, we'll be seeing him again a bit later,"' says Sean Kelly now. 'But we didn't.'

On the Tour of Ireland that October, as is normal for an end-of-season race, all the talk was of the following year. Irish and British riders were well represented there and, after Stephen Roche's stellar year had brought cycling into contact with a whole new audience in the British Isles, there was massive excitement about his new team.

After his run-in with Visentini and the team management, the likelihood of Roche remaining with Carrera was always going to be slim. That said, when he told me he was coming to Fagor I couldn't believe it. The team was a mess.

He explained that Fagor was actually ideal, because the deal he had struck involved him bringing his management team of Philippe Crépel and Patrick Valcke with him to sort it out. The Fagor team owner, Agustin Mondragon, was apparently all too aware of the poor management, and saw Roche's team's arrival as an opportunity to have a thorough sweep of the old system. Crépel would be the new general manager and Valcke would be the new *directeur sportif*. That suited me. I had no time for Bazzo's bizarre meanderings and having the new World Champion, Giro and Tour winner as the leader we'd been lacking was brilliant news, especially as he'd been a good friend to me. It got even better when he told me that Robert Millar would be coming too, as would Eddy Schepers, his faithful Carrera sidekick. Now I knew what those three had been talking about all the way through that Rorke's Drift effort to win the Giro. The best of the ANC–Halfords riders, Malcolm Elliott, would further strengthen our English-speaking hardcore. Fagor would be the new *galacticos*, a Real Madrid-type star line-up on the biggest budget in cycling, a fair chunk of which would be heading directly into the bank account of Stephen Roche. It was very exciting.

Patrick Valcke was a surprising choice as *directeur sportif*. He'd been our mechanic at Peugeot when I'd turned pro and had stayed with Stephen ever since. In his twenties, he was the same sort of age as us, and didn't have a background in racing like most, but by no means all, *directeurs*. He was clearly going to be working for Stephen rather than the other way round, but there was no reason that shouldn't work.

After a Christmas at home, training and catching up, we all headed down to San Sebastián for the team photos and presentation. It turned into an absolute débâcle.

The general gist of it was that Fagor said that Bazzo was still in charge and there was no role for either Crépel or Valcke. Essentially, they were saying that we were going to carry on just as we had the year before, but with Roche, Millar and Elliott added to the roster. They failed to realize that the overhaul of the team was an essential part of the deal for us being there. Mondragon came in and told us all to get ready for the photos. Of the eighteen riders, sixteen of us refused, under Roche's leadership. The other two were Spanish guys who were closer to the old management. We couldn't see the point in having our photos done if the team wasn't going to ride and refused to get our new kit on. Mondragon said, 'Either you all leave, or you all stay.'

We all left.

The team all wanted to stay together; we felt we were on to a good thing and we liked the idea of Stephen, Crépel and Valcke running things, so Crépel put the word around that Fagor were pulling out, and would anyone like to sponsor us? I did my usual trick of sitting back and waiting to see what happened, then Stephen announced that he'd sat down with Mondragon and everything was OK and we could start as intended. It wasn't the most traditional way of starting a season.

Stephen was on the way back to fitness after putting off a knee operation until after the end of the previous season, making sure he was able to ride that Tour of Ireland where he had finished second to Sean Kelly. The crowds had been incredible to the pair of them everywhere the race went; it was important for both of them and Irish cycling as a whole that they were able to race so well in their own country. However, the knee meant that when we got to the start of Paris–Nice for our first major engagement, we discovered that Stephen would not be riding. It was a blow, especially as Johnny Weltz had just been ruled out with appendicitis. It felt like nothing was going right.

The first stage was through Beaujolais country down to Saint-Étienne. It was freezing and there was snow on the ground, and then it started falling in flurries as we rode along. The bunch was really grumpy about the whole situation and the race began to split on a climb with about 75 kilometres to go thanks to a big effort from one of my French teammates, Robert Forest. I had the idea that they wouldn't be too keen on chasing down an attack on a day like that, so I launched a bit of an effort over the top of the climb and got myself a little gap. It was like Kerry again: I concentrated on the rhythm of the pedals, the countryside around, and tried to shut everything else out. I pulled the lead out to six minutes before Sean Kelly put the whole of his Kas team on the front and started driving to bring me back. He'd won the race six years on the trot and had the strongest team he'd ever had for it, so there were no prizes for guessing who was favourite.

'Once again, Sean Yates disappeared up the road,' says Kelly. 'On this occasion, though, I was a bit more wary. I knew he was one of those guys that you might not see again so we all got on the front and started pulling.'

I had time for a bit of the old victory salute in Saint-Etienne, remembering the days of Divisional Championship Road Races and the like, and allied to the much appreciated stage win, I got to pull on the white jersey of race leader. I was pretty unaccustomed to the podium stuff but it felt good, the first British leader since Tommy Simpson twenty-seven years earlier. Brad would wear the leader's jersey as well, twenty-four years down the line, which feels quite neat now.

I knew that keeping it would be nigh-on impossible,

with plenty of long stages and climbing to come, plus Kelly's unbeatable record in the final mountain time trial up the Col d'Eze. However, the team rode really well and we hung on and hung on, Robert especially keeping the big guns in check on the slopes. I finally lost the jersey at the end of a horrible day where I belted myself to try to stay within contact with Kelly's group over Mont Faron and ended up losing it on time bonuses. Or had I? By the time I was back at the hotel, showered, changed and eating, someone came in to tell us there had been a mistake, I still had the jersey and Kelly was a couple of seconds behind me overall. It didn't make much difference, and he unsurprisingly took what he needed and more into Saint-Tropez the next day.

'I'd forgotten that,' says Kelly.

There was great morale in the team considering how the week had started, and I got a chance to lead Malcolm out for the sprint on the stage into Nice. He was edged out by Andreas Kappes but second was a great return in our first effort at a bunch kick.

As we find ourselves in Nice, I suppose this would be a good point to tell you about one of the less edifying periods of my life. I got a letter from the Inland Revenue back at Forest Row asking me for the small matter of unpaid tax for each season that I'd been a professional. I replied that I had been paying tax in France, but they pointed out that the £40 or so a month I'd been so generously shelling out to *la Mairie* in Tours or Lille since 1982 merely covered my social security payments. It was not, and was nowhere near, an income tax payment. Furthermore, as I was paying my money into an English bank and living in Sussex, I owed the UK taxman six years' worth of income tax, plus a fine for non-payment that would double the amount I owed.

After the obligatory shitting my pants and punching myself in the face for having my head in the sand for so long, Dad and I went to see an accountant to sort it out. It became apparent that, for once, it was fortunate that I had been on such terrible money at Peugeot, so the amount wasn't anything like what it could have been. In fact, the current season would be the first where I was earning anything reasonable, which would help pay off the debt I'd built up. The accountant forged a deal with the Revenue that meant I avoided the fine on the basis of being an ignorant fool. It also involved me leaving the country. Under this arrangement, I could only spend sixty days of the calendar year in Britain.

I packed two suitcases, one full of my normal clothes, one of cycling kit, climbed into the 2.8-litre Bodie and Doyle-style Ford Capri I'd bought, and drove to Nice. I went to a hotel I'd stayed at a few times when we'd been racing down there and negotiated a deal on a room. It wasn't a luxury suite. It wasn't a double. It wasn't even a single. It was like a broom cupboard out the back that they only rented out when the hotel was full. I agreed to pay them about 30 francs a day to live there – about £3. When it came time to go off to a race, I'd put one of my two cases in the car so they could let the room, take my other case and my bike and get a cab to the airport, leaving the Capri at the hotel.

It was a miserable time. I knew nobody in Nice. I would sit on the beach and watch British Airways planes taking off from the nearby airport and feel like crying: they were heading back to England and I wasn't. It didn't have a detrimental effect on the racing, though. I trained like I did when I'd been a kid in Sussex: long rides in the hills behind Nice every morning and sitting on the beach in the afternoon. Then it would be a baguette or something: I had no cooking facilities or anywhere to store food. I stayed skinny and fit and concentrated on being a professional cyclist.

One of the other guys on the team, Charly Bérard, turned out to be a local. We started meeting to ride if our programme meant we were both in Nice at the same time. When he realized how I was living he took pity on me and took me back to his parents, who had a good-sized house in the town. They took me in and I was able to have my own room and a cooked meal occasionally. In that fashion I paid my debt to British society and came out of that year a chastened and wiser 28-year-old man than the 27-year-old teenager I'd been masquerading as previously.

In April, Fagor sacked Patrick Valcke. Again. Stephen Roche's knee was still sidelining him and, as a result, he was becoming marginalized. To rub salt in the wound, they reappointed Pierre Bazzo to take over as *directeur sportif*. The team was an absolute joke. There was this guy from Fagor management called Miguel Gómez, who came in over Bazzo's head as general manager. He used to drive round races in the car screaming at us to do stupid things. It was like hiring the landlord of a pub near a Premiership football ground to run the team. He didn't have a clue. There were no team talks. Your programme would be changed at the drop of a hat. He'd get lost driving to the start every day, then get lost again looking for that night's hotel. We got used to just looking after ourselves.

In despair, I rang my dad and told him what was going on.

'Dad, you've got to get me out of here. It's a fucking madhouse.'

'Well, what do you want me to do?'

'Phone Dag Otto, see if you can get me in at 7-Eleven.'

'Yes, I remember that call from Roger,' says Dag Otto. 'I was very pleased that Sean wanted to come to us and I spoke immediately to "Och" to try to sort it out.'

7-Eleven were a pretty exciting set-up. They'd been the main sponsor in US domestic cycling for years, and this year they were going to be the first American team to compete in the Tour de France. Their leader, Andy Hampsten, was just about to pull off an incredible feat and win the Giro d'Italia with one of the bravest acts in modern cycling, winning a stage over the infamous Passo di Gavia in a complete blizzard.

Fortunately, their manager, a guy called Jim Ochowicz, universally known as 'Och', seemed to think that a rider like me would be a useful addition to what was a small and young squad. Dad struck a deal with him for 1989. There were no agents in those days.

In Stephen's absence, Robert got completely stitched up. He'd hated the pressure of being leader at Panasonic and was looking forward to his designated role as wildcard and specialist climber for the hilly Classics and the Tour. There was to be no Vuelta or Giro for him in his quest to be at his peak to ride at Stephen's side to a glorious defence of the Tour that July. He'd been very clear that he would never go back to the Vuelta again after what had happened to him in 1985. As soon as Valcke was fired, they told Robert he would be leading the team at the Vuelta after all, starting in a few days' time. It was a real kick in the nuts, and a horrible reward for his good form. He'd come third in the Critérium International, third in the Route du Sud, then a really superb third in Liège–Bastogne–Liège just before the Vuelta. You could see the motivation leak out of him and he sank into his shell.

We managed to win three stages of that Vuelta. I got away with Deno Davie on the run into Jaca in the Pyrenees and outsprinted him to take a stage in a Grand Tour for the first time.

A couple of days later Johnny won, then Malcolm won the sprint in Toledo with a display of pure class. Me, Johnny and Robert executed the perfect lead out and Malcolm finished it off, beating no less than Sean Kelly. It remains one of my most satisfying Tours, with three stage wins between us. Robert managed to sleepwalk to sixth in the overall classification too, keeping his head down and riding alongside Kelly wherever he could. The Irish legend was at the peak of his powers after a decade at the top.

We went to the Midi Libre to warm up for the Tour. Marc Gomez had joined the team that season. He was a bit of a legend on the French scene after winning Milan–San Remo as a new pro in 1982. He'd got away with Alain Bondue in a torrential rainstorm and then won alone when his more experienced breakaway partner crashed coming down the Poggio. He had taken to wearing the biggest glasses you could imagine. Dennis Taylor wouldn't be seen dead in them. He was instantly recognizable and had a big fanbase as he was a bit of a rebel. He turned up at the start of the Midi Libre with a beard, which was pretty much unheard of in cycling. Miguel Gómez (no relation) told him to shave it off. Marc told him where he could stick the razor and went straight home. It was that sort of team.

The Midi Libre turned out to be OK. On the fourth stage of the week-long tour of the Languedoc region, I got away as half of a duo with my old Peugeot teammate Jérôme Simon. There were 80 kilometres to go to the pretty little town of Quillan in the lovely Aude valley. We were a minute or so up on Claude Criquielion and Laurent Fignon, who were contesting the overall, so we couldn't hang about as we got near the finish. We came round the last corner and I was full of confidence that

I could beat my smaller breakaway partner in a two-up sprint, but I hadn't reckoned on a puncture hitting me at that precise moment. Second would have to do.

The next day I got in a move again, this time alongside Criquielion and a couple of others. We wound our way up into the Pyrénées-Orientales a few kilometres from the Med on one side and the Spanish border on the other. Crique, who had been World Road Race Champion just over the mountains in Barcelona a few years previously, was on fire, the ideal person to be driving the break with. I beat him in the sprint at Céret and he wrapped up the overall victory, leaving everyone happy.

Two road-stage wins that spring. What was happening to me?

It's hard to imagine that anything good could come out of Fagor's visit to the Tour de France that year. Unlike with most teams, money wasn't the problem: Fagor were throwing it around with gay abandon – but largely to run the team as a big jolly for the company management and their friends. We would go to get on the team bus at the end of a stage and it would be full of drunk Basques in suits, half-eaten sandwiches everywhere, beer cans rolling around. Malcolm and I found where they stashed the beer and would shake all the cans up in the morning before the stage start. That should have given them a nice surprise with their lunch.

We arrived on the Côte d'Amour for the start of the 1988 Tour without our glorious leader. Stephen's left knee was still not right. People were questioning his attitude, saying that he'd piled on the pounds over the winter, wasn't interested in putting himself through the hardship again, would rather go to the endless dinners and interviews that are the province of a popular sporting superstar in Ireland. I couldn't see that, to be honest. He'd historically followed a good year with a bad one through his career, his body a little too fragile to support his intense will to win and his sublime technique on a sustainable basis. If he'd been around, maybe Fagor would have run a bit more smoothly, but with Miguel Gómez going round shouting things like, 'Where's your famous World Champion now?' and Valcke and Crépel shunted out of the picture, we'd pretty much all given up on the team. But we all liked riding our bikes and wanted to do a good job for each other and ourselves. The French call it *faire le métier*, which probably translates best as 'taking care of business'. And, paradoxically, as my results that spring showed, I was in the shape of my life.

The prologue was a strange affair. As I recall, we did a sort of team time trial and prologue combined: we all rode until there was a kilometre to go, then one rider from each team went on alone. That must have been me on our team, as the results I'm looking at now say I was sixth, but I can't say I remember anything about it. Perhaps I was just too busy smiling, as before the stage I'd put pen to paper with 7-Eleven for the following season.

The long time trial at the end of the first week was over some pretty dull roads that I knew well from my time in Lille. Lying in 129th place overall, I had a pretty early start time in Liévin, but as soon as I got into a rhythm I knew I was on a ride. There was a tailwind blowing and when I got the big gear rolling over it felt like I was back on the Q10 Tonbridge Bypass. It was 52 kilometres to Wasquehal on the far side of Lille, not far from the famous old velodrome at Roubaix. I covered it in an hour and three minutes to take the provisional lead, but with all the big names still to come. Fignon came in two minutes slower than me, then Kelly at a similar margin, and I began to think that I just might hang on. Charly Mottet and Jeff Bernard, the best French testers at that time, lost a minute or so to me. The wind began to drop off, which was giving the later starters less of an advantage, and then, to put the icing on the cake, it began to rain. While there might be some truth in the theory that there is 'more oxygen in the air' when it is raining – it certainly often feels faster on those days – the bends towards the end of the course would certainly have to be taken at slower speeds in the wet.

All in all, I had to wait four hours from my finish until Jelle Nijdam came in. He'd been faster than me at the first time check, putting a bit of fear in me and cranking up the tension, but faded to finish fourth behind me, Roberto Visentini and Tony Rominger.

I was a Tour de France stage winner, the fifth Briton to win a stage, the first Englishman since Barry Hoban in 1975, and the first British rider to win a time trial in the Tour. It also turned out that my average speed of 49 kph was a record for a time trial. It remains the fastest time trial without tri-bars in the history of the race.

A couple of days later we headed down towards the Alps and into the hilly country of the Vosges along the German border. I was near the front of the bunch as we went over the last climb of the day, a couple of minutes behind the break of the day. Descending being particularly enjoyable for me, I pulled away from the field and realized that if I could bridge across to the move, I could actually have a chance of taking the yellow jersey. My time trial had moved me up more than a hundred places into 18th spot, and I was about two and a half minutes behind Steve Bauer, who was in yellow. It took me 14 kilometres to get across the gap, but I latched on to the back of the group and we set about working together to maximize the gap back to the peloton. Jérôme Simon was in there too and he was better placed than me on the general classification so I knew I'd have to put some time into him as well if the plan was going to come off. With a couple of miles to go I counter-attacked after we'd caught a move by a Système–U guy, but despite my giving it the berries, Simon knew what was at stake and hauled the break back up to me before countering himself to win the stage. I was eighth. Bauer's Toshiba team had spent the last 20 kilometres chasing furiously on the front so that neither I nor Jérôme Simon could nick the jersey off them. I finished the day in fourth overall. With the real mountains ahead of us I knew there was no chance of sustaining that kind of position, but I was well satisfied with the week's work.

Robert's season hit a new low in the Pyrenees. He had singled out the stage that had mirrored his 1984 victory at Guzet-Neige as his big target and duly approached the finish on the wheel of Philippe Bouvatier – their final breakaway companion, Massimo Ghirotto, having been dropped on the upper slopes of the mountain. As Bouvatier lifted the speed to try to distance Robert, who was well known for a surprising little kick at the finish of stages, he mistakenly headed into the *déviation* for team vehicles instead of swinging left up the last slope to the line, taking Robert with him. Ghirotto, treading water in third, couldn't believe his luck and took the stage.

Just to rub salt in the wound, he admitted his good fortune and apologized to Bouvatier, generously donating the Peugeot 205 he had won to the Frenchman. That caused a chorus of disapproval amongst those of us who had fancied Robert to have pipped him in the uphill sprint.

The team was in utter shambles. Robert went home a few days later, barely having spoken since that finish. I made it to Paris for my baguette from Monsieur Boucher in 59th, by far my best finish in a Tour de France, an hour behind Pedro Delgado. The second half of the race had been ruined by a couple of high-profile doping cases. In stark contrast to today's attitudes, Pedro Delgado tested positive while wearing the yellow jersey but didn't get thrown out of the race as the substance, a masking agent for steroid use, was on the Olympics banned list but not the UCI's.

I'd been telling anybody who would listen that I was on my way to 7-Eleven. I didn't want Fagor taking any credit for the results we achieved as a team that year.

The best time we had that year was at the Tour of Britain. Stephen was finally back racing again, though not at his full-speed 1987 version – something that would only be spotted fleetingly for the remainder of his career. Malcolm was going really well and Robert was there too. I was in the post-Tour groove that I seemed to find every season by this point – my best results in the second half of my career were often in August or later – and our five-man team was completed by Bernard Richard, our only non-British Isles rider. We developed a style that would provide a useful template for later smaller stage races with 7-Eleven and Motorola. In the bigger races, you could use a nine-man team to control events. When you've only got five, you need a worker on the front to do a lot of the donkey work on his own, which was right up my street. A lot of week-long stage races are decided by time bonuses, so sprinters can often find themselves competing for the overall positions that would be beyond them in longer or more mountainous races. After Malcolm took the jersey with some rapid finishing, I rode on the front all day every day, with Richard there to give me a break if I needed, Stephen and Robert riding shotgun to cover any moves that went, and Malcolm sitting in behind us in the leader's jersey and conserving energy. People cheered us wherever we went. I've rarely had more fun on a bike. The irony is, of course, that we were doing it in promotion of a company and team organization that had failed us completely. We told ourselves each night that we weren't doing it for Fagor, we were doing it for each other and for the masses of British cycling fans that had come to the roadside to cheer us on.

Malcolm won, I was fourth, Stephen was sixth. It was a fitting epitaph to a totally topsy-turvy year.

Chapter Ten

If 1987 was the season that I began to understand my potential as a rider and 1988 was the year I started to fulfil it, then 1989 was the year I found the team in which to do it.

I'd had a great end to 1988. With the cushion of having signed for 7-Eleven beneath me I'd ridden well, then set off for Australia with a Swinnerton mountain bike, panniers and a tent. I flew into Brisbane and immediately set off for the Gold Coast. After riding several miles along what turned out to be a dead-end, I found myself on the Pacific Highway. Not ideal. These massive articulated lorries were passing within inches of me and I wondered if I would ever make it as far as Surfers Paradise. It was looking more like a one-way trip to Naïve Tourist's Graveyard.

Fortunately for me, a guy came past in a pick-up, or 'ute' as the Aussies call them, and offered me a lift. I slung the fully laden bike in the back with difficulty and jumped gleefully into the cab. I can honestly say that nobody has offered me a lift like that in Britain, or anywhere else for that matter, and I was eternally grateful to the Samaritan.

On the Gold Coast I camped, swam and explored every day. Determined to rid myself of the cycling season's tan lines, I am ashamed to report that I wore nothing but a pair of yellow budgie-smugglers and my Brancale cycling shoes for a month. Walking round supermarkets. Cycling through towns. People of Australia, I apologize unreservedly.

After a few weeks of eating one meal a day and camping without speaking to a soul all day I was going a bit stir-crazy, but fortunately I was scheduled to meet Allan Peiper and his mum. We stayed in a five-star hotel, as a complete turnaround from the previous month. Allan and I were as competitive with each other as ever and devised two-man *Superstars* tournaments every day. I may have earned a reputation for giving my all in bike races, but I never tried any harder to win a race than I did to beat him at hotel tennis, sea swimming or beach long jumps that winter in Australia.

I finished off my trip in Melbourne visiting my aunt. My grandfather on my dad's side emigrated to New Zealand many years ago, where he became a lumberjack. His daughter, my Aunty Brenda, decided pretty swiftly that a lumberjack's daughter's life in the backwoods of New Zealand was not for her and hopped across to the cosmopolitan delights of Melbourne. There was a great cycling scene there, hundreds of people tearing it up in a massive chaingang on what they called the Bay Ride. I was sitting in a café on the waterfront there one day and the American cycling legend Jonathan Boyer came strolling past. 'Bloody hell,' I thought, 'what's he doing here?' A few days later, I saw Eros Poli as well. It was the perfect place for winter refugees from the European bike season to hang out.

Back home at Mum's, I had a crazy Christmas. I could not stop eating. Could. Not. Stop. I was chugging bowls of cereal every five minutes. Compulsive behaviour again; it was the behaviour of somebody with an eating disorder, eating until I was genuinely and physically sick. I must have been very thin when I arrived back, though, as I was still pretty slim when I arrived in Santa Barbara for the 7-Eleven training camp, despite a couple of weeks abusing muesli.

There's a picture of me with Eddy Merckx on the front of an old *Cycling* from January 1989. The legend was at our camp with his bikes, which we would be riding for the coming season. The funny thing about that picture is that at the moment it was taken I was actually complaining to him that my bike was the wrong size – I'd always had a 60-centimetre frame and they'd given me a 61-centimetre. I still rode it all through the spring, another pointer of how things have changed since then. These days Sky would phone Pinarello and there would be five new bikes at the hotel the following morning.

I also got a cover shot of me smiling brightly on *Winning*, which was a cool Anglo-American magazine then. I say smiling brightly – my improved financial situation had persuaded me to part with a few quid and get my teeth done. Basically, my entire set of gnashers was screwed; maybe I'd spent too many years eating chocolate, I don't know, but they needed doing. The pearly whites on the front of *Winning* were all new. I soon reverted to type and gave up on the refurbishment plan, though, deciding it was costing too much, tight git that I am. As I write this I'm running my tongue over the huge gap in my lower gum where there used to be a line of teeth that I've never had replaced.

That training camp was the beginning of the golden days. The team was a dream. Our leader was Andy Hampsten, after his eye-catching Giro performance, and he was weighing up the Tour. Davis Phinney had been the long-term main man, and he was the biggest character. There were Americans like Jeff Pierce, Roy Knickman and Bob Roll; then the Europeans: Dag Otto, me and Gerhard Zadrobilek. Jim Ochowicz was the boss and he set a perfect tone. We had fun, were laid-back, but we were serious too. On that camp we rode regularly to Solvang, this Scandinavian community in the hills behind the coast that Dag Otto loved. We ate muffins and massive Mexican meals, went to the cinema, had a golf day . . . I remember wondering why not every training camp was like this. Afterwards, Dag Otto and I headed down to La Jolla near San Diego and carried on the vibe of training hard but hanging out, this time with his family. We hit Disneyland, SeaWorld . . . all while getting fit.

'That camp in Santa Barbara and the stay in La Jolla were an absolute blast,' recalls Dag Otto. 'My wife and kids adored Sean. Line and Stian seemed to treat him like a pet that comes and goes. He spent most of that spring at our place in Gullegem near Kortrijk. They went so far as to actually get a pet and name it after him: Sean the cat. It was a stray that used to come and go, which was pretty much how Sean lived too. We had a little gang round there: us two, Steve Bauer and Greg LeMond all lived pretty close to each other and we used to ride together between races.'

I hit Europe flying. I wasn't too happy about our early programme as it was in Italy, where the racing in February and March is always faster than in France. With Milan–San Remo being the first big Classic of the year, all the Italians are super-motivated for Tirreno–Adriatico, the week-long stage race that precedes it, and the attendant one-day races in the sunny south of Italy. Nathan Dahlberg and I stayed for a week at a hotel in Caserta outside Naples, a place where you're best advised not to talk too loudly about the *Cosa Nostra* or *Camorra* as they are known in those parts, and the team left one of the *soigneur*'s vans with us. That was a bit of a touch for us as we were both tight and were able to live off the PowerBars in the van for a week without spending any lire on real food. I went well at Tirreno and then went up to Milan and finished in the front group in San Remo, which I think was the only time in my career that I managed to do that.

As a result, I arrived in northern Europe for my favoured races in great form. I was a little unlucky at the Tour of Flanders when Dag Otto, who was our leader that day, punctured when we were together in the front group. With no team cars allowed to follow after the ascent of the Paterberg – there had been a major fuss a year or two before when the Danish rider Jesper Skibby had been run over by the race *commissaire*'s car when it tried to overtake him on the narrow Koppenberg – I gave him a wheel. It didn't work out too badly, as Dag Otto got third, but any hopes I had of a personal good placing all went on him. I found myself in a two-up chase with the Belgian Jean-Marie Wampers that didn't get us back to the front, but must have done us both some good, as the next few days would show.

'If I could only say one thing about Sean, it is that you can trust him 110 per cent,' says Dag Otto now. 'He'll always put you first.' I think he's being kind; he was designated leader that day and I knew that he had a better chance than me. It was the right thing to do, and I'm sure he would have done the same if our positions had been reversed. There is no point in having a plan if you don't do everything you can to execute it.

It is only very recently that Gent–Wevelgem has been moved to the weekend before Flanders. That week was always the week that the cobble-lovers spent all year waiting for: Flanders on Sunday, Gent–Wevelgem on Wednesday, Paris–Roubaix the next Sunday.

My chase with Wampers had given me enough hope

that I could do a good ride at Gent, and the appalling weather was no hindrance. I've done a lot of my best rides in the rain, motivated by the knowledge that plenty of others hate it. The race is a full 276 kilometres long and it rained for every one of those.

I got away after just 30 kilometres with Gerrit Solleveld, Bruno Cenghialta and Louis de Koning, all good riders. Breaks are often allowed to go early in the day at that race because there is a difficult long headwind stretch along the coast which saps the speed from an escape, and the real racing starts after you swing back inland. On this occasion, though, the field had misjudged the mood of the breakaway, and they were in for a long, hard day of chasing through the rain, spray and debris of Flemish roads in spring.

'I covered a move by Sean Kelly to pull them back,' remembers Dag Otto. 'He was not only World number one and on superb form, he was the defending Gent–Wevelgem champion. He chased really hard and a few of us gritted our teeth and held on to his wheel. He had two Norwegian teammates at PDM then and they were both neighbours of mine in Kortrijk: Atle Pedersen and Dag Erik Pedersen. They told me later that they got an absolute bollocking from Kelly for letting that break get away.'

The cobbled climb of the Kemmelberg is covered twice in Gent–Wevelgem, and on the first time up, Solleveld and I left the other two behind. The final 80 kilometres turned into a two-up time trial much like the one I'd had on the Sunday with Jean-Marie Wampers, except this time we were going for victory. In hindsight, I should have attacked him, but with the chasers not far behind I thought it best that we worked together to make sure we stayed clear. I climbed on a smaller gear than most in those days; I liked to use a 24-sprocket on the cobbled climbs, when most had a 21, and I think I could have dropped him the second time up the Kemmelberg. In the wet, his bigger gear would have meant it was harder to prevent his wheel slipping on the cobbles if I'd given it everything, but we stayed together, and then to my great and eternal surprise he outsprinted me easily in Wevelgem. We were only 11 seconds in front of the bunch so who knows, maybe we both would have been caught if I'd dropped him anyway. It remains simultaneously one of the best results and biggest disappointments of my career.

'Sean is being a little modest,' says Dag Otto. 'Solleveld's team offered to do a deal with him, but he turned them down as he wanted to win. Then Solleveld told Sean he was exhausted and couldn't do his fair share of work, but suggested he could help with small turns to give him a breather and enable them to stay away and would be happy with second place. Sean's mistake was doing more than his fair share and taking Solleveld's word at face value.'

From there we went to Paris–Roubaix where I was to enjoy protected status on the team for the rest of my career thanks to the form I was showing at those races.

Paris–Roubaix was destined to become 'my' race; the day when I would be leader, when the others would fetch bottles and chase down moves for me for a change. To be honest, there's not an awful lot of that at Roubaix. The broken old cobbles and narrow cart tracks make it more a case of every man for himself. The trick is to ride at the front of the race as much as you can. I was doing exactly that as the race entered the business end, but was baulked by a motorbike and crashed when I tried to attack on the penultimate cobbled section before the horrible run through the Arenberg forest. I chased back with Jean-Claude Colotti, who was also going well, and hit the Trouée d'Arenberg in the front group. The crowds are behind barriers now, but back then you had to push your way through the spectators like you were climbing Alpe d'Huez in the Tour, meaning you couldn't really see the road in front of you. There is also the problem of huge clouds of dirt and dust from the preceding cars. As a result, I didn't see a massive hole in the *pavé* and hit it hard, blowing out my front wheel. The neutral Mavic motorbike with spare wheels attended me and I managed to get a change – the team car was way behind, held back by the many small splits and groups that form at Roubaix. I got back on my bike and hammered off after the motorbike, which had shot off to help other victims. I'd only gone a few yards when I realized that I had a rear puncture as well. Shit.

At that point, my head fell off. 'That's it,' I thought,

chucked the bike down and abandoned. For somebody who somehow has a reputation for being calm, I had a remarkable temper. I remember doing the same thing in a time trial years before after a car cut me up on a roundabout. I probably lost all of two seconds, yet I felt my race was over and abandoned immediately. With a calmer state of mind I may well have waited for another wheel and chased back, but instead I found myself back in the team hotel that evening cursing my luck and myself. The race had been won by my chasing partner of the previous weekend, Jean-Marie Wampers, just to prove that it is always worth persevering.

After my semi-successful Northern Classics campaign, I headed for the Ardennes and my one and only Liège–Bastogne–Liège appearance. I remember thinking to myself, 'Fuck this for a game of soldiers.' It was so damn hilly. I absolutely hated it and abandoned at the first feed, determined to never return.

These days, squads are big enough so that you can fine-tune each rider's programme to provide him with individual targets and the ideal run of races to prepare for those targets. At 7-Eleven there simply weren't enough of us for that, so we had an 'A'-team that rode together pretty much constantly for the big races. The upside of this was a real togetherness within the unit that is hard to achieve if you're swapping the side around with regularity. It's something we tried to recreate at Sky by keeping the same group together right through from the start of the year to the Tour de France. That includes managers, mechanics and *soigneurs* as well as riders, and extends to training camps as well as racing.

The team spirit at 7-Eleven was never greater illustrated than that spring when we headed back to the USA for the inaugural Tour de Trump, America's biggest bike race. I got second in both the time trials, but the story of the race was Dag Otto taking the leader's jersey in a first-stage break, then us working to protect it for the rest of the race which, at ten stages plus a prologue, was quite a feat. Eric Vanderaerden was on storming form for Panasonic, and we had our work cut out to prevent him from snatching the overall lead by gobbling up the many time bonuses on offer to sprinters. While I and the others rode hard on the front all day it was left to Davis Phinney to take on Vanderaerden in the sprints and keep some vital seconds away from him. He edged out the Belgian in the last road stage with a brilliant sprint to give Dag Otto some wiggle room for the closing time trial.

In the final time trial in Atlantic City, with us all using the brand new triathlon-style bars we'd been given, Dag Otto managed to hold off a charging Vanderaerden to take a famous win for 7-Eleven on home turf. It wasn't without controversy, though, as Vanderaerden had been led off course by the official motorbike he was following and lost valuable seconds. Panasonic protested, but the race organization ruled that the result hadn't been affected.

We were treated like millionaires by the millionaire in Atlantic City. There was a tour of Donald Trump's yacht, limos to pick us up from hotels, champagne, cheering crowds . . . good times.

The Hell of the North cobbles came back to haunt me for the second time that year when the Tour de France organizers pulled their perennial trick of dropping those roads into the first week of the Tour de France. My job was to look after Andy Hampsten in the early stages, and while looking for him over my shoulder I touched a wheel and came down. I ended up chasing for the second part of the day – not ideal with the long time-trial stage that I'd won the year before coming up the following day. I performed OK, fifth place, and held fifth place overall for a few days too. But instead of everybody talking about an American team in the Tour, it was an American rider on a Belgian team. Greg LeMond, the 1986 champion, was making his comeback after that shooting accident a couple of years previously. Using the triathlon bars he'd seen us using in America, he won the stage and took the yellow jersey.

If that wasn't enough of a fairytale, his main challenger emerged as Laurent Fignon, another former winner on the comeback trail. Over the three weeks they slugged it out toe-to-toe all over France in the best Tour of all time. Fignon had the measure of LeMond in the Pyrenees, only to lose the jersey again to the American in the Alpine mountain time trial. LeMond held it for two days this time until Fignon spanked him on Alpe d'Huez. They swapped stage wins in the final week but Fignon went into the final day's time trial on the

Champs-Elysées with 50 seconds in hand on the second-placed LeMond.

7-Eleven were actually in trouble. Not the team, the company. They were filing for Chapter 11 bankruptcy in the States, their business undermined by the number of gas stations jumping on their late-night convenience-store bandwagon. I'd been going well, holding that top-ten spot for a few days after that first time trial, and being within spitting distance of yellow for the second year running before we got into the high mountains. In an effort to put a spotlight on the team's Tour de France coverage to attract a new sponsor for the following season, Jim Ochowicz took me to one side before that last time trial.

'Sean,' said Och, 'we need a big result. You're in great form. A win here could be worth millions to us and save the team. So, if you win this time trial, which I know you can, I will give you $20,000.'

That was twenty thousand little pieces of motivation for me, but, to be honest, it didn't really bother me as I always did my best no matter what. My motto has always been 'An honest day's pay for an honest day's work', whether it's cutting a hedge or winning a bike race. I always hoped that people would pay me what I was worth and never haggled or even wanted to discuss money.

I was unlucky in that this was the most fiercely con-tested time trial in the long history of the Tour thanks to the general classification situation. LeMond and Fignon also happened to be two of the best time triallists in the world. Greg had the tri-bars, Laurent did not. Estimating that they would save him a minute or so over the 25-kilometre course, Greg took 58 seconds from Laurent, winning the whole Tour by eight seconds, the closest winning margin ever.

I was fifth again. Pretty good, but no cigar or $20,000. Greg also took my record of the fastest ever time trial in the Tour. I finished 45th overall, an hour and 27 minutes behind LeMond and Fignon, my best Tour performance. Och managed to persuade 7-Eleven to extend for another year, so the axe was lifted from over our necks anyway.

As was becoming the norm, I had good form after the Tour de France. 7-Eleven sent a team to do the week-long Tour of Belgium, with me as leader, and I won the first two stages. They were on the same day; in the morning I got away from a group including Fignon, Johan Museeuw, Visentini and the World Champion Maurizio Fondriest with a Russian guy called Sergei Uslamin and outsprinted him in Verviers. That afternoon, Allan and I pulled the old one-two when he attacked Frans Maassen, Maassen chased him down, and I came off the Dutch champion's wheel to take the win. Allan and I had chatted before the prologue and he thought I would win that, but I'd punctured and lost a few seconds. By the end of the split-stage first day proper, I was leading, Maassen was second and Allan was third.

We were a very inexperienced team – I was leader, so it was obviously not our best line-up – and there were some really good riders in the race, so we had our work cut out to hold it together. In the days before riders' radios and TV in the *directeur sportif*'s car, the team captain's role was an important one and I learned a lot that week that would stand me in good stead when I went into management years later. Knowing that we weren't strong enough to boss the race on our own, we had to second-guess what other teams would do and use their ambitions to help ours.

On the fourth stage, for instance, after loads of attacks that we'd been trying to deal with, a group went away with Johan Bruyneel in it, and he looked likely to take the lead. We were in pieces, but we knew that Maassen's Superconfex team stood to miss out too, so we let them do the lion's share of the chasing. At the end, my future boss Bruyneel held on to take the lead by a few seconds, but it was manageable enough for me to get it back in the afternoon time trial despite another puncture. The real problem wasn't Bruyneel, it was Frans Maassen. He'd won the time trial and now, with two hefty stages remaining, he was only one second behind me overall. He was Dutch national road race champion – the jersey looked good – he had the might of Jan Raas's Superconfex team at his service, and he'd won this race last year.

The next day was a 240-kilometre epic that combined a whole bunch of cobbled climbs from the Tour of Flanders with a finishing circuit that was over Paris–Roubaix-type *pavé*. It was evil. I clung on to Maassen like a fly on a turd, knowing that if he didn't drop me and we finished near the front I would take the jersey into the final day. He couldn't shift me then and he couldn't shift me the next day either. I'd won the Tour of Belgium.

There was some kind of weird tie-in between the race and the big rock festival in Werchter they have every year – maybe it was the same organizers, or something like that. As a result, my prizes on the final victory podium, in addition to one of the most garish leader's jerseys in the history of cycling, were an electric guitar and a gold disc.

I've just had a look to see who's on at this year's Werchter festival: Green Day, Kings of Leon, Depeche Mode and Blur . . . I might go.

I went from there to the Worlds at Chambéry in France, where Greg LeMond managed to rub Laurent Fignon's nose in it again, but also fabulously outsprinted an in-form Sean Kelly, something not many men can lay claim to. I was going well, but had another one of my 'fuck it' moments and climbed off in the latter stages. I never really did a good ride in the Worlds. I often had good legs, but I could never climb with the best guys, and it's such a long race. It's usually 260 kilometres and fifteen or so laps of a circuit. You'd do ten laps and think, 'Yeah, this is cool, I'm going well here,' then the big guns would start to ride properly on the eleventh and twelfth laps. In addition, you have to ride past the pits on every lap, so the temptation to pack after the race has split is immense. A lot of the time in races you might as well keep going as you need to get to the finish just to get back in the car or get to the hotel. The Worlds, a circuit race, has a greater dropout rate, and it's no mystery why.

A couple of weeks later I was back in Belgium for the Eddy Merckx Grand Prix, an invitational time trial like my early rides at the Grand Prix de France and the Grand Prix des Nations. It was held on a circuit based around the national stadium at Heysel, in Brussels, a tragic site for football fans since the death of thirty-nine Italian fans there in crowd trouble before the 1985 European Cup Final between Liverpool and Juventus.

This was an important race for us because Eddy was supplying our bikes, of course, and Andy Hampsten and I got to stay at the great man's house. It was wet again, as it had been in Gent and for much of the Tour of Belgium, and I fancied my chances. I like corners in the wet on a time-trial bike, it's fun to see how far you can push it, knowing that half the others are cornering like Bambi on ice.

There was still a fuss about tri-bars going on. Laurent Fignon, amongst a few others, turned up with a pair of clip-ons attached to his lo-pro and was told he couldn't use them. Believing he was on the receiving end of an injustice – he thought LeMond should have been banned from using them in the Tour – he promptly got back in his car and disappeared in the direction of Paris. We'd heard that this was going to be the rule, and so Andy and I had full one-piece triathlon bars instead, which were permitted. Made by Dave Scott, specifically for tri-bikes, they look absolutely ludicrous by today's standards, but were cutting edge in September 1989. I must have liked them, though, knocking out the 60 kilometres more than two minutes quicker than anybody else. I wish there had been a World Time Trial Championship then. It came later, in the late nineties, but my form in the late eighties, combined with the late-season date of the Worlds, would have put me in with a good shout of a medal.

Unfortunately, as good as 1989 had been for me, I was unaccountably crap by comparison in 1990. Our Tour de France was exciting, though. The first stage was split between a road stage in the morning and my favourite event, the team time trial, in the afternoon. Steve Bauer had joined us for 1990 and was a popular member of the gang, a trier who always gave his best. He'd been squeezed out at Paris–Roubaix in an incredible sprint with Eddy Planckaert that was given to the Belgian on a photo-finish, but everybody thought was a dead heat. On that first day of the Tour he got in a move with Frans Maassen, Ronan Pensec and Claudio Chiappucci that was somehow allowed to steal ten minutes on a bunch waiting for the afternoon team time trial. Steve found himself in yellow thanks to a quicker prologue than Frans Maassen, who won the stage.

That left our nine-man team super-motivated for the team time trial. We had to hold off the challenge of Carrera, Z and, more awkwardly, Jan Raas's Buckler team if we were going to keep Steve in yellow.

Davis Phinney had flown to America and back for the birth of his son – Taylor, now a successful pro in his own right – and was knackered. Andy Hampsten hated the team time trial. We didn't have a strong team, to be honest, but Dag Otto and I thought that we could pull out something good. Always before the team time trial in any race, the others would start saying, 'Oh no, the TTT, Sean's gonna kill us, we're gonna get destroyed.' What they didn't realize was that they were just building up my own motivation to do just that. I felt I had a reputation to maintain. On that day around Futuroscope, the bizarre theme park near Poitiers, Dag Otto and I did nearly all the work. Andy was actually crying. Davis was hanging from the moment we left the start. At one point I turned round to my pal Bob Roll, who was supposedly one of our stronger riders, and said, 'Hey, Bob, what's the chances of you doing a fucking turn on the front?' Our efforts kept Steve Bauer in the yellow jersey for ten days, when he could have made obscure Tour history by spending the morning in team kit, the afternoon in yellow and then be back in team strip by the evening.

'Sean really was frightening in the team time trials,' says Dag Otto now. 'He would pull for half of the entire time the team were out, and his turns would be harder than anybody else's too. There was one team time trial – I think maybe it was in the Tour of Burgos, or somewhere like that in Spain – and there was a cross tailwind. I don't like to exaggerate but we were genuinely clocking 60 kph and he was doing full ten-minute turns on the front. We'd all tap through and swing off one after another after a few seconds, then he would be back on the front for another ten minutes. He's right, I remember the Americans crying. Sean turned round from the front and said, "What the fuck's the matter now?" On another occasion, in the Giro, we were wiped out when a black cat ran into the road. Everybody hit the deck, there was yelling, cursing, injuries . . . When we re-formed there were only five of us left, the minimum number needed to make it to the finish, so he coaxed us all through, doing double and triple turns. I had a puncture near the end but he just screamed at me to keep going, so I did. We never found out what happened to the cat.'

Before the Tour that year, we had gone to the Dauphiné for the traditional form-honing warm-up. There was a time trial at the end, with the bizarre qualification that only the top fifty riders on general classification would start it. I was desperate to be in there as I thought I could get a result from such a small field, so I crucified myself to make the top fifty in what has always been a horribly mountainous race. Brad won there in 2011 and 2012, and Froomey has carried on the good work for Sky in 2013 – and they both had to dig in on some major Tour de France climbs to do so. Anyway, somehow I did qualify for the time trial, though only just, as I was one of the first starters. It was a really grotty day and I did what I used to do back as an English amateur on cold Sunday morning time trials. I covered myself in Cramer Red Hot warm-up grease before I put my skinsuit on to ensure I didn't freeze. Dag Otto saw what I was doing and said, 'Hey, what's that?' I explained and he, always ready to try something, wanted some too, so we coated ourselves in it. The only thing was, he was right up on the GC and had a much later start time. By the time it was time for him to start, the sun had come out, it was a hot day and he had been stewing in the equivalent of turbo-charged Deep Heat for a couple of hours. He was in agony on the start ramp, absolutely purple, dripping with sweat and hyperventilating. I came third; I don't know how he got on but I imagine he made for the showers in double-quick time afterwards.

That reminds me of doing that Sealink International race with Doyley when we were amateurs. Before the start, we were putting our kit on and Doyley was putting some Vaseline in his shorts to soften up the old-fashioned leather chamois. A fan asked him, 'What's that you're putting in there?'

'Capsicum cream, you should try it,' Doyley told him. Capsicum cream was the most powerful hot cream you could imagine, ten times the power of Cramer Red Hot, which in turn was twice as strong as Deep Heat. If the bloke tried it, he's probably still crying now.

The only funnier thing I've seen in a time trial was Chris Froome in the Tour de France prologue in 2012 in Liège, when he flew across the finish line shouting, 'I can't breathe, I can't breathe!' He'd done the whole thing without taking out the cotton-wool buds doused in Olbas Oil that riders stuff up their noses to clear their passages in the warm-up.

I did my customary good ride in Ireland later that season, getting a couple of second places on stages and finishing third overall behind Kelly's teammate Erik Breukink, leading a powerful PDM selection.

By the time we got to the Tour of Lombardy at the end of 1990, Och had lined up Motorola to take over from 7-Eleven, but the deal was yet to be sealed and their representative, Sheila Griffin, flew out to be his guest in the team car at the race. I've never seen him so tense. On the way to pick her up from Milan he must have checked the route a hundred times, he was so scared of getting lost; not something he ever did as far as I remember.

Thanks to Och's hard work, 7-Eleven morphed into Motorola pretty seamlessly. It turned out that Sheila was really passionate about the team and Och hadn't got lost when he went to pick her up for Lombardy. She didn't even seem to mind that it was misty or wet, or that we didn't win. She flew us out to the US in the New Year to visit some of their plants and installations and the scene was set for a fruitful relationship that continued until 1996, my last season.

There was little pressure at Motorola, just the pressure we put upon ourselves to get results. We weren't strong enough to steamroller races like Sky, but we were a decent outfit and we always picked up enough results to keep our sponsors and fans happy, and people liked us. A lot of that was to do with Och's attitude. He liked to do things differently and he liked to have fun. It was a very Californian approach to a sport that was still largely living in a post-war European era. What differentiated Och's approach from other American teams that have

busted their way into sports around the rest of the world
is that he wasn't brash, he didn't make out he knew
everything, that everybody else had been doing it wrong.
But he was quietly innovative and inclusive. They were
great years.

My first Tour de France in Motorola colours was interrupted by a couple of crashes. I fell somewhere in the
first week in the company of Phil Anderson, one of those
tumbles that you get early in the Tour when a wheel is
touched and people come down. It seemed innocuous
enough at the time, but the bruising that I got on my left
thigh led to me sitting unevenly on the bike and sciatica
setting in that gave me problems for many years, maybe
a decade.

In that Tour, though, the second crash I had would be
the decisive one. There was a difficult hilly stage through
the Cévennes to Alès that was won by the maestro
Moreno Argentin. I was with Phil again, right at the front
of the main field, when some idiot came up the outside
of the bunch and just cut straight across me. It happened
so quickly I don't even know who it was, but both Phil
and I hit the deck. I jumped straight up, but something
had punched a neat hole in the crook of my arm – I don't
know, a brake lever, perhaps – and blood was literally
squirting out. Motorola were the first team to use rider
radios and Phil was on his, alerting Och in the team car.
He was standing there with his helmet – Phil was one
of the first riders to always wear a hardshell helmet –
hanging in tatters around his head, held together by the

straps, saying, 'Sean's down, Sean's down, there's blood everywhere.' For some reason, Och's guest that day in the car was some kind of big security guy, an ex-forces type, who raced out of the car as if he was a bodyguard. I thought he was going to throw himself on top of me to protect me from a sniper.

Gérard Porte, the long-term doctor on the Tour, bandaged my arm up and I chased to the finish in Alès, where Paul Sherwen tried to interview me for Channel 4. I was in a foul mood by then: 'For fuck's sake, Paul, the only time you want to talk to me is when I've fucking fallen off!' He left me alone, and a crash meant I was forced to abandon the Tour de France for the second time in my career.

Graham Watson has a slightly different angle on it: 'Gérard Porte told him he'd punctured an artery and would have to quit. Sean was having none of it and demanded that he bandage it up. He had to use tape, like electrical tape, to hold it together.'

It was the 1991 visit to Ireland and the Nissan Classic that brought me one of the results that people still ask me about today.

'Now that was a horrible, horrible day,' remembers Sean Kelly. 'We went from Limerick down to Tipperary and up the Glen of Aherlow. It's a beautiful place, a long climbing valley called "the Vee", but we saw none of it that day, just sheets of Irish rain blown flat by the wind. I was in contention for the jersey, which Johan Museeuw had at that time. The race split to pieces up the Vee and

I was in the front, knowing those little roads and climbs would be a handful on a day like that. I remember coming to a T-junction and Yates came flying round the outside, barely making the corner. I thought to myself, "He's in one of those moods today."

'By the time we got to Fermoy the race had sorted itself out a bit and we were both in a break. It was hard out of the town on lumpy roads in the wind and rain, and Yates took off. I thought, "There goes my taxi," and jumped on him. He was going so hard I couldn't work and sat on for ages. Eventually I felt able to come through but I was doing maybe 150-metre turns; he was doing 400, 500 metres each time. There was a hill as we came into Cork and he struggled a little bit, but I decided to wait for him because of the form he was in. We spoke briefly and agreed to ride together to the finish.

'I think there were three circuits of Cork city centre going up St Patrick's Hill each time. It's a very hard hill and often proved to be the turning point of the Nissan. The first time up it I paused for a moment over the top and he came past me for the descent. I thought to myself, "Jaysus, we're not going to get down this hill alive." He was going down there like an absolute madman. The second time, I took a deep breath and thought, "Well, we might crash and die, but at least we'll both die." I couldn't just let him go.

'He took the stage and I took the jersey and held it for the rest of the race. That was my fourth and last Nissan

Classic win, but it wouldn't have been possible without a ride on the Yates train.'

The Nissan Classic, as the Tour of Ireland was named, and the Kellogg's Tour of Britain were happy hunting grounds. We won the Kellogg's three times on the trot at Motorola following the pattern we had devised during that 1988 race with Fagor. We'd work hard to try to take the jersey near the beginning of the race, then I would ride on the front for the rest of the race to keep the pace high while a couple of teammates rode shotgun on my shoulder to reel in breaks or give me a breather, and the other team members looked after the leader in the jersey. It was perfect for me. I was always highly motivated racing at home; there were always big crowds who recognized me and gave me bags of encouragement, and the smaller teams – I think the Kellogg's were six-man teams – meant that having one strong rider to do the donkey work was very useful. I felt valued and there was a point to all the effort: when Phil Anderson, then Max Sciandri, and then Phil again, won the race for us, I felt very proud.

I had a corking ride at the '91 Dauphiné – in the rain, naturally – when I won the stage into Orange. I attacked into the last corner with Viatcheslav Ekimov on my wheel and he crashed, taking out virtually everybody behind him and leaving me a clean sprint up to the line. Lovely.

By the end of 1991 I felt like I had really got to the peak of where I was going to be. I wasn't going to pull up any trees by winning the Tour de France or anything like that, but I was a valued, useful member of a decent team. I had a fantastic girlfriend, Pippa, and was earning proper money. I began to think about the future, maybe getting married, maybe starting a family, maybe packing up. I'd be 32 in 1992, an age when a lot of top riders' careers had wound down. I was aware that I couldn't expect Pippa to hang around indefinitely while I carried on my peripatetic lifestyle, and that if we were going to be together and turn out a baby or two I'd better be at home.

I began to relax and enjoy this new-found cash. I bought a Honda RC30 motorbike. It was seriously quick and I loved the way you could lean it over; I just wished that I had more opportunity to ride it. By the time I sold it in about 1998 it was still virtually new. I dreamt – still dream – of going to the Isle of Man for the other kind of TT, but I'm still waiting.

My other purchase was a 2.5-litre, long wheelbase turbo–diesel Land Rover Defender. Now that has seen some action. I was driving that right up to a few weeks ago, when I migrated to a van with two rows of seats to let me take the kids away cycling.

Virtually the first thing I did when I picked it up was to drive it to Norway to spend some time with Dag Otto that winter. We went cross-country skiing ('He was absolutely fucking useless' – Dag Otto) and walking in the snow along the coastline from his place, looking out across the Skagerrak towards Denmark and Sweden. One day I was coming downhill to a T-junction and lost control on the ice and slid out into the main road straight into a bus. My new car! I was gutted.

'When I got there he was just standing in the road resting his head against the driver's door gently banging his forehead rhythmically against the glass,' says Dag Otto. 'There's a certain way of driving in the ice that English people rarely get to try out, even in a four-wheel drive. There was nothing I could say apart from commiserating with him about his lovely new vehicle and getting it to a garage.'

Dag Otto was great. He got the Landy to a body shop and it was good as new – it was bloody new! – in no time. Dag Otto is a bit of a legend in Norway. He has faced some problems with his heart, like me: I can't help thinking that the type of rider we both were had something to do with that, the readiness to go the extra mile. He's a well-known figure on TV at home these days, covering the Tour de France and presenting a show called *On the Wheel with Dag Otto*. His real claim to fame with the Norwegian public, though, is not winning the Tour de Trump or taking a Tour de France mountain stage at Luz Ardiden, it's coming third in Norway's equivalent of *Strictly Come Dancing*.

Life was about to get more exciting at Motorola. We were getting a raw recruit from Texas, a kid called Lance Edward Armstrong.

Chapter Eleven

When Lance Armstrong came on board the good ship Motorola in late 1992 after the Barcelona Olympics, he found his English teammate wasn't wearing the same blue and red jersey as him. Since June 1992 I'd been allowed to wear a specially made white jersey with a red and blue band around the middle. I'd earned the right by becoming National Road Race Champion.

I'd never been a fan of the National Road Race, despite my love of racing on home roads. It always turned into a grudge match, the home-based pros ganging up on the Continental riders like Robert Millar, Malcolm Elliott and myself. I wasn't bothered when the team didn't want me to go – each country's national road race often falls on the weekend before the Tour starts – and had rarely had a good ride there, so I travelled up to Kilmarnock more in hope than expectation.

As is often the case in British races, it was pretty negative, everybody chasing moves down rather than trying to instigate things themselves. I could never fathom why riders with no hope of themselves or their teammates winning a bunch sprint spend so much effort trying to keep things together, but there you go.

It was three big circuits with a hill on, I think, then a smaller finishing circuit round the town. There was a Canadian guy called Sean Way, who was there because he used to race on a British passport, and he attacked on a descent and I went after him. I dropped him when we went up the hill the next time, but was caught by Brian Smith, who was the defending champion.

'I saw Yatesy go and I thought I'd better get on it,' remembers Brian. 'I waited for the hill then gave it a hundred per cent effort to bridge across to them. I passed Way and caught Yatesy. I went past him too, but he came back up to me and we worked together.'

We had to work really hard to stay away as the bunch chased and chased. I don't think we were ever much more than a minute in front.

'Keith Lambert, my *directeur sportif*, came up and told us what was going on,' says Brian. 'There were nine or ten guys behind us going through and off at full gas to reel us in. When we got on to the finishing circuit in Kilmarnock, my family had all come down from Paisley, just up the road, and I could hear them shouting for me, but the chasers were inside thirty seconds. I thought, "We've been out here for eighty-odd miles, we can't get caught now." We hadn't really spoken in that time – we'd been working too hard – but Sean turned to me and said, "Right: all or nothing." He had that kind of authority that you just thought, "Yes, Mr Yates, sir," and you knew you could trust him. We rode eyeballs-out from that point on, knowing that if we succeeded we would be first and second; if we were caught we would both lose out.'

With a lap to go, they were into the finishing straight behind us by the time we'd hit the line for the bell. There was no point in weighing each other up, we had to get there in front and not worry about the end until we reached it.

'I often think when I'm commentating on races and I see a little group getting caught before the finish because they're fannying about, why doesn't somebody just say, "Come on, all or nothing," like Sean did that day,' says Brian. 'We hit the last corner about ten seconds ahead of the chasers. Yatesy was in front and I thought I could take him. In hindsight I was a wee bit excited, bursting off his wheel with three hundred metres to go and gaining a couple of lengths' advantage. With every pedal stroke, though, he clawed back until he was alongside me, then gradually, painfully but inevitably, pulled in front. With fifty metres to go, I sat up, beaten. Keith Lambert, who knows a thing or two about winning sprints, told me that I'd gone a hundred metres too soon and he was right. Sean was stronger than me in the final reckoning, but maybe he would have run out of road to overtake me if I'd have waited a second or two before jumping him.'

I was bloody happy with that win. I thought that the extra distance would play into my hands, as I was used to racing further than the UK-based riders, but Brian was pretty strong. It had been fought for and earned over every one of those eighty miles we were away. You can see how pleased I am by the pictures of the finish.

'I can still see him now, an emphatic, ecstatic win, both arms up, fingers stretched out. Also, he'd been wearing this white lycra helmet-cover from the race sponsors stretched over his old-fashioned leather helmet. He looked like he had a pair of knickers on his head.'

I have worn some funny headgear over the years – the aero-balaclava, the Paris–Roubaix headband – but that helmet-cover probably takes the prize as most ridiculous, though the sponsor's trucker's cap I wore on the podium was nearly as bad.

'Though I was disappointed to lose, I was happy that the jersey had such an illustrious wearer. I'd worn it in Italy the previous year and I'd had Italian riders coming up to me all the time and asking what it was. I won it again on the Isle of Man two years later when I was Sean's Motorola teammate, and his spell wearing it in the big races had made it much more recognizable. Bradley Wiggins, Geraint Thomas and Ian Stannard wearing the jersey proudly at Sky over the last few years can all point back to 1992 as the year that it became a genuine honour, thanks to the man who won it.'

Lance had been on the Motorola radar for a little while before he joined full-time. I met him at our Santa Rosa training camp in January 1992, when he was US Amateur Road Champion. He was being treated as part of the gang already, a prodigy whom the team wanted to nurture. He was earmarked for greatness after winning that jersey at the age of 19, but he was also the US's big hope for the Olympics later that season, which were only open to amateurs then, so he was brought into the Motorola family without actually competing in our races.

We were staying at the Fountaingrove Inn, as had become our custom, and getting in the long Californian rides on roads that we had got to know well. It had become a bit more serious since the first 7-Eleven camp – no more stuffing our faces with Mexican food. I always loved riding on those roads, whether in a group or solo. In fact, I've always been the same: I like company on the bike, but I like my own company too. If a training ride is going for four hours at, say, nine o'clock, I'm going at nine o'clock, whether anybody else is there or not. Get there at one minute past and you won't see me, as the press guy we had at Discovery in 2006 found out one morning when he arranged to ride with me at six in the morning. He got there at 6.01 a.m. and there was no sign of me. See ya, bye.

Lance was a breath of fresh air at the team, a coiled-up bundle of energy and fun, full of the joy of riding his bike. I looked at him and saw the ACBB-era me, just loving being out there and racing and winning. He was winning national and international amateur races and he'd already been a national triathlon champion before he took on the bike full-time at 19. On one of those long rides we found ourselves in a convenience store in the back of beyond in the Californian Mayacamas Mountains. Lance was goofing around and messing about. I turned round and said, 'We'll see who's laughing when you turn pro, boy!', a tale he took great delight in telling and retelling years later, usually after we'd been grovelling in the gutter all day on some windswept grim Belgian roads.

I'd been telling anybody who would listen that the 1992 Tour de France would be my last. My girlfriend Pippa and I were engaged and this was my eleventh season as a pro and my fifth of living out of England as a tax exile, which was long enough in my book. I'd been squirrelling cash away through an offshore company that my dad had administered for me and had enough to buy a house for us in Sussex and live off as long as I continued working after my proper money stopped with the racing career. I wasn't considering stopping bike riding – I'll always do that – but it would be good to finish with the roving itinerant lifestyle and put down some roots with Pippa.

That viewpoint began to change in the latter part of the season. Lance turned professional for us immediately after Barcelona, where he had been disappointed to come 14th behind Italy's Fabio Casartelli, another young prospect. His first professional race was the Clásica San Sebastián, where he was stone-cold last, but finished nonetheless. He followed that up with an eye-catching podium placing behind Ekimov at the Championship of Zurich, a tough World Cup event. A couple of improving performances later, we were rooming together at the Tour of Lombardy, the last big rendezvous of the season, and getting on like a house on fire. I gave him one of my GB champion's jerseys as a souvenir of our trip and as a reminder that this was the start of something big. Having this punchy, brash Texan to guide and assist was like a shot of adrenalin for me and I was in love with racing all over again.

Och recognized that I could be a useful asset in what he expected to be Lance's breakthrough season, and he made me a terrific offer to stay on with Motorola. It was too good to turn down, so I extended happily but unexpectedly into 1993.

I was just looking through Phil Anderson's *palmarès*. Christ, that bloke had a few results, eh? I remember the Nissan in 1992, when he was in the jersey and we were pulling our perennial Britain and Ireland trick of me nailing it on the front all day to make attacks hard, a couple of guys riding on my shoulder to chase any moves, and the jersey, in this case Phil, protected in fourth or fifth wheel. It worked a treat. On one day in that Nissan I must have ridden literally a hundred miles on the front, like I was on a lone break, but with the whole race behind me. I loved it.

Two Danish guys that were always good fun to hang out with were Brian Holm and Søren Lilholt, who were at the Tulip team with Allan. One by one, those two bastards attacked me again and again. When I caught Brian Holm for about the fourth time, I said, 'What the fuck are you playing at?' He just grinned and said, 'We just love watching you chase, Sean.' When Lilholt attacked for the umpteenth time a minute later, I turned round to Lance who was riding on my wheel and said, 'Any fucking chance of you doing a turn, Lance?'

Pippa and I were married in East Grinstead in November 1992. In fact, when I was up on the forest having my picture taken for this book, I pointed out the tower of St Swithun's to Phil Ashley, the photographer. We Yates types don't fly far from the nest, really.

I'd never been great with girls, to be honest. I don't know what this says about me, but I just hadn't really been interested, certainly not like the other guys always seemed to be, talking about girls all the time. My romances had barely got beyond the teenage holding hands in the High Street and snogging in the park type of thing; I was too independent for grown-up relationships. One case in point was back when I first went to France. At ACBB, John and I went to ride this track meet on the old Saint-Denis velodrome. We won virtually everything between us, including a hilariously mismatched Madison: he was half the size of me and his handslings had no effect whatsoever, whereas I was chucking him halfway round the track. For each event I won, I was given a bouquet, which in turn I daringly handed over to a nice-looking girl in the front row of the crowd. A year later she wrote to me via Peugeot, when I was in Tours, and I suggested meeting up at the upcoming Four Days of Dunkirk, as it wasn't so far from her home in Compiègne, north of Paris. She did so, and I did the normal thing of promenading up and down the seafront with my arm round her for an evening.

When I got back to the hotel I was eager to impress my roommate Stephen Roche – in my eyes a hoary old man of the world – with what a stud I was, saying that she'd invited me to go and stay with her before the following week's Tour de l'Oise. 'Brilliant. Did you say she lives in Compiègne?' asked Roche. I nodded, trying to look like a cool old hand. 'Perfect, that's on my way back to Paris, I can drop you off.'

Shit. Of course, she'd said nothing of the sort. Roche dropped me off at her front door, waving from the car as she opened the door, wide-eyed. 'Errrr . . . hello. It's me. Can I stay?' She was 20, she lived with her mum and dad. And, it turned out, she had a boyfriend. But they kindly put up with me for a few days.

I stayed in touch with her, and she actually came to the 7-Eleven end of Tour dinner as my guest in 1989. I sat between her and Eddy Merckx, proceeded to get extremely drunk and talk about Eddy's daughter Sabrina for most of the evening, which went down really well, as you can imagine. I capped it all off by throwing up red wine all night. Considering myself well and truly dumped, I didn't go to meet her the next day as we had previously planned, though she told me a year later that she'd waited ages for me. Like I said . . . not so great with the girls.

Pippa was the exception. We'd actually had three periods of going out: that first abortive teenage thing, again when I was at Peugeot, and the last couple of years. She was the only girl I'd felt truly comfortable with, and

I didn't want to lose her again, so I thought I'd better get her hitched up.

Brian Phillips was my best man, with Conall a page boy and my sisters as bridesmaids. We had a brilliant honeymoon in Colorado, where my teammate Ron Kiefel generously paid for a couple of nights at the fantastic Hotel Boulderado as a wedding present. After that, we headed down to Durango and hung out with Bob Roll and went mountain biking with John Tomac. Well, I went mountain biking, Pippa didn't. Bob and I got caught in a blizzard in the mountains down there and were out until all hours . . . Pippa was well pissed, as the Americans say. Not for the first time, nor the last. I was always happy to be on my own and never made any concessions when we were together. When she came down to Nice I would go out on my bike all day and couldn't understand why she just couldn't go to the beach or the shops, or whatever.

The deal was that Pippa would run the household and I would just ride my bike. With my earnings we bought a lovely place up the lane from Mum and Dad, called Cherry Cottage, and she took care of everything. Within a year, Liam would come along and make us very proud parents.

After a bit of toing and froing, Pippa also took over running the financial side of my career from Dad. He was working as an investment advisor for Allied Dunbar and had invested money for some of the guys – Robert Millar, Eddy Planckaert, a few others. I mentioned it to Sean Kelly when we spoke recently for this book.

'Yes, Roger invested some money for me at that time,' Kelly said.

Oh shit, this could be bad. What happened to it?

'Actually, he did brilliantly for me, he made me about forty per cent on the money I gave him, and he advised me to take it out at just the right time.' Phew. 'Unfortunately for me, after I took it out I left it in a US dollar account and forgot about it, then the dollar crashed and I lost pretty much all the gains that Roger had made for me.'

The old boy wasn't all bad, then.

I carried on living at the Bérards' in Nice and visited Pippa for the short time I was allowed to be in the country after taking off the days for racing the Kellogg's Tour and things like that. I had a good mate in Nice who lived just up the road. His parents were in some kind of dispute with a neighbour, and the neighbour tried to get them in the shit by stitching them up, reporting them to the French customs for some kind of invented scam. I was driving up to see him one day and found myself surrounded by *douaniers* (customs police) who escorted my car down to their offices on the docks and took the thing apart. There was nothing for them to find – the malicious neighbours had fabricated the whole thing – but I ended up on a ludicrous tax charge for leaving my car at the Bérards' while I was off round the world racing. I didn't understand it then and I don't understand it now, but I paid it and put it down to experience.

The Tour DuPont had taken the place of the Tour de Trump after Donald Trump's empire had crumbled. We went into the 1993 race with Lance and Frankie Andreu as our hitters, and I was trying to keep the pace high so that it would come down to a sprint finish for Frankie on the third stage in Maryland when I found myself off the front with a couple of other guys on the finishing circuit. There was a drag up to the line that suited me, so I attacked them and managed to hold on for a solo win. It was good to have enough time to put my arms up and show off the Great Britain champion's jersey. Lance picked up a stage two days later and came second overall to make it a good week for the roommates.

I liked racing in America, which was quite surprising because so many of the events were circuit races, which have always been uninteresting in my eyes. I got a massive win there the following year at the US Pro Championship in downtown Philadelphia; the Core-States, as it was known. Unlike the Europeans, their professional road race championship was open to all nationalities and I took advantage of everybody marking Lance to solo off again, much as I'd done in Maryland the year before. The open status of the race meant they had to give the US champion's jersey to the guy who came fifth, as he was the first American over the line. The race paid out a stunning $25,000 winner's cheque, plus a tidy unexpected bonus $10,000 for being the best-placed rider over the three-race series that the CoreStates completed, thanks to second place in the preceding Thrift Drug Classic. The team were pretty pleased with that – we always pooled winnings – but not quite as pleased as we had been the year before, when Lance had improbably collected all three races to win a cool $1 million. We had fun that night.

Wearing a white jersey with the colours of the rainbow in a band round his middle, Lance was easy to spot for all those riders who wanted to mark him so tightly in that 1994 CoreStates Championship. On a rainy Sunday in Oslo, he had become the youngest post-war winner of the World Championships with his stunning breakthrough performance.

I was in Norway that day, but only indirectly for the race. Dag Otto was retiring and had invited some guys to his place in Grimstad that weekend to celebrate. His last race was to be the Worlds on home soil, then a party the following day. Pippa and I had already been there for a week or two, hanging out with him and enjoying the fag-end of a Scandinavian summer. She was expecting Liam and we were trying to time things so I could spend some time in England with her when he was due, as I was still a tax exile.

Dag Otto went off to the race and we watched it on TV. As the rain came down, the course got very slippery and people were falling constantly. Improbably, Dag Otto got in a move, and then, with not far to go, found himself alone at the front. Surely not . . . but he was swept up by a desperate chase before Lance escaped to win alone from the mighty Miguel Indurain. Olaf Ludwig won the sprint for third, with Dag Otto seventh. We nearly roared the roof off his Grimstad home.

We had a fantastic evening that following day, the carousing heading long into the night, celebrating my favourite Norwegian's incredible and varied career. He had the final laugh, though, when he dropped the bombshell that, due to his surprisingly excellent form, he was going to carry on riding! Some retirement party.

That's just got me thinking about what a dude he's always been. That winter we went and stayed at the Lauritzens' place in Belgium for a couple of months while they were in Norway; Pippa, me and the infant Liam. No bother. I basically lived on and off with them for about ten years, coming and going as I pleased. If we were bachelor boys that would be one thing, but he had a young family. What fantastic people.

It was an honour for us all at Motorola to spend 1994 riding in support of the rainbow jersey, and we all have happy memories of that season. Brian Smith had joined the team, which was great. He remembers an Italian training camp we were on:

'Hennie Kuiper was a *directeur sportif* there then and he was pairing us up for an intervals session. I was thinking, "Please not Yatesy, please not Yatesy," as I expect everyone was, but I inevitably got him. During the ride we had a session where we had to do twenty seconds all out, each three times, rest two minutes, then repeat. Until death, I think. Nobody wanted to be paired with him; he used to love that kind of shit more than anything, more than winning races, I suspect.

'Later in the ride, Hennie had us ride up this big hill in

pairs to see how we were going. I was on the front next to Phil Anderson and we were pulling so hard my knuckles were white. It was all quiet behind us so I thought we might have dropped some, but as we came past where Hennie was watching from his car bonnet, with his arms folded, George Hincapie came flying round us and shot down the descent. It all started bunching up, and I was back to about tenth in the line, but Yatesy went after him. I thought I'd better go for it too and we all started plummeting down this hill. I was picking up places here and there on the hairpins until I came round one and saw George lying in the middle of the road looking a bit dazed. That's what you get for trying to take on Yates on a descent – it just can't be done. Needless to say he hadn't waited, and, as the other guys were stopping to check on George, I thought I'd best press on after him. He was sat up and soft-pedalling when I eventually caught him on the flat and we rode together for another hour or so, half-wheeling each other. When we got to a junction and I thought we'd be heading right to head back to the hotel, he went left. "What are you doing?" I asked, riding up alongside. "A bit extra," he replied, putting his head down. We rode for another hour on the rivet, then he suddenly peeled off into a café and ordered two cappuccinos and two giant pieces of cake. He held up the cake in front of my face before he gave it to me and said, "This is why you do extra, boy!"'

Whenever you see old pictures of Paris–Roubaix it seems to be wet, the riders streaked with mud, their dirty faces etched with pain, the grime obscuring their features. But, my abortive 1989 challenge apart, all my Roubaix appearances had been dry-weather days, until 1994. I was just shy of my 34th birthday, but Roubaix was one of those races where older riders could still prosper, based as it is around experience, stamina and durability rather than exuberance and raw speed. When I'd turned pro with Peugeot all those years ago, one of my established leaders had been a guy called Gilbert Duclos-Lassalle. Now I lined up alongside him at the start of a race we both loved, with him as defending champion at the age of 39.

That race was a true epic, the sort of day that cycling fans live for and reminds them of why they remain addicted to the sport. The weather split the race early and most of us were riding in twos and threes from a long way out. A little-known Ukrainian guy called Andrei Tchmil attacked more than 60 kilometres from Roubaix and resisted all attempts to catch him. Johan Museeuw came closest. The Belgian was at his peak in the mid-nineties, but was yet to take one of his three Paris–Roubaix victories. I had been too far back on the earlier sections of cobbles when the splits happened and fell twice, skirted a crashed motorbike by way of a ploughed field, overtook numerous victims of accidents and mechanicals, but had good luck in that I didn't have a single puncture. Duclos and Franco Ballerini, another pre-race favourite who had been travelling well, both got ruled out by flats at bad moments. I chased on to fifth on the velodrome, the closest I ever got to winning my favourite race. I'm pleased it came in such a memorable edition of the old Classic.

The 1994 Tour de France was set to be an exciting race for British fans, as it was coming to England. More specifically for me, Sussex – almost past my front door. There was all sorts of fuss in the build-up to the event: that it would be a damp squib, nobody was interested, *Daily Mail* readers would wreck the event in umbrage at having their roads closed for a summer's day. The naysayers couldn't have been more wrong: an estimated million British fans lined the Wealden course from Dover to Brighton in the race's first week. It was an extremely proud moment for me when I was allowed to ride clear of the bunch as we crossed the Ashdown Forest to stop and greet my folks at the roadside. That's the sort of thing that happened a lot in the old days, but the Tour de France post-Hinault has always been a breathless event, so I was touched, as a veteran of eleven Tours, to be allowed such an honour. After asking Johan Museeuw for permission – he was in yellow, so was the *de facto* boss of the race – I big-ringed it up the climb to where Mum, Dad, Uncle Michael, Chris, Ella, Conall and Oriana were all waiting for me with a bottle of champagne. I can hardly get up that hill in 39 x 25 these days.

The British public were already well fed on glory before the race even got to England, when Chris Boardman won the prologue in Lille with a phenomenal 55-kph ride that remains the fastest prologue in Tour history. Chris was already a household name thanks to his Barcelona Olympics Individual Pursuit gold medal. Despite some definite similarities between us – he'd made his name in domestic time trials, had been our selection for the Olympic pursuit, and was setting records against the clock in the Tour – his career path had been totally different to mine. His scientific approach under the watchful eye of Peter Keen had served him well enough that there was no need to flog his guts out on the French minimum-wage circuit to make a name for himself. From the Olympics he went on to take the World Hour Record and then turn professional as effectively a Tour de France team leader with Gan, all without having to leave his base in the Wirral. He'd won his first race as a pro – the previous autumn's Grand Prix Eddy Merckx, as it happened – and now he had set the tarmac on fire and worn the yellow jersey in his first appearance at the Tour.

His team managed to undermine his achievement slightly with a scruffy team time-trial performance a couple of days later, robbing Chris of the chance to take the yellow jersey to England, but he, and by extension Britain, had already overachieved in the Tour's first week. We, on the other hand, almost pulled off what would have been one of my proudest moments as a Motorola rider when we lost out to the Italian GB–MG squad by six meagre seconds in that team time trial. Gutted. The day before, Hennie Kuiper had sent Steve Swart off on a lone break that never had a chance of succeeding. Steve was screwed the following day, and we dropped him early on, which must have cost us at least the six seconds that we lost by. It was madness and would never happen now. As a professional *directeur sportif* you have to be looking at all the possible futures, thinking about what will be happening in five minutes' time, in five hours' time, in five days' time. Sending a guy on a suicide break the day before a team time trial you have a chance of winning was just plain silly.

The two stages in southern England were an absolute delight and I went back to France sat in the top ten overall thanks to our team time-trial performance. The first stage back in the Tour's mother country was a flat run south from Cherbourg to Rennes that was animated by an attack by Frankie Andreu with 20 kilometres remaining. There had been a break for much of the day containing Johan Museeuw, who was threatening to snatch the overall lead, so there had been a big effort in the peloton to bring it back. In the confusion that followed the escapees being recaptured, Frankie launched a move and I went after him. A break of seven riders formed, with Motorola being the only team with two riders. We were thinking of the stage – Frankie was a fast finisher – but the quick Uzbekistani sprinter Djamolidine Abdoujaparov was in there too. Och did a quick bit of calculation in the team car and realized that at 38 seconds off the lead, I was the best placed rider in the bunch. If we could reach Rennes with a buffer of 39 seconds or more, I could take the yellow jersey.

This was a situation I knew well, having come very

close to the lead in Strasbourg back in 1988, then within a few seconds again in 1989, and I was determined that today would be third time lucky. There were plenty in the break who wanted to succeed, which helped, as did the fact that six teams were represented and therefore unlikely to chase. The exceptions were GB–MG, who were going to lose the jersey worn by Flavio Vanzella, with his teammate Museeuw close behind. They chased and chased, but it was a quality break of just the right number of riders, and we held them off.

Then Mapei hurled a huge spanner into the Motorola works when Gianluca Bortolami attacked the rest of the break two kilometres out from the finish. He was 23 seconds behind me on general classification, with a 20-second bonus on offer for winning the stage. Frankie and I weren't aware of that, and Och didn't inform us, so what happened next was purely down to luck. We were just trying to busy ourselves to stay away from the peloton, but in doing so we closed the gap on Bortolami, a classics rider of true class, so although he won the stage, we had closed to within two seconds of him.

There was an anxious wait at the finish line while the authorities checked, but then the news came through that I was leader of the Tour de France by the narrowest of margins. I was in yellow by one precious second from Bortolami.

You wait thirty years for a British leader of the Tour then two come along at once. I was only the third man from these islands to wear the *maillot jaune* after Tom

Simpson in the sixties and Chris Boardman a few days previously.

Graham Watson was another British face on that Tour, and he often seemed to be looking at me, facing backwards from the pillion seat of a *moto* in front, with that huge round white helmet that he always wears.

'My memories of that day are bit blurred,' confesses Graham now. 'It was right after the boat transfer to Cherbourg after two days in the UK; it was the longest stage in years, about 300 kilometres plus a neutralized section of 20 kilometres and bloody hot. I was a bit knackered, and didn't appreciate he'd taken the jersey until suddenly, there he was: all shy and proud at the same time on the podium in yellow. I was next to Paul Sherwen in the photographers' pit. I almost didn't take enough shots because we were both so happy.

'The next day was the best,' continues Graham. 'Boardman was so happy that Sean too had taken the jersey – two Brits in a week in yellow – and I got some exclusive shots of them together. Jean-Marie Leblanc was the race director then and a real Anglophile, and he handed me a glass of champagne during the stage to help celebrate Sean's and Chris's spells in yellow.'

I had my photo taken more times in the next twenty-four hours than in the rest of my career put together. In fact, an overview of my career in pictures might lead you to think that I had won many Tours and worn that fabled golden fleece for weeks on end over the years, but the truth is that I wore it for just one day. GB–MG squeezed me out in the following day's time-bonus sprints along the route, allowing Johan Museeuw to grab the jersey back. It was a case of literally squeezing me out too: when I tried to follow Museeuw's wheel, I was physically baulked by his teammate Rolf Sørensen. We protested and Sørensen was fined, but there was no sanction against his team or Museeuw. That was that.

Motorola were delighted, though. The yellow jersey and the rainbow jersey side-by-side in the Motorola ranks was a dream come true for them, and I had my photo taken alongside Lance to commemorate the day. My preference for normal drawstring-waist shorts over the more popular bibshorts worn by most riders came to haunt me, though. In the picture taken by Graham Watson before that day's start my belly button is clearly visible between the top of my shorts and my jersey, which had ridden up. Sigh. No matter, I still have that picture hanging proudly in my living room.

For a rider who had found delight and fulfilment in riding in support of teammates for the vast majority of my career, the yellow jersey was something else. Also, it had come late enough in my career for me to properly savour and appreciate. It may have only been one day, but it was one day that I never thought I would see, and one I wouldn't trade for anything.

There was a lot of talk in the papers and magazines about how nice it was for me to wear the yellow jersey in my final Tour, but looking through a contemporary *Cycling* I can see a certain amount of prescience from

Chris Boardman. 'I find it hard to believe this is his last Tour de France,' he said about me. 'He's beginning to avoid the question, so I think he might do another one.'

He was right. Lance's development meant that I was of more value to the Motorola set-up than ever before, and he personally entreated the management to persuade me to stay another year.

One of the last races of the year was Paris–Brussels, and I got into a break with Franco Ballerini and Rolf Sørensen. I hung on to them – they were two of the best riders in the world at that sort of race – while Lance tried to bridge up to us. He couldn't make it, so I clung on to the other two for grim death and got third outside the stadium in Anderlecht where it finished. On the way back, I was in one team car and Lance was in the other. He came on the radio and said, 'Hey, Sean . . . one more year, then?'

I was going as well as ever and the money was good . . . I just had to persuade Pippa. We had a baby at home and Liam's arrival had changed my view on life. However, one of those changes was to begin to see the value of my salary as more than just a nice personal stash; it was my means of ensuring a good start for my family, providing a steady home life, eliminating the need for his mum to have to go to work, that kind of thing. We talked about it and I signed on one more time.

The team was evolving. Phil Anderson had retired and Max Sciandri had moved on, but the old guardsmen like Steve Bauer, Frankie Andreu, Johnny Weltz and myself were still around. Youth was being invested in, with George Hincapie and Axel Merckx joining Lance as the team was rejuvenated. We'd also landed the signature of the 24-year-old Olympic champion Fabio Casartelli, a classy young Italian who was going places.

My Tour de France career ended with a whimper rather than a bang. After the heights of '94, I came into the 1995 version suffering from the sciatica that had plagued me on and off since 1991, and a growing pain from tendinitis in my left shin. In an effort to be ready for July, I'd been resting since it flared up at the Tour DuPont, where Lance had swept all before him, but it wasn't great and got progressively worse over the first two weeks of my final Tour de France as a rider. The first 20 kilometres of the unlucky 13th stage from Mende to Revel were absolutely flat out and the pain was just too great to continue. My Tour de France final statistics read: started twelve, finished nine, one stage win, one day in yellow, best finish: 45th.

I'm often asked what the hardest day on the Tour was. For me, I would always answer immediately it was stage 13 of the 1992 race from Saint-Gervais to Sestrière over the Italian border in the Alps. That was over eight hours in the saddle over no fewer than six Alpine passes, including two of the top-ranked HC climbs and two first-category passes. I remember coming down into Bourg-Saint-Maurice and passing the sign telling us how far it was to the top of the climb we were about to commence, the Col d'Iseran, the Alps' highest pass. It said 'GPM 45 kilometres'. Now that's a climb. By the top, with three hours still to go, my teammate Ron Kiefel was already 50 minutes down and had to abandon. Claudio Chiappucci scored one of the great Tour de France victories that day. He'd broken away near the start – I was in the move too, trying to build a buffer for the attritional later part of the day – and held off a chasing Miguel Indurain in his pomp to win 255 kilometres later.

I rate the hardest climb as Mont Ventoux, just for its relentless nature, but the climbs to Superbagnères and Plat d'Adet in the Pyrenees are tortuous. Ones that just go up to ski-stations rather than natural passes are always harder.

The hardest Tour was probably the 1987 race. It was so ridiculously long, and the absence of Hinault was like throwing the gates of the asylum open. People went from the gun every day. To abandon on the day before last was a crushing disappointment after battling all the way through the carnage.

It was a love–hate affair for the whole time I was a professional, and probably still is. When you're not there you love it; then when you get back to the Tour you remember why you hate it. Before the race began in '95 I'd agreed – I know, don't start – to do one more year with Motorola, but it would definitely be my last, and I was adamant there would be no Tour ride in '96.

I'd headed home a day before the '95 race reached the Pyrenees. The second big Pyrenean stage took the race from Saint-Girons to Cauterets. To get there, the bunch had to negotiate the tricky descent of the Col de Portet d'Aspet in the beautiful *département* of Ariège. On a fast left-hander as the road narrowed, a number of riders came down. One of those was my teammate Fabio Casartelli, and he collided at high speed with one of the concrete blocks that line French mountain roads. Medical people were there within seconds, and it was clear that Fabio had suffered serious head injuries. Our doctor, Max Testa, was with him as he was rushed into an air ambulance, but he died before he could be brought to a hospital.

Lance rang me in Nice, where I'd headed back after withdrawing. We talked it through, everything we remembered about Fabio, talking to him a few days earlier about his brand new baby, his *bambino*, his lovely wife . . . it was too much. There were tears shed, but we both needed to talk, especially Lance, cosseted in the hermetically sealed world that is the Tour. The whole thing seemed so unreal. We'd never see him again. Lance talked about pulling out, about the team pulling out, but we decided it would be best to ride for Fabio.

The effect of Fabio's loss was absolute devastation at Motorola. Though we all knew that cycling was inherently dangerous, no rider had died at the Tour since Tom Simpson's collapse in 1967. We were all more frightened about being hit by cars while training; in the big races we were masters of own destinies. Fabio was popular, a thoughtful, caring guy who was liked and respected as well as rated. In the following day's neutralized stage, the seven remaining Motorola riders were allowed to ride clear of a respectful soft-pedalling peloton to cross the line in his memory. It's not being overdramatic to say that something went from our team that day on the Portet d'Aspet that we never got back.

I met up with Och, Max Testa and Bjørn Stenersen on the shores of Lake Como to represent Motorola at Fabio's funeral. The other guys were unable to come because they were still trying to complete the Tour in his honour. I was one of the coffin bearers on what was a desperately sad occasion, a full requiem mass with the kind of anguish reserved for Italians who have lost somebody special before his time.

There was another sad postscript, as Bjørn himself died a few years later. He was riding in what was scheduled to be his last ever race when he had a heart attack and died, aged 28.

Supercharged with emotion, Lance won the stage two days after Fabio's tragic accident with a blistering attack into Limoges. The tears that had flowed in the camp for days intensified as he pointed to the sky in his victory salute, leaving nobody in any doubt to whom he was dedicating his victory.

It's hard to remember the kind of rider Lance was in those days. He was a barrel-chested powerhouse who seemed capable of winning any one-day race or short-stage race, but he was never considered suitable for the high mountains and long time trials that decide the Tour de France. He was favourite for the Olympic Road Race in

Atlanta in 1996, on home roads amongst national fervour in the first 'open' Olympics. He arrived on a hot streak too, outwitted by the canny Swiss rider Pascal Richard in that spring's Liège–Bastogne–Liège when he had been the race's strongest man, and the winner of no fewer than five stages and the overall classification of the Tour DuPont. His 12th place finish was a disappointment.

Lance and I flew to Germany for what would be the last race for a while for him and one of my last races ever. We were riding the Breitling Two-up Time Trial together and had been looking forward to it for ages. We were hopeless on the day; he was treading water. Chris Boardman and Uwe Peschel caught us for a whopping six minutes and we finished nowhere. Lance fell asleep in the car on the way back to the hotel and then missed dinner and went straight to his room to crash out: absolutely unheard of.

I was at home a few weeks later when I got an unexpected call from Och. 'Are you sitting down?' he asked.

Lance was suffering from advanced-stage testicular cancer that had spread to his lungs, abdomen and brain. He was 25 and almost certain to die, according to his doctors.

Lance's return from that to win seven Tours de France remains, in my mind, one of the most enduring stories in the history of sport. Say what you will about Lance, make your own mind up about being stripped of those titles for doping, I won't ever be dissuaded from my opinion that his seven Tour de France victories after recovering from cancer is the greatest achievement our sport has ever seen. I don't believe for one minute that many previous winners of the Tour or Lance's rivals for victories in those years were preparing for the race in any different way. How can anybody know how many previous Tours de France before 1999 have been won clean? All of them? Some of them? None of them? We'd be pretty naïve to think that the Tour heroes of old rode their careers without some outside chemical assistance; many of them have gone so far as to admit as much in their retirement. It's a great thing that the culture has changed so much, that people care whether their champions are cheats, and that today's riders are as motivated to ride clean as they are to win. So why single out Lance? A baddy to carry the sins of a whole sport, so that everybody else can sleep easy? It's a joke.

The twist in the story of Lance's comeback is, of course, that without cancer, he never would have won the Tour. His shape meant that he would have carried on his path to being a classic Classics rider, a Sean Kelly of his generation blessed with outrageous power and determination. Lance Mk II was lighter and slimmer without any discernible loss of ability. He also had the power of anger and retribution on his side thanks to, amongst other things, his disgusting treatment by Cofidis, the French team who picked him up after Motorola left the sport at the end of 1996. Mk II Lance was angrier than the original.

As for me, my final year was a quiet one. A long trip

to the Far East and the Japan Cup were my last as a professional cyclist. After fifteen years as a professional, sixteen seasons living abroad – nine years as a tax exile – I was coming home. I had a lovely wife waiting for me, and now I was the father of two beautiful bouncing boys, Jesse coming along to join Liam shortly before I packed up.

It had been quite a ride.

Chapter Twelve

I've been a bit belligerent with my bikes and kit over the years. People often ask me why I used to do this or why I used to do that, when half the time everybody else was doing something different, so I've been having a look back through the old photos and trying to fathom out what the hell I was playing at.

Bike design didn't actually change a great deal through the first few years of my career. To be honest, the biggest problem for me was going from having everything custom-built and prepared for me at home to using very ordinary off-the-peg kit when I turned professional. This wasn't unusual. Sky have actually broken the mould a little bit with their approach to bikes, kit and that much-maligned pursuit of the marginal gains. Their bikes are as good as you can get. Most other teams I've known work on the premise that you get what you're given – now go and win some races.

Tony Mills, Mick Coward and my dad always conspired to get me the best stuff. My original time-trial bikes from 1979 weren't so different from my road bikes, but that was before the advent of the low-profile 'funny bikes'. As well as the hours of messing around filing things off to make them smooth, Dad would do things like remove every last scrap of grease or oil in the bearings and replace them with graphite dust. It was all the rage. He would strip my bike after every race and put it back together. When he was finished prepping my bike on the workstand he could spin the pedals, go upstairs to make a cup of tea, bring it back down to the workshop and the pedals would still be going round. There were a few differences between time-trial bikes and road frames. The angles were a bit steeper to get you a little further forward on the saddle and keep you on the drops for longer. '76 parallel' was the watchword, meaning that both the head tube and the seat tube were at the relatively steep angle of 76 degrees. The wheels had fewer spokes and the chainrings were massive for forcing a big gear round, before the advent of tiny 11-tooth sprockets made that less important.

At Peugeot I had an off-the-peg 60-centimetre-framed racing bike. That was it.

Throughout my whole career, frames were pretty much made of various types of steel. Peugeot were innovative enough in the mid-eighties to have a carbon-fibre bike as their top-of-the-range model, and I think I rode one in the Tour de France in 1986. It wasn't the whole moulded carbon that everybody rides today, but carbon tubes glued into polished aluminium lugs. It

SEAN YATES

looked great. There used to be scare stories of carbon frames snapping, and I suppose in those days of narrow tubes that might have been an issue, but I don't remember ever seeing one snap. I remember finishing a stage of the Circuit de la Sarthe in a big bunch sprint, thinking that my bike felt funny, and noticing afterwards that one of the fork legs was snapped right through. That was as close as I got to a catastrophic failure.

I didn't ride an aluminium bike for my whole career; they were gaining in popularity when I packed up in the mid-nineties. The only deviation to our steel rides were some titanium Litespeeds that we had branded as Merckx or Caloi in the last couple of seasons at Motorola. Those steel frames were lovely, but they weighed a ton. Cycling was obviously going through one of its phases where weight is less important than something else. It's just fashion half the time.

Just having one bike in the old days was a pain. You had a spare one, but that stayed at the *service course* so the team could take it to races and carry it on the car. You had to clean your bike yourself after every training ride and turn up with it pristine or you'd get a bollocking. You could see where you were in a season by the state of the bikes on the start line. If it was March, they'd be sparkling. By September, people were losing interest and there would be a layer of grit and grime coating everything.

I think the main reason for only having one bike was because there were no trucks to carry the team's stuff around back then. If it was cost reasons it was a false economy, because you were always toing and froing for new bits or repairs, and they sold the bikes off at a profit at the end of the season anyway.

It was only when the lo-pros became popular in the late eighties that teams began to lug more kit around. We had a truck at Fagor, and I suppose I had a race bike, a training bike and a time-trial bike then.

The lo-pros were a waste of time, really. If you compare my position on a lo-pro to my old time-trialling position from 1979, it's no different: the triangle of hands, feet and bum is in exactly the same place. OK, perhaps there's a little bit less bike in the wind, but that's fractional. It wasn't until tri-bars hit the scene in 1989 that things really changed there. At 7-Eleven, we were the first team to really use them, when we worked with Dave Scott at the Tour de Trump. For an American team it was a massive event, second only to the Tour de France in importance. There was a decisive time trial along the boardwalk at Atlantic City, where we used them for the first time. We had disc wheels on front and rear with a 26-inch front wheel, and trying to keep the bike in a straight line along a windy seafront was like kitesurfing in a hurricane. Nightmare. Fast, though, and Dag Otto won the race, beating Eric Vanderaerden, who was renowned as the fastest tester at that time. Mind you, he'd been busted while beating Francesco Moser in a time trial somewhere – for the team car pushing him along with the help of a surreptitious broom handle – so maybe he wasn't that good, after all. Greg LeMond saw us using these new bars and immediately set about utilizing them to seal his comeback, using them in all three lengthy time trials in the '89 Tour. Andy Hampsten wasn't happy – he wanted us to keep our powder dry and save the tri-bars for the Tour – but we won the Tour de Trump with Dag Otto, and Andy was never seriously likely to win the Tour de France, so it wasn't a bad decision to unveil them in Atlantic City. That said, it can't be denied that they saved Greg a lot more than the eight seconds he won that Tour de France by.

To be fair to Greg, he didn't stop at the tri-bars. He completely evaluated his position, aero-helmet and everything, to gain his advantage at that Tour. If you compare his position in that race with that of another great time triallist like, say, Sean Kelly, he has more in common with Brad in 2012 than with us in the same race. He was a true innovator.

The biggest and most useful new addition to cycling technology in my time as a professional was, in my opinion, clipless pedals. When I was a junior, Brian Phillips and I saved up and bought these beautiful Duegi shoes that were the envy of everyone. They were super soft Italian calfskin, with wooden soles. But then you had to put them into metal toeclips and pull the straps up tight to avoid slipping out, losing all the comfort the leather had given you. I used to use an extra toestrap to try to keep my foot from twisting in the pedal. Our feet used to kill us. On long hot training rides around Sussex

Above: Riding the way I like it: full gas, off the front. This was with my new 7-Eleven team at the Tour of Belgium in 1989. Rolf Sørensen, Alfons de Wolf and world champion Maurizio Fondriest are behind me.

Left: Flat out again at the Tirreno–Adriatico in 1989 with my double disc wheels.

Below: I was flying in my favourite wet conditions at the 276 kilometre long Gent–Wevelgem and got away for 247 of them with Gerrit Solleveld, only to finish second.

Above: Showing off my shiny new teeth with Eddy Merckx. They were happy days at 7-Eleven, which then morphed into Motorola.

Above right: My first Tour in Motorola colours in 1991 was a painful one though, and a crash on stage fifteen, when I punctured an artery in my arm, meant I had to abandon for only the second time in my career.

Right: The Nissan Classic that year brought another famous victory though, in a stage ending with three circuits of Cork city centre; I'm climbing St Patrick's Hill here. Sean Kelly told me he thought he was going to die on the Yates train that day.

Top: Becoming British National Road Race Champion in 1992, beating Brian Smith in Kilmarnock, with more dodgy headgear.

Above and right: Sporting the National Champion's jersey in 1993, with Franco Ballerini and Edwig Van Hooydonck on my shoulder over the Orchies pavé at Paris-Roubaix, which was always a favourite race of mine, and in winning a stage of the Tour DuPont, another happy hunting ground.

Left: On crutches in Austin, Texas with (left to right), Max van Heeswijk, Lance Armstrong, Steve Bauer and Johnny Weltz.

Above: Jim Ochowicz was a great *directeur sportif*, and I learnt a lot from him that I would use later in my career.

Below: Lance was, and remains, a good friend, and those years before his cancer were just fun for everyone at Motorola.

Above: Typical conditions at Paris–Roubaix in 1994, a true Classic, when I came a best-ever fifth. Note how Johan Capiot behind me is covered in shit because he never put his nose in the wind.

Right: The team time trial at the Tour de France in 1994 was one of our biggest disappointments, as we missed out on the stage win by just six seconds.

Below: The Tour crossed the Channel that year and passed through the Ashdown Forest, where I was allowed to greet my family: (left to right) Ella, Conall, Dad and Mum at the roadside. What a day.

Left and above: Things got even better at the 1994 Tour when getting into the break on stage six into Rennes gave me the ultimate honour for one precious day: the *maillot jaune*.

Below: Chris Boardman had worn yellow after the prologue, so it was an incredible year for British cycling and unheard of at the time.

Left: Me in yellow; Lance in the World Champion's jersey he won in Oslo with a stunning performance.

Above: Winning the Giro d'Italia in 2005 as a *directeur sportif* with Discovery put Paolo Savoldelli in the pink jersey – another great achievement.

Above: Getting Bradley Wiggins to Paris in yellow in 2012 was another career highlight.

Left: I had to raise my voice in the Alps though, when Chris Froome went off on his own, as Marty McCrossan's cartoon shows!

Above and below: Leading friends and family on my annual ride through the Sussex countryside to the top of Firle Beacon. On the summit: (left to right) my friend Luke Evans, my brothers Chris and Con, me, my kids Liam and Jesse, friends Charli and Paul Divall.

we'd stop at various petrol stations and fill the sink in the toilets before putting our feet in the water to cool off. Blessed relief.

Peugeot had a deal with adidas to use their pedal system when I was there, but the pedals were hopeless, basically the same as the old Cinelli ones I'd used on the track years before. You had to pull a lever to get your foot in and out. There was also a halfway setting that was pure peril: you didn't know if you were going to get your foot stuck in when you stopped, or pull it out in the middle of a sprint.

The day before the Giro d'Italia started in San Remo in 1987, I rode down the coast to Ventimiglia. I knew there was a big bike shop there, as Allan and I had found ourselves stranded there one day a few years earlier, when a petrol-station attendant had mistakenly filled our car up with diesel. While we had hung around, interminably waiting for the system to be pumped out, we'd spent an hour or two rowing a boat along the shoreline waving at girls on the beach then looking at everything in this very bling shop.

I walked in with my team bike and had them fit a set of Look pedals and bought a pair of Brancale shoes to go with them. It was the best thing I'd ever done. The team weren't happy, as we weren't sponsored by Brancale or Look, but I was getting used to not doing what I was told by then. I spent the rest of my career getting told off for wearing the wrong thing or using the wrong stuff by team management, but I just ignored them and they usually relented and let me get on with it. As long as I was going OK, they reasoned, it was probably more hassle than it was worth to talk me out of it.

After I crashed in the Tour in 1990 and developed the sciatica down my left leg, the only way I could pedal was to have my heel in and toe out on that side, which caused a problem with the pedals I was using at the time. I got myself Time pedals and shoes, as there was more flexibility in their position, and had a longer axle fitted in the left one so that my heel didn't hit the frame of the bike. That was the only way I could ride at the time, but the long-term effect was that over time my whole body twisted to face the way my left foot was pointing. I had to have a reinforced seatbolt fitted because, by the end of a long ride, instead of pointing towards my handlebars, my saddle would be pointing to mid-on. My pelvis was completely out of line, but I carried on rather than try to fix it and end up missing time on the bike.

I didn't address it until after I packed up in 1996. I thought, 'Right,' and used fixed pedals and shoeplates to pull myself straight again. Even then, I had to have my left shoe looser than the right to give it a bit of wriggle room. In fact, I think it was ten years between that crash and riding my bike without making some sort of provision for it. The tendinitis in my shin that forced me to abandon my last Tour de France was a direct consequence of this, even though the original incident had happened five years earlier.

My basic standpoint throughout my riding career was

a simple one: I hated change. From being a cutting-edge iconoclast as an amateur with my aero-balaclavas and rear-facing front brakes, I turned into a complete Luddite.

One thing that got people scratching their heads was my handlebars – twisted forward and down, with the brake levers pointing back down the road the way I'd come. Contrary to popular belief, it wasn't just that my stembolt had once come loose and I'd grown to like it like that; there was actually some thought behind that position, however misguided. In my early days, I felt that I could generate more power from my beefed-up top half if I could stretch my arms out more when I stood up on the pedals. I liked to ride in a big gear and having the brake levers further away gave me a bit more leverage when I pulled on them, bringing the pecs and biceps I'd been subjecting to hundreds of press-ups into play. I also liked the feeling of security of the hooks on the bars coming back round and compressing my hands into the crook of the bend when I was descending; I felt like my hands wouldn't shoot off the ends of the bars if I hit a bump. I remember going to the Four Days of Dunkirk in 1982 as a neo-pro and the mechanic had moved them up to a more acceptable position.

'What's going on? What have you done to my bike?'

'It's not me, it's not me,' he said, waving his hands. 'Maurice de Muer told me to do it!'

'Put it back and don't touch my bike again!'

He got out his spanners, muttering something under his breath about '*putain d'Anglais*'.

Every time I got a new bike, the handlebars got a little bit further down. When I look at the pictures now, I think it got a bit out of hand. By about 1993 it just looked like I'd had my bike put together by a dad who'd bought it from a catalogue for his kid and built it himself.

When STI levers came out, most people were very excited about them. You could change gear without taking your hands off the bars, or even riding out of the saddle. I didn't want them; it was different. Change, aaaarrrggghhhh! I didn't ever change gear anyway. What's more, if you'd set the bike up with the levers twisted round as far as I had my old traditional brake levers, you'd probably not even be able to change gear.

These days I just do it all normally, by the book, and wonder what was the matter with me. I was a nightmare for a team: 'Yates, this year we're using these.'

'No.'

Unlike every other cyclist, I didn't like bibshorts, the type that come up over your shoulders to ensure everything stays where you put it. I wanted the little shorts with a drawstring waistband that normal people wore, because the bibs made me too hot. While I was living in Nice and windsurfing, hanging out on the beach, etc., I used to wear board shorts that were a bit shorter in the leg than cycling shorts. To get rid of the white band that was developing on my thighs in between where my board shorts came down to and where the lycra cycling shorts ended, I began to pull up my shorts when I was racing. I started rolling them up, or folding the bottom bit up, or more often than not just hoiking them up so that the sponsor's name on the side of them would be rumpled and lost. 'Yates, pull your shorts back down so we can see the sponsor's name.'

'No.'

Even my Oakleys became resistant to change. Every time they brought out a new model of sunglasses, the guys would get really excited, trying out new lenses and frame combinations. 'Yates, take those old Oakleys off, we've got some new ones for you.'

'No.'

Laurenzo Lapage was a funny guy. Later, he was a fellow *directeur sportif* with me at Discovery, but I first remember him as a rider with a Belgian *kermesse* team. I remember doing the Kellogg's Tour of Britain in the 1990s and I'd stand there on the start line with my Oakleys on and my shorts rolled up. He'd be next to me looking me up and down as if to say, 'What the hell do you think you look like? Are those swimming trunks?'

People think I didn't wear gloves because I wanted to show the world how hard I was. In reality, they were just another bit of kit that I'd have to wash if I wore them. Better off keep them nice in their packet and flog them to a fan for a few quid. What was the point of them anyway? If you were worried about hurting your hands if you crashed, why not wear elbow pads and knee pads too? I wore them sometimes. I even remember buying a silky-backed lightweight pair of gloves to wear in the Tour in '86. They're in some pictures from the mountains that year, but then there is also a headband on display, so I think I'll keep those pictures to myself, if you don't mind.

I didn't like computers then. I preferred to ride based on feel and the amount of time I'd been out rather than how far I had gone or how fast I was going. Avocet computers sponsored us at 7-Eleven and Motorola so the team insisted I had one on the bike, but I took the mounting kit and sensor off and just had the computer on my bars, picking up nothing from the front wheel. I set it to the clock setting and just ignored it. I did use a heart-rate monitor a little bit in my latter years as a pro. I finally became aware that overtraining was a bad thing and I used it to check that I wasn't low or sick on training rides after races.

All this is in stark contrast to the use of new technology and having the best of everything at Sky. I guess I have mellowed in my old age, or you might call it growing up – I don't know.

Generally speaking, at the teams I rode for, if I was going all right, they'd leave me alone to do my own thing. That was fine by me.

Chapter Thirteen

It's not easy sometimes to talk about your life, your family and the people close to you. Writing this has made me realize that very clearly, and also demonstrated that it's hard to keep a sense of perspective. I started talking to Pippa, my ex-wife, as she knows me better than anyone, and I'm trying to get a feel for things that I've rarely, if ever, stopped to think about.

Once we started talking about stuff, it was clear that she has a much better memory and a much better understanding than me. I thought the best way was to let her talk to you directly and keep my nose out, so this chapter is hers and hers alone.

Pippa's Story

I was 13 when I met Sean. I was spending most of the summer hanging out at King George's Hall, now called the Kings Centre, in East Grinstead. I loved roller skating, and I got free sessions on the rink there if I helped out on the counter. I spent the school holidays handing out rental skates to other kids and feeling pretty cool.

I'd seen this guy coming and going. In fact, he seemed to be there every day, pumping iron in the weights room. One day, I sauntered up to him.

'So, what are you up to, then?'

'I'm training for the Olympics.'

Wow!

Autographs were big in those days. I don't really know why, but whenever you saw somebody famous, everybody would say, 'Ooh, did you get their autograph?' like they would be worth money or something. Kids had autograph books that they would take to football matches or pop concerts. I reckoned that if this fellow was going to the Olympics his signature would be cool so I asked him for it and he wrote it on a scrap of paper.

After that, he would send me postcards. It wasn't what you might call regular correspondence, but I'd get a card out of the blue every now and then, always from some spot around the world. Later, he sent me reams and reams of letters. I still have every one of them in the cellar. When we divorced I said, 'Here, you can have these back,' like you're meant to, but they've somehow found their way back here.

We didn't actually start going out until I was 16, and then we had a romance that lasted a full two weeks. He used to walk or hitch up from Forest Row to East Grinstead and we'd sit in the park, pretty standard fare.

I can still see him now, always wearing the same clothes: a pair of combat pants with a bar towel sewn across the seat. I think he got fed up with having to trawl three and a half miles to see me and started going out with a girl in his village instead.

It must have been another four years until we went out again, though the postcards kept dropping on to the mat sporadically during that time. I was walking down East Grinstead High Street on a Saturday morning, when Sean came parading along in the other direction. I say parading – he used to call his Saturday jaunts up to the huge metropolis the 'Grinstead Strut', strolling along the road like a peacock, checking out who was around. It was great to see him after such a gap, we'd both grown up a bit – in years, if not in mentality – and we went to the pub to catch up. This time, we carried on seeing each other.

I remember going on a day trip to Brighton beach with his youngest brother and sisters. Oriana was just a toddler and little Conall was about five, I suppose; Ella was eight. I remember laughing my head off at Sean's funny tan lines and shaved legs when he stripped down to his trunks. Even then he had a huge wiggly varicose vein winding across his right shin that he seemed improbably proud of.

He invited me over to France to a race he was doing, a gentleman's two-up time trial, where he, as a younger rider, had to lead an old pro round. I sat down to wait for him and a man I vaguely recognized as one of Sean's teammates sat down next to me and began to chat in French. My French was pretty hopeless, but I appreciated him trying to make me feel welcome and stammered back as best I could in a language that was almost totally unknown to me. After five minutes of stumbling difficulty I realized that the man talking to me was Stephen Roche and English was our shared mother tongue.

Back in England one day, Sean and Chris turned up at my parents with a bike of Chris's that I could ride. I'd not ridden a racing bike before, only a pass-me-down that was old, tatty, clunky and with no handlebar tape. This one had a saddle much like the proverbial razor-blade. Sean and I trundled off for a jaunt in the Sussex countryside carrying a picnic I'd made. This was the day I discovered his true sadistic streak, cajoling, nagging and bullying me up hill and down dale for hours on end; I couldn't walk for a week. I lay down in a field hoping to just die quietly while he ate every morsel of the picnic.

He was so hard on me, just toying with me and teasing me whenever he could. I don't even want to think about the first time he persuaded me to get on a motorbike with him. Needless to say, I endured the journey out but refused the ride home.

A few months later our relationship ended but we remained firm friends as usual. Then in 1992 we started dating again. This time we were much more grown up. I had a flat of my own and Sean lived in Nice. I was working for a company of civil engineers and worked long hours and extra days so that I could have a holiday with him down at the Bérards' place. We had a truly lovely summer. By June of that year we were engaged, and married in the November. We were married, by chance, on the same day as Miguel Indurain. That Christmas Sean bought me a bike. He had got it from a supermarket and it appeared to have been made from scaffolding pipes, judging by the weight of it, but he'd written 'Pip' in nail varnish on the top tube. So the following February, in Nice, I thought I'd give it a go. Sean kitted me out with a heart-rate monitor and all the cycling kit – no helmet in those days, of course. Just getting the bike out of the shed the monitor rose to 93; I was quite excited. Well, it was straight up from the off, up into the hills behind the house. He might have thought it was a gentle leg-stretcher, but the Col de Turini was a bloody big mountain as far as I was concerned. If you watch *Top Gear* you'll have seen it when they went in search of the world's best driving road, a tiny ribbon of hairpins climbing high above the Med. I was in a bit of a state; my heart was at 175 after about five minutes. He rode up to the top then rode back down to see how I was doing, then again . . . and again, each time finding me in a greater state of distress, discarding another layer of clothing. We finally got to the top and I ate a Mars Bar like a condemned man enjoying his last meal. On the way down, he left me behind, leaning his bike over at a crazy angle into the corners. I didn't want to be up there on my own so I pedalled for all I was worth to catch him up.

Inevitably I went too fast into one of the hairpins, pulled both brakes too hard and lost control. I came down hard on my arm and slid on my side all the way across the road, through the gravel, and ended up with my head an inch from the rock cliff. A bus swerved around me and I lay on my back staring at the sky, panting. A lady who had been passing by ran over to see if I was OK, then hollered down the mountain to alert Sean.

He came flying back up almost as fast as he'd gone down.

'What the fuck are you doing?' he bellowed. I must have looked up in shock.

'How the hell could you fall off on a road like this? What's the matter with you?'

'Sean,' I sobbed, 'my arm really hurts.'

'Come on, hurry up, get back on, it's getting dark.'

The saddle was twisted and so were the bars, so he pulled it all straight and we set off again down the mountain into the gathering dusk. The crash had put the wheels out of alignment so that now the brakes squeaked whenever I used them.

'Stop braking!' he shouted every time I tried to slow down.

Back at the Bérards' in Nice, I tried to clean myself up. In Sean's little apartment he had a hotplate next to the sink. When you were cooking you had to be careful not to touch both at the same time or it made a circuit and you electrocuted yourself. My arm was really hurting and he eventually took me to the hospital, where they agreed it was broken, set it, put it in a cast and sent us away.

'Well, that's it; you'll have to go home now,' he said, 'you're broken.'

I was gutted. I'd spent weeks working to earn the time and money for my holiday.

'Can't we just take it easy and stay on the beach for a week?' I asked.

'This is not a holiday!' he growled. Miserable old git.

Neither of us knew that I was expecting our first child, Liam, at the time.

And despite all that, Sean was great fun. A total clown. A visit to the shops became a circus act; tangling himself up in the clothes rails so that he'd have shirts and jumpers hanging off him; running up the down escalator. He always played the fool and we laughed a great deal.

Money isn't important to Sean. He likes earning it; he's not really into spending it. It bothers him about how much he has but he certainly doesn't sit at home counting the pennies. Money is the one thing that Sean and I have never argued over. When we found out that we were expecting Liam, we decided to buy a house. We bought a beautiful cottage in Forest Row. I would run the house and all that that involved so Sean could concentrate totally on his career. He'd get back when he could and Liam and I would go out to Nice whenever he had a gap in his race schedule.

Up until that point, Roger, Sean's dad, had been

director of the offshore company they'd set up to handle Sean's money, so we agreed to change it round so that I would be in charge. I asked Roger for all the bank paperwork so I could take over the administration and run the accounts. He came back to me with a bizarre story of how, somehow, they had all been burnt by mistake. I told him not to worry and got the bank to supply us with copies of everything without too much bother. It became obvious at that point why he didn't want me to see any of it. At that time, Roger was working at a local college as a sculptor and selling stonework. It was apparent that he'd been dipping into Sean's cash at regular intervals to fund his activities, buying the stone he needed for his sculptures.

I obviously informed Sean and left him to deal with Roger. Next time Sean was home I remember looking out of the window at Cherry Cottage and seeing him in the garden outside with his hands round his dad's throat, shaking him like a rag doll. That was it. It was never mentioned again.

To be honest, Roger was a lunatic. He controlled his family and put them through hell chasing his pie-in-the-sky ideas. The real victim of Roger's antics was Jenny, though. Our first Christmas as a married couple was a big celebration. We had both sets of our parents over and Roger was being particularly fractious. My dad, who was always a very polite man, said to him, 'You must be very proud of Sean, Roger.'

'No,' he replied.

My dad gave him a look and decided to not speak to him again. He was obviously not worth the effort.

I remember another Christmas at Roger and Jenny's, where she'd gone to town beautifully – pixies, elves, candles all over the house, all very arty and Steiner, really gorgeous. They even had real candles on the tree. Roger was having a bath while the rest of us sat there, enjoying the moment, when we noticed a pretty golden light playing on the ceiling above the staircase. Sean and Chris ran downstairs to find the dresser on fire. All those candles had come at a price. They ran to fetch buckets of water to douse the flames, but all in silence lest they alert their father. When Roger returned from the bathroom, he was none the wiser, even though we all had secret expressions on our faces.

Eventually, Roger just upped sticks and left for Portugal with his Swedish girlfriend, painting henna tattoos for tourists on the beach. As with most of his schemes, it didn't last that long and they moved to Sweden. He still rings Jenny up regularly, and I wouldn't be surprised if he showed up again sometime. Ella, Conall and Oriana have been out to see him, but as far as I know neither Sean nor Chris have spoken to him in a long time.

Jenny has an inner strength. She has dedicated her life to her family. She's an amazing woman. She regularly visits my mum in East Grinstead – we lost my dad three years ago – and they have tea together and chat about the grandchildren. Never about Sean and me, though; according to Mum that's the unspoken rule between them. There's a lot of Roger in Sean, but there's plenty of Jenny too.

When I was eight months pregnant with Liam, we were somewhere on the French Med with Phil and Christy Anderson. We hired two catamarans between us and, of course, it turned into a race. Sean just headed straight out to sea under full sail with me hanging on for dear life. A rescue boat came up alongside and asked if we were OK, if we'd ever sailed one before. 'No,' Sean shouted back over the spray, 'but these things are all the same!' and we caned it out into the open sea. I looked forwards at the water breaking over the bows, then back to the helm, and he'd gone. Disappeared overboard. I hadn't a clue how to sail and I had a buoyancy thing on, so I thought my best bet would be to abandon ship and bob in the water until somebody realized we were missing and came looking for us. I was on the verge of jumping over the side when I saw eight white knuckles clinging to the other side of the boat. It wasn't until very recently, when I was telling somebody this story, that he confessed he'd done it deliberately just to see what I would do.

Similarly, we were out on Dag Otto's speedboat in Norway once and he just stood up and jumped off the back while we were speeding along at full pelt, just to make everybody laugh. It cost him a new pair of Oakleys, but he didn't seem to mind.

The deal we had when we got married was that Sean wouldn't be away for long, a year at the most he had said.

We were a young family, and the money he was earning was giving us a great base, but it was never our intention to carry on like that indefinitely. Certainly, the last two years of his racing career, '95 and '96, were both extra time as far as I was concerned. Motorola didn't want him to retire and kept extending his contract. That last year, 1996, was at the personal request of Lance, who was beginning to come into his own as a bike rider and saw Sean as something of a wingman.

The Motorola gang were great. It really was like a big family. The wives and girlfriends met at the Tour de France and various get-togethers throughout the year. Och went out of his way to make sure everybody felt involved. There was Frankie Andreu and Betsy, who was still just his girlfriend in those days, Phil Anderson and Christy Valentine, Sean and myself, and various others coming and going, and we all went out together. The Americans, or specifically the American WAGs, were nervous when Lance joined the team. They knew he was supposed to be the boy wonder and they were all worried about how it would affect their men's standings in the pecking order. You can imagine that that kind of team politics didn't bother Sean in the slightest, and I always felt a bit like an outsider looking in at those guys anyway. It was probably that as much as anything else that drew Lance to Sean, and they got on like a house on fire. Motorola took Lance to the finish of the Tour de France in 1992 as a non-riding member of the gang to give him a feel for the world's biggest race. With all the riders out at a team presentation and the girls all getting ready for their big night out, Lance was bored and turned up at our hotel room on the pretence of needing shampoo, or something similar. I was about seven months pregnant and we chatted very naturally. He was always very respectful and loyal to me and all the other members of the group. At a later time he came to stay at our cottage and was the perfect house guest. At a couple of Tours later, we were at the usual team dinner. One of the riders was quite drunk, as can be excused amongst very skinny men who've spent three weeks hauling their bodies around France at a rate of knots. Anyway, he decided that it would be a good idea to unzip the back of the dress I was wearing for the occasion. I was shocked and just stood there with my mouth open. Sean didn't react at all. Instead, it was the youngest member of the party, Lance, who calmly stood up, zipped my dress back up and let the culprit know in no uncertain terms that was no way to treat a lady.

I don't think I'm letting too many confidences slip when I say Lance was clearly the up and coming man and as such was targeted by teammates and their partners to be the one to hang out with. I found him incredibly loyal to his teammates and their women. He spent an awful lot of time in the company of Frankie and Betsy near Lake Como and then later in Nice.

Sean retired around the same time that Lance got ill, so we weren't around during the years of his great comeback and subsequent success – therefore I can't really comment on the illegal methods used by the team to win those seven Tours beyond giving my opinion of the man I knew before then. He was a decent, respectful, driven and ambitious man. Brash and loud, but, God, he's American. I can't help but be thoroughly confused by a sport that reveres his rival and similarly disrobed champion Marco Pantani yet goes to such lengths to vilify Lance at every available opportunity. I just don't get it. His loyalty still extends into his isolation too: I don't hear Lance accusing any of those around him in those glory years of any fault or blame for their roles in the saga.

Sean finally packed up at the end of 1996. We had a second boy now, Jesse, and we prepared for life at home as a family. It wasn't easy. Sean had problems adapting to life in his own house – he didn't know where the electric meter was, he didn't know which cupboard the plates were in – whereas I had difficulty adjusting to having him around all the time when I had day-to-day life at home down to a fine art. He took to spending most of the time in the garage on the turbo trainer.

His compulsive behaviour was a pain. I would make a cup of tea and leave the spoon by the sink, which used to make him mad. He would lecture me and lecture me, but I wouldn't be bullied and carried on doing it as a point of principle. After a while, I started hiding the spoons in different spots round the kitchen to watch him go mental when he found them. He had a thing we called 'Wet Cloth Syndrome'. I would cook a meal, wash up and wipe the surfaces down, but he would have to get up and go over everything again with a wet cloth. Now, in his own house, or if he's in a restaurant, he will be continually wiping imaginary crumbs from the table into his hand. He says that my house is a mess; too many animals for a start. He regularly comes round to see us and, every now and then, we still all go out as a family.

In 1998 we had a chat about what we wanted to do and agreed that living in France would be very attractive. I set to work finding properties in the Dordogne and the Lot that would suit us and we put the house on the market. Sean sold his boat and his motorbike; I sold a family heirloom piece of furniture that I shouldn't have sold – but we were preparing to move wholesale.

A little alarm bell began to ring in my mind. Life at home as a single parent in Sean's absence was hard enough. If he started off on his travels again – I thought it was virtually inevitable – I would be on my own with two young children in a foreign country. Where would the boys go to school? How would I get by at the shops and the town hall? What if the boys needed the dentist or the doctor? When would I see my parents? I started to think I wasn't sure I wanted to go at all. Plus, buying and selling a place in France was more complicated and expensive than here; we couldn't afford to turn around and come back after six months if it didn't work out – there was no safety net. In the end I pulled the plug on the idea. Shortly afterwards, Julian Clark came calling, dangling the promise of a job back in cycling with a

British team and, of course, Sean left home again. We ended up moving to Buxted. After six months, we realized we had made a mistake leaving Forest Row and set about moving back again. By now our gorgeous daughter, Bathsheba, was born. In 2000, we were very lucky to find another cottage in the same lane that we had lived on before. It was just perfect. Sean became *directeur sportif* with a few teams over the next years. Then in 2005 we were divorced. I was fortunate to be able to keep the cottage and still live there today. Our divorce was calm and straight to the point with no arguments. The traumas had been in the years leading to that point. I have never regretted marrying Sean and I certainly don't regret divorcing him either. Finally, I no longer flinch when he makes a sudden movement.

All in all, in the thirteen years we were married, Sean only had a concerted period of eighteen months at home in between being a pro cyclist and going back to the game.

As I say, to this day we speak to each other on more days than we don't, even when we want to kill each other. I firmly believe we've been together in former lives and we'll be together again in future ones. He always turns to me when he is confused or the going gets tough. I have always been his rock and he knows that I will never let him down. It is important for family to stand by each other and I am proud that we can do this as it shows our children the correct morals of life. I always talk things through with them and they are in no way hidden from the facts of their parents' lives, however hard some of the news is.

To demonstrate that some ties go beyond marriage and divorce, whenever Sean has been ill with his heart, I have been the first person he has called. I immediately take care of things for him and, if he is in the UK, turn up with a basket over my arm like Little Red Riding Hood, full of all his favourite bits and pieces from the health food shop in Forest Row. He just hates hospital food. Even when Sean had his stroke in Germany a few years ago, I looked after things this end – sorting out the DVLA and ringing doctors, etc.

He'll always be all right. Sean has the golden ticket to life. He'll always be OK because a) he has the golden ticket, b) he works bloody hard, and c) he's not greedy.

It's hard for people to understand his attitude to work. Everybody seems to accept that he loves grafting and loves the concept that good things have to be earned, but they have a problem understanding that to Sean, being a professional cyclist, being a Tour-winning manager and being a gardener are much the same. They're jobs. The key thing to making sense of it is to recognize that none of them are *just* jobs. They are all jobs that demand his 110 per cent effort and application and they will all reward him with the same satisfaction.

Sean is basically a simple man. You go to work, you work hard, and you get paid. If a problem comes along, you fix it, or should I say, you get me to fix it. He's a country boy, really. People who have only heard him talking in recent years on TV might be fooled into thinking that his stroke has made him talk the way it does. Granted, you can hear it sometimes, especially if he's tired, but essentially he's always had that slow Sussex way of talking. It's almost a drawl. Because the Sussex accent isn't a country voice like, say, a Somerset or Devon tone, people don't recognize it, but it's a different way of speaking to the estuary English that it can be mistaken for. It's slower, with longer gaps, much more like these West Country brogues in pattern. You can take the boy out of Sussex, but nobody's ever got near to taking Sussex out of that boy.

For his birthday this spring we went up on to the golf course just across the way, with the kids, and lit some Chinese sky lanterns. The first one lurched off at a mad angle – we'd lit it wrong – heading for the houses. We all raced after it and it disappeared into the gardens somewhere. 'Shhh!' he shouted, 'Leg it!' and we all ran home giggling, hoping we hadn't been seen and hoping he hadn't set the forest alight. Again. Just like when he was a kid. But then, he is a kid.

I'd like to leave it there, but I should really tell you about what happened last year when everything went belly-up at Sky. Sean was really shaken, very upset in the face of scandalous gossip and tittle-tattle. He came straight round to me and we talked his options through. He was worried about the kids and me and how we would get by without the Sky salary coming in with him in retirement. I said it would be OK, I would get a job. He said he would leave his girlfriend, as his family was more important. We talked and talked and eventually agreed that it would be good for him to move back in and for us to pull our strengths together as a family. I was left to explain to the children the plan and, obviously, they were delighted, absolutely over the moon. They had waited all their lives so far to have their dad at home and not going away all the time. It was like Christmas come early.

Unfortunately, a few days later Sean told me he'd changed his mind. I'm used to it; I know what he's like. The kids deserved better from their dad, though, and I should have protected them better. You see, he had found his confidence again and therefore his rock could be put to the side once more.

Chapter Fourteen

There are few ex-professional cyclists who still go bike riding. In the old days it was virtually unheard of. Once you were done, you were done, and the years sacrificed to careful eating, abstinence and sport were quickly regained through face-stuffing, boozing and chain-smoking. It seemed unnatural for me to stop, though, and I kept riding every day, because I enjoyed it, and because I always had, I suppose.

If I was going to ride, there might as well be a point to it. I tried to keep my weight down in the mid-70s like it had been for the second half of my career and resolved to spend my late thirties doing a few time trials and domestic road races. Which is how I found myself in Hertfordshire on a cold and windy February morning in 1997. I was riding the North Road Hardriders 25-Mile Time Trial. I'd done it before, of course, but that was eighteen years previously, in 1979. It was a wild day with the wind blowing me around on the tri-bars and a couple of spooked horses threatening to put me in the ditch, but I hung in there and got my first win of my second amateur career, holding off the younger long-distance specialist Gethin Butler. He went on to break the Land's End to John O'Groats record in 2001 with something just over 44 hours, which remains the fastest time. There are nutters, and there are nutters.

I got a nice result on local roads when the National 50-Mile Championship was held around Crawley. I put a couple of minutes into Gethin on that occasion and walked off with a gold medal. A National Time Trial Champion again, seventeen years after my 25-mile title in 1980! Being retired was easy!

I was sponsored by a great guy called Vic Haines, who had a cleaning company called Fresh Start, which seemed appropriate: an old bloke home from France racing around with Fresh Start written all over him. I rode the tandem with Vic as well – we broke the 30-mile record up on the A12 in his home county of Essex. I'll have to check if we still hold it. Tandem records are great to set because so few people ride tandems, so they're much less likely to get broken. Oh bugger, I've just looked it up, and not only did we lose the record to Zak Carr and Glenn Taylor, I've been reminded of Zak's cruel and untimely death. He was killed riding to work when some fucking idiot was half asleep at the wheel and wiped him out. It makes you sick to think you can race all round the world and then something as dumb as that can take you away for ever from the people who love you. Zak and I hold a tandem record ourselves when we did 304 miles in twelve hours in 2005, just before he was killed.

I re-established the gardening round I'd had as a teenager. I did a house a day five days a week, and rode my bike on a turbo in the garage afterwards. That brought in a little bit of cash, and Vic covered all my racing expenses. With the money I'd put away over the past few years at Motorola we were doing OK: Pippa and I were pretty frugal people and didn't need much. We weren't into going out a lot or buying fancy gadgets every two minutes. I couldn't see me doing it for the rest of my life, though; I needed something to get my teeth into. I was aware that after spending my entire adult life on the road I wasn't the easiest character to get on with at home, and I wanted to get out there and do something.

Graham Watson is cycling's best-known photographer. God knows how many frames he's fired off pursuing cyclists round the globe for the past thirty-odd years. A good cycling photographer needs a good pilot, as the snappers call the motorbike riders that drive them in and out of the peloton all day on the big races. Graham and I began to talk about the possibility of me driving him on the pro race circuit.

'I'd hinted to Sean about driving me and staying in the sport that way – he was interested,' says Graham now. 'But as his career ended he had other things on his mind, and I sensed he needed to spend time away from races. Eventually he got back into the sport as a *directeur sportif*, and I realized in hindsight that was what he was really good at – which has been proved. I also realized he was a mad driver anyway, and that I was probably better off not having him drive me in races.'

At the same time, Pippa and I were wondering about our next steps. A new family life in France would be an exciting adventure, and we both thought that the countryside around Cahors in the Lot would be a great place to bring up a family. But the sale of Cherry Cottage moved slowly, and we began to cool on the idea. It was going to be a big deal to uproot the boys, and Pippa started to get cold feet about bringing them up abroad when I was away working.

Our unravelling plans were shelved indefinitely in May 1998 when I got an unexpected call from a guy called Julian Clark. He was a newcomer to cycling, having ridden for and managed professional motocross teams previously, but now he was running the most eye-catching domestic cycling team in the UK: the Linda McCartney squad. Formed on a ticket of vegetarianism to spread the word that Linda's philosophy could benefit anyone – even competitors in some of the world's toughest sporting events – and to promote the range of frozen meals bearing her signature, they were selected to ride the inaugural PruTour.

The PruTour – a shortened form of the Prudential Tour of Britain – was the replacement event for one of my favourite old stamping grounds, the Kellogg's Tour. It was a nine-day race starting in Scotland and taking in as much of the UK as possible between there and London. Julian was ringing me because he had a problem: the race was about to start and he was a rider short after one of his guys, Scott Gamble, had unluckily had an untimely accident. He offered me £1000 to join the team for the duration of the race as a guest rider.

I wasn't sure. I'd been retired for two years and had just turned 38. I had continued riding, but mainly short time trials – hardly ideal preparation for a grade-one international stage race against teams from Festina, US Postal and the likes. Also, Pippa's brother was getting married on the penultimate day of the race. Pippa and I talked about it, reasoning that the £1000 Julian was offering was what I had been earning a month tending gardens and, if I could finish on the Friday night instead of the Sunday to make Crispin's wedding, that had to be worth it for a week's work. That night I went up to the loft, dusted down my old kitbag and prepared to fly up to Edinburgh.

I got picked up at the airport and was taken to the hotel where most of the teams were staying. It was like walking into a time-warp, a dream-like stroll through my past and all the people I'd cycled with in the peloton over the years. Over there was Chris Boardman, there was Stuart O'Grady, look, there's Viatcheslav Ekimov.

I went fine in the race, enjoying the lack of pressure and discovering I was still fit enough to ride the Tour of Britain, if not drag it round the country like I had years ago. I roomed with Julian and he pummelled me for information, hungry for knowledge. He was a pretty amazing character, having taken up riding only a few months previously and now riding a big-budget professional stage race. I couldn't help but be impressed with his energy.

A couple of things stand out in my memory from that race. Julian was very wary of a climb on the Yorkshire stage called Rosedale Chimney, that is purported to be the steepest road in England. We weren't exactly blessed with limitless resources and it looked like some of the riders would have to use a 21-sprocket to climb it. I'd been up it several times on the Kellogg's or the Milk Race, or some race or another, so I gave him a couple of tips on how to tackle it.

That night, back in the room, he said, 'Shit, you must be strong.'

'What do you mean?'

'Well, I did what you said, tried to use the speed and momentum coming down to the foot of the climb, but there was such a long drag up to the first hairpin I was dying by the time I got there. God knows how you beast it up there. I had to zigzag all over the road just to get round it.'

'Ah, sorry about that. It wasn't the climb I was thinking of.'

On the next day's Pennine moorland stage, the peloton split, leaving Julian and me as the only McCartney riders in the front. I looked for him, in my old habit of always looking for my leader, and saw he was hanging near the back of the long single line, grovelling in the crosswinds. He wasn't the world's prettiest bike rider, but he was clinging to the wheel in front with all his might. I dropped back until I was alongside him and said, 'It's going to split again and you're in the wrong half, you have to move up.' He looked sick at the thought but swung across on to my wheel and I towed him up to the front. When we got there, naturally there were no gaps, and there were some serious guys pulling hard. I saw Jean-Cyril Robin in about fourth place and had a quick word with him in French and he pulled back to make a gap that Julian manœuvred himself into with gratitude.

'What did you say to him?' he asked me that night.

'I just told him you were my boss and that if he didn't let you in I wouldn't get paid.'

I ended up getting tenth on that stage in the big sprint on the prom at Blackpool, and was 39th overall when I pulled out on the Friday night in Reading, I think. The best-placed McCartney rider, anyway, so I hope he got his money's worth. During the week he told me of all his big plans for the team, how there was loads of money available, how he was thinking big and trying to build a British Tour de France team, and how would I like to be the *directeur sportif*? I jumped at the chance.

At about the same time, I got a call from my old Motorola teammate Steve Bauer. Lance had called him offering him a job at his US Postal set-up assisting another of my old pals, Johnny Weltz, who was their *directeur sportif*, but he wasn't interested. I called Lance and we had a chat, but I wasn't sure about it. It sounded like there was some politics: Lance had come in a year after they'd begun and had gone directly to pretty much running the show as his comeback gathered pace. I wasn't sure how well he got on with Johnny and didn't want to get caught up in that if there was a power struggle. I should probably admit that I was a bit put out that he'd called Steve Bauer first, which made me think I hadn't been first choice. In that last year at Motorola before Lance got ill, Och was trying to find a new sponsor to keep the team going, and it was understood that I would get the assistant *directeur sportif* job if it came off.

Julian was keen for me to sign and the Linda McCartney team would be an ideal place to learn, somewhere I could grow with the team. It would mean less travelling as well, as we were still going to be based in the UK, with a *service course* actually not far at all from my home, so Pippa preferred that too.

The first year was a bit static, with us being easily the strongest UK team but often losing out to good riders from smaller teams who used our strength against us to poach wins. When we did venture abroad, notably to some French Cup races, we got a good hiding. For the second season we aimed big and restructured. In came Max Sciandri, one of my old Motorola hitters, as leader, and with him the Olympic champion Pascal Richard. They were two of the three medallists from the Atlanta road race, and had won countless other things between them. We were looking to make a splash.

McCartney was ramshackle. None of us really knew what we were doing, but it was fun, and some of the friendships formed there have lasted for many years. Take Craig Geater, for instance. He was a Kiwi guy who was over to ride in Europe with his mate Scott Guyton, who'd found a place on our team. We were presented with a bit of a crisis when our mechanic went AWOL before a big race, and Craig stepped in to help out. He's been a pro circuit mechanic ever since, working for CSC, Discovery, Astana, RadioShack and now Orica– GreenEDGE.

I had slipped into the lifestyle I've continued since those first days with McCartney, of going out to ride every morning before the race began.

'I'm not sure when exactly I started riding in the mornings with Sean,' Craig thinks back now, 'but it was some time during that first year at McCartney. He'd get me up at the crack of dawn, or earlier, and we'd be off. I remember going to Canada for this race called the Trans-Canada Tour, or something like that. Considering it was Canada, it was about the flattest race I've ever been to. My mate Scotty won the King of the Mountains jersey there, which showed how hilly it was as he had trouble climbing the stairs of a night. There was one hill to speak of at the whole race and, needless to say, Sean headed straight for it, then blasted off and left me. It was dark, I didn't know where we were and there were squirrels running across the road under my wheels. "He'll be back," I thought. No, he won't. The next morning, he dropped me before we got out of the car park. The morning after that, I said, "I'm not riding with you any more."'

I remember that race – damn, it was flat. I'd been really looking forward to seeing beautiful Canada, but we got mile after mile of featureless highway. Scott got the jersey through virtue of being in a break all day. The day after that, he was so keen to get up that hill Craig was talking about, and get some points to keep the jersey, that he blew his doors off completely. The whole race came past him after the summit and he nearly got eliminated by the time limit.

'Sean and I established a pattern that would last many years,' says Craig. 'We would sit in the car all day bitching and moaning about everybody and everything. He's crap, look at his position, he's fat, he's a cheat, that *directeur sportif* couldn't drive a milk float, their bikes are ugly . . . One morning I got to the car and Sean threw the back door open for me and said, "Welcome to the Bitter Zone!" That was about right.'

Craig had this trick that I have never seen anybody else master. He would sit motionless in the back seat not saying anything – he was the silent type anyway – with his mirrored Oakleys on. I came to realize over the weeks, months and years that he was often asleep, but he looked no different, asleep or awake. Great trick.

'Yeah, at one race he got me good, though,' says Craig. 'I was woken by the car screeching to a halt and the boss shouting, "Puncture! Quick, Craig, rear wheel!" I leapt out holding the spare wheel only to be met by silence and no bike rider in sight. Just Sean sniggering like Muttley. "Gotchyer! That'll learn yer to sleep on the job, boy!"

The sleeping trick is a good one, though obviously I don't do it now if anybody from Orica–GreenEDGE is reading this. The clincher is to keep your mouth shut. Not many people can sleep like that. The only person it never fooled was Johan Bruyneel. That man has spidey sense.'

My riding in the mornings got me into trouble in South Africa, where we were doing a pre-season race called the Rapport Tour. I was already getting funny looks from the other *directeurs sportifs* and the older riders for my unusual habit. When I got back after my ride, the *soigneurs* told me that the race officials were looking for me because someone had tested positive. It turned out to be a fuss over nothing – the rider in question had left his certificate proving his naturally high testosterone level at home – but as I hadn't been there, the team management and sponsors had been rung back in England in the early hours to try to find somebody in authority. I got a right bollocking and was told in no uncertain terms that I had to be there at all times to look after the riders. I think this was meant to stamp out my bike riding once and for all, but instead I just went earlier each day, getting back at the time the riders were waking up. I couldn't be needed while they were asleep.

'Later on, when we were at CSC,' Craig continues, 'there was a Danish mechanic called Jonny, who always wanted to take him on in the mornings. The two of them would ride and ride, trying to drop the other one all the time. On one misty morning, Sean was hanging on to

Jonny's wheel as he tried to sprint off when the mechanic suddenly flicked out of the way of a bollard that loomed out of the mist at the last moment. The boss hit it head on and Jonny never even realized, he just kept going. The cuts and bruises kept us amused over breakfast.'

Another friend from those days is John Deering, who's been helping me with this book. He was our press guy there and he remembers my nocturnal miles.

'We were sharing a room at a race somewhere in Italy,' says John now, 'when I woke up in the dark in the middle of the night to see this figure in bike kit creeping past the end of my bed. When I woke up in the morning, at about 7 a.m., Sean was just coming out of the shower. I had to ask him if I'd dreamt it.'

We managed to wangle a start in Tirreno–Adria-tico thanks to our newly raised profile, and rode really strongly to make sure we were on the front when live TV joined the race in the last hour each day. We didn't win anything, but Pascal and Max came close, and our Irish sprinter Ciaran Power ran Cipollini close once or twice. As a result, we were invited to be the first British team ever to ride the Giro d'Italia.

We scored a huge success at the Giro when David McKenzie took a stage win after a 100-mile solo break. 'Macca' was a canny rider, a sprinter who wasn't quick enough to threaten the fastest guys when he had moved up to the top level, and had reinvented himself to find another way to win. He had asked me about long solo efforts the night before, what I'd thought about to keep me going over those long lonely miles when I'd tried it.

'Sean told me that you think about all those miles of training you put in as a kid when your mates were out enjoying themselves, and how everyone was laughing at you and thinking you were wasting your time,' said Macca afterwards. 'The long break is when you think about payback, proving to everybody that it was worth it, making them sit up and notice.'

Max nearly made it a double for us the following day when he got second behind Axel Merckx, son of the legend himself, in Prato. Merckx had crashed on a descent just before the finish and got back on to Max's small group without him knowing, using the element of surprise to jump away for the win. Max was inconsolable in second, but there was no doubt that whatever happened now, our Giro would be considered a success.

We pushed on with massive plans for 2001, signing riders like Juan Carlos Domínguez and Íñigo Cuesta from Spain, the former World Junior Champion Mark Scanlon, and a young Londoner fresh from the Sydney Olympics by the name of Bradley Wiggins. Neil Stephens was also joining as another *directeur sportif*. There had been some problems with funding in 2000 and some of the guys had gone for stretches without being paid, but that was all in the past thanks to new co-sponsors Jaguar and Jacob's Creek.

When we assembled for our first get-together before the official team launch in London, there was a mood varying between general unease and open rebellion.

There were a lot of people owed money – Max was claiming that he hadn't been paid at all for the previous year – and there had been rumblings about the validity of our new sponsorship deals.

Over the course of the next twenty-four hours at the Cricketers hotel in Bagshot, the whole sorry story unravelled. It seemed that Julian – who had failed to show up – had spent all of the 2000 budget by May and had persuaded the McCartney organization to forward the 2001 money in the summer on the understanding that there was no more to come after that. In his desperation to bring in new sponsors to cover the shortfall and to cover the team's rapidly mounting debts, he had jumped the gun and announced the Jaguar and Jacob's Creek partnerships as done deals when they were just at the early stage of talks. There was no money. In fact, there was less than no money thanks to the debts already run up. It was the proverbial house of cards.

I was so angry at Julian. He'd had the idea and the drive to go for it, but he'd let so many people down with the bullshitting and promising. The more we found out about the situation, the more foolish we felt for being taken for a ride.

The day after leaving the Cricketers and the rest of the stranded Linda McCartney riders and staff, I was labouring for my oldest friend Paul Divall on a building job in Nutley.

I worked for Paul's company for a year on various sites and did a bit more bike riding. At the end of that year, I got a call from David McKenzie. He and his wife Susan were setting up an Australian-flavoured team to be based in Belgium. It would be unique in that it would be based on individual subscriptions – a revolutionary idea to bring cycling to the people who loved it; a team actually owned by its fans: iTeamNova.

They were upfront from the start about how much money was involved, and they were open about the fact that they needed more money to come in during the season for the project to be sustainable. I had no illusions that it was anything other than a shaky proposition, but the McKenzies were great people, and their honesty was music to my ears after what had gone before. I had a year's perspective on my management career now and realized that I had enjoyed it, was OK at it, and could see where I could improve. I didn't need to be stressed out. Racing was a circus anyway, stay calm – *tranquillo*, as they say – let the madness go on round you and concentrate on the job of racing. Also, I recognized, from my new position of hindsight, that where in my first days I had found it difficult to manage riders like Sciandri and Richard, who were bigger achievers than me when we were riding together, now I was a bit older and more experienced. I decided to get back on the carousel.

There were some familiar faces from the McCartney implosion, with Russell Downing, Alan Iacuone and Craig's mate Scott Guyton riding, as well as Macca himself. We were doing the sort of races you'd never have believed existed, let alone heard of. Craig had landed a job at Bjarne Riis's Danish CSC team and we struggled for regular staff.

Vic Haines came with me to do the Tour of Serbia, or Slovenia, or somewhere, and we got hopelessly lost. He was map reading, so I'm blaming him. I was so flustered that when we stopped to fill up somewhere – we were so lost I couldn't even tell you what country we were in – I filled the car up with diesel instead of unleaded. That took some sorting.

Then we got a start in a race down in Montenegro, of all places. The peace-keeping forces were still there after the war, and the race was designed as an international event to show that Montenegro, Croatia and Bosnia-Herzegovina were all decent places to visit. The riders and I flew down, but we had to get the team car there, and a Londoner I knew vaguely called Jas helped us out. He was officially the mechanic, though he'd never fixed more than a puncture in his life.

'On the way down there, the *soigneur* and I stocked up with cigars and cognac,' remembers Jas. 'I thought he was just buying them as duty free, but he was smart, we needed them for oiling the wheels at border posts and hotels to get anything done.'

The hotels were absolutely atrocious and so was the weather. It all came together on one nightmarish day that I'll never forget. It started with punctures. Puncture after puncture after puncture. The roads were a bit shitty anyway, and this torrential rain had washed every sharp bit of grit down from the surrounding mountains out on to the surface. Before long, we'd used up all our spares and Jas was trying to fix the ones we'd taken off riders.

'I had towels trying to dry off inner tubes and find the holes in them,' says Jas. 'Sean looked in the mirror and said, "Do you know what you're doing?" I said, "Not really," so he said, "Right, you drive," and we swapped over, me chasing after the race, him fixing flats. Then we heard on race radio that one of our guys had flatted again. By the time we got to him, he was bedraggled and pissed off and chucked his flat rear wheel off the road as Sean slotted the spare in. When we went to drive off, Sean said, "We need to get that wheel!" I hadn't realized there was a drainage ditch about ten feet deep next to the road, and this wheel had ended up at the bottom of it. "Leave it!" I shouted through the rain. "We can't, we haven't got enough spares!" Sean scrambled down to it, but it was too far down to get out and he was stuck. He had to swing the wheel round for me to reach in and grab the other side of it, then use it to haul him out.'

I know. That wasn't even the worst of it. Diarrhoea was sweeping through the race like wildfire, thanks to the appalling hotels we were staying in. Scott Guyton couldn't ride more than a few yards without it coming out of him, the poor bastard. I asked him if he wanted to pack it in, but he tried to continue, only to have another attack a couple of minutes later. We got him in the car. He was drenched, freezing, upset . . . and sitting in those shorts in the passenger seat. And it hadn't stopped. I'm not talking about the rain, but that hadn't stopped either.

Jas carries on the story. 'Next, with the rain coming down like stair rods, a wheel fell off the wheel rack overhanging the windscreen and broke one of the windscreen wipers. By this time, there were four of us in the car, as Dominique Perras had also been forced to stop, and we were miles behind the race. The road was closed for the event, though, so there was nothing in front. Sean was flooring it now: 90 mph, one windscreen wiper, biblical storm, four guys, awful smell. All of a sudden, it felt like the car took off. We were aquaplaning, and we were aquaplaning straight towards a hard rock wall. "That's that then," I had time to think, then the tyres bit at the last moment and we lurched on. Though he might have killed us, I prefer to think that Sean saved us, because if he hadn't been so cool and wrenched on the wheel we would have certainly crashed.'

As we'd feared, iTeamNova's budget didn't see out that year, but we could look back with our heads held high and say that we'd given it a good go. Macca is working at the Tour for Australian TV these days, and it's always good to see him. Brett Lancaster is a survivor from those days too, still knocking out quick rides for Orica–GreenEDGE.

After iTeamNova wound down I went back to gardening and started to build up my round in Sussex again. I got these special hedge steps that enabled you to adjust the legs separately for moving them up and down banks and the like. They were fucking cool. Then I had a custom roof rack made for the Landy to carry them. I loved that, too. I was getting right into it and decided that if I was going to expand my little business I could do with a trailer. I drove over to see this guy in Kent and bought his trailer, hooked it up behind the Landy and struck out for home. I was about five minutes out of there when my phone rang with an unknown foreign number. It was Bjarne Riis offering me an assistant *directeur sportif* job at CSC. My first thought was, 'I wonder if I can take this trailer back?'

It turned out that the 'in' at CSC had come through Craig. 'I was at a race with Bjarne Riis and Alex Pedersen and they asked me if I knew any English-speaking *directeurs*. I said I sure did.'

It was a proper set-up, with great riders like Tyler Hamilton, Ivan Basso, Frank Schleck and Carlos Sastre. There were some older hands whom I'd ridden with too, like Andrea Tafi and my Motorola teammate Andrea Peron. Tyler won Liège–Bastogne–Liège with a really beautifully timed late attack, and then went straight to Romandie and won that too. That was the platform for a stunning long mountain break in the Tour and fourth overall, all achieved with a broken collarbone. In fact, we won three stages at that Tour, thanks to Tyler, Carlos Sastre and Jakob Piil. I was down the pecking order of *directeurs*, behind Bjarne, who was moving on to be more than a *directeur sportif* – a sort of team principal; a Dave Brailsford type of role – by then, and my old friend Johnny Weltz, who was driving team car one at the big races. I got to like not having to worry about all the other shit that you had to deal with every day at smaller teams. I turned up, drove the car, helped the guys race, and went home. That's the bit I was good at, so it suited me. I didn't really have ambitions to run things like Och had, Bjarne did, or Dave later would. I had found my place in the scheme of things and was determined to be a useful, valued member of the team, much in the same way I had been as a rider.

I had some health issues that year, which I'll come to, but when I got back on my bike I was determined to never stop riding again. It was more acceptable for a *directeur sportif* to ride then than it had been a few years previously – managers were getting younger and healthier, it seemed, and I began to feel like more of a trendsetter than a weirdo.

'He always rode. Always; every day,' says Craig. 'In Lucca on a CSC training camp in January one year, maybe 2004, there was a massive snowstorm one day and the riders were given the day off. Around lunchtime, after we'd finished eating, I was wondering where the boss was, as I hadn't seen him all day. He swung through the door in full winter kit soaking wet. "Five hours," he said, teeth chattering.'

I had a couple of great years at CSC, but in 2005, the UCI unveiled their grand plan for cycling, the ProTour. It was to be a cross between the old calendar of races and a shift towards a Formula One-type moveable feast. If a team wanted to be involved – which everybody did – they would have to commit to sending a team to every

ProTour-listed event. For most, this meant an expansion so that they could support up to three teams on the road at any given time. That's not just an expansion in riders, but in management, coaches, *soigneurs*, mechanics, press guys, vehicles, bikes . . . all sorts of things.

Bjarne needed to bring in another *directeur sportif* or two, so Kim Andersen and Alain Gallopin were signed. It was clear that I was getting shunted down the pecking order a little, and I was a bit put out by that, having put a good couple of years in. I'm not one to blow my own trumpet; sometimes that works in your favour, sometimes it doesn't. At the same time, I was contacted by Lance, as his victorious US Postal squad was morphing into the Discovery Channel and they were facing the same ProTour issues. He recommended me to Johan Bruyneel, who was running things, and they made me an offer.

When I told Bjarne about it, he offered me more to stay, but my mind was made up. I'd always wanted to work with Lance again, watching him go from talented youngster to his deathbed to multiple Tour champion had been one of the most amazing experiences of my life. And I felt I'd be valued a bit more there, so off I went.

It was an exciting start to life at Discovery, travelling to the government buildings in Washington for a presentation. Then we flew by private jet down to Santa Barbara for the training camp. I think it was Lance, Johan Bruyneel, Laurenzo Lapage, Dirk Demol and me on that plane, getting buffeted about all over the sky because of terrible weather over California. It looked like we might not be able to land, but we got into Santa Barbara eventually, only to find that the others wouldn't be able to join us for a couple of days due to a landslip.

I hadn't taken my bike – I didn't know if the new team would be cool with it – and spent a few days on that camp going stir-crazy. I joined a gym next door to the hotel and went ballistic on the cross trainer for hours at a time. On the rest day I hired a bike and went out wearing trainers, board shorts and no shirt. I did about six hours, then when I was coming back, I saw Stijn Devolder, our Belgian Classics rider, going the other way. I can still see his, 'Was that . . . ? No . . .' facial expression as I rode by.

As it happened, Johan was cool about me riding the bike. He even bought me a set of Dura-Ace SRM power monitor cranks when he was buying the team's stuff. I was grateful – they cost a packet – and I still use them today.

Johan lives in London these days, so we met up to catch up and see what we could remember.

'I didn't turn professional until 1987, but I knew you from TV,' says Johan. 'The first time I really became aware of you as a rider was when you won that Tour time trial. Shit, you were flying that day. After that we came up against each other a few times in time trials. In that one in the Dauphiné I remember us both desperately hanging on in the mountain stages to qualify for the time trial, as we both thought we could win it if the other specialists had been eliminated. I was looking out for you and Edwig Van Hooydonck, as you were the other fast guys. When I finished, quicker than you, I thought, "Yes! That'll be enough!" then that Colombian guy Mejía beat me. I wasn't amused.'

'I remember Álvaro Mejía from our Motorola days,' I reply. 'He was a nice guy. Weird, but nice. He just smiled, never said anything. On his own little planet. He's a sports doctor with the Movistar South American development squad, I think, which is a unique career path in my experience. When we were at Motorola he lived in a hotel on Lake Como. He never got an apartment, just lived in the hotel. Like the Major in *Fawlty Towers*. I remember you on that stage into Liège in 1995 . . . man, Indurain was going like a train and you stuck to his wheel like a bit of dogshit on his tyre. And you got to wear the yellow jersey for a day.'

'Just like you the year before.'

'Yes! What about when you fell down that ravine in the Alps? Was that 1996?'

'Yeah, on the Cormet de Roselend. Where Iñaki Gastón had fallen a few years before. You were with him, weren't you?'

'I was right on his wheel, missed him by an inch.'

'I went down a long way. Took me ages to climb back up. It was on that same corner that I crashed the car.'

'Ahhh, in 2005! That was hilarious.'

Johan had Thomas Weisel, the Discovery Channel team owner, with him in the car. Weisel was jetlagged, having just got off a flight from the States, and Johan was trying to keep him interested. The Roselend is a narrow, winding descent, 20 kilometres long with a drop on one side.

'I was trying to remember which corner I'd crashed on as there are a few that look pretty similar,' says Johan. 'I was saying, "This one. No, this one." Then [Yaroslav] Popovych came back to the car for some reason. I leaned out of the window to talk to him and BANG! Straight into the back of Bjarne Riis in the CSC car.'

The first I knew of it was Johan radioing me. I was in the second car with Dirk Demol, and we drove up to him. He had us get out and nicked our car. When the tow truck turned up, saw the damage and the driver started giving me the knowing look, I was like, 'It's nothing to do with me, pal.'

I was in the hot seat on my own for the Giro that year, however. As you can imagine, with Lance going for a record seventh straight Tour win, there wasn't much focus on the Giro, and I was handling a weakened team led by Paolo Savoldelli.

'Nobody wanted Savoldelli,' says Johan. 'He'd gone to T-Mobile as Giro champion but had endured a terrible couple of years. We'd picked him up just to have a leader for the Giro, really – thought we'd give him a chance.'

And then as soon as we signed him, we went to the training camp and he broke his collarbone on our favourite old ride to Solvang. No way would you put any money on Paolo winning anything in 2005.

I was backed up by my old friend Laurenzo Laparge

in the second team car. Laurenzo is one of the funniest guys I've ever known and could have me in stitches with his stories, facial expressions and knowing looks. We had a little trick up our sleeve at that Giro that I'll reveal later, if you behave yourselves.

The race began inauspiciously when I couldn't find the team car at the start of one stage. Giro stage starts and finishes are notoriously ramshackle affairs. Laurenzo and I walked into the start area, expecting the mechanics to drive the cars round to meet us. They couldn't find the way in and were still looking when the race started, so they set off in their allocated places in the race convoy. Allocated, but without a *directeur sportif* in either of them. We had to get lifts in neutral service cars until we caught up. My one was behind the race and found my team car quite easily, and I slipped in without too many people noticing. Laurenzo had the misfortune to be in the neutral car in front of the race, and got dropped off at the side of the road for the whole race to ride past him. He was covering his face when I drove past. Shameful.

After that, though, it could not have been sweeter. Nobody took Paolo or Discovery seriously, and we let Gilberto Simoni, Ivan Basso, Danilo Di Luca and José Rujano kick lumps out of each other all round Italy, just carefully and quietly following the right wheels. Even when Paolo rode himself into the leader's *maglia rosa* with eight days to go they weren't worried about us, assuming that he was keeping it warm for one of the challengers. We let them think that, not being strong enough to control the race, and allowed the rivals to go about each other while we hung in. The other teams realized too late that, instead of fighting each other, they should join forces against the common enemy. On the last proper stage, Paolo was not on a good day. We had to go up and over the brutal unsurfaced white slopes of the Colle delle Finestre and then on up to the finish in Sestrière. Di Luca, Simoni and Rujano rode away together on the Finestre and by the top, all of Paolo's precious two-and-a-half-minute lead had been eaten up. It was thanks to a supremely gritty ride and some help from Lotto that he ground his way up the haul to Sestrière just two minutes behind his attackers to sew up the overall win by 28 seconds.

However, in my mind, he'd won it the day before that stage when he made up 30 seconds on everybody else on the descent at the end of the time trial into Turin. He was so fast down there it was breathtaking. We'd recce'd the route in the morning and he'd said, 'When I point at a corner, make a note of it.' Following him in the car, I'd jotted down all of his gestures to shout them out to him over the radio when he flew down there in the pink jersey that afternoon. I'd never seen anything like it. On one section, I missed giving him an instruction and he rocketed through a chicane like he was on rails. People often talk about how fast I was downhill, but I tell them that Paolo Savoldelli was better than me.

'That was the first time a British *directeur sportif* won a Grand Tour,' says Brian Smith, now in his capacity as

Eurosport commentator, 'and he doesn't get the credit for it. In fact, ask yourself this question: how many British *directeurs* have won a race of any size at all? Ever? There's only one. And he's won two Giros and a Tour.'

The last stage, a promenade through Milan, passed off without incident for Paolo, but not for me. I was trying to do the traditional winning *directeur sportif* thing of handing out glasses of champagne to the peloton when I hit a kerb and burst a tyre on the team car. We changed the wheel and then I got lost trying to get back up to the race. I stopped to ask a *carabinieri* officer directions and he said, 'You're on the route – but you're in front of the race.'

'I was so pleased for Paolo,' says Johan, 'and so pleased we'd decided to give him a chance. But most of all I was pleased for Sean. He showed just how much of a nose he has for racing, understanding not just how to motivate your own team, but understanding what is important to the other riders, knowing how they are likely to react. It was a true *directeur*'s victory.'

While I was becoming the first British *directeur sportif* to win a Grand Tour life back home wasn't so rosy that spring, unfortunately. Pippa had long been accusing me of having affairs and since I'd been away more and more with CSC and now Discovery it was getting worse and worse. I wasn't. But nothing I said made any difference. With my cycling commitments, I'd never been able to be the regular dad to my kids – we had three now, Bathsheba joining the boys in 2000 – and the man about the house that she'd wanted me to be. I knew that I made few adjustments to allow for things. I basically lived how I always had as a bike rider, working hard to provide for them but not committing time and effort to being around the home. In the end, I foolishly had a fling while I was on the road.

I was getting ready to go to the Tour of Romandie, sorting my kit out, preparing to be away for a while when my phone bleeped with a text from the other woman. Pippa asked what the text was and that was it. In her eyes it provided her with proof that all the years of doubt were correct. I left immediately for Romandie. When I got back after the Giro, a few weeks later, my Land Rover was on the drive with all my belongings in it. Our marriage was over.

I didn't really want to stop and think about it. Whenever there have been changes in my life, I haven't mulled them over, it's just been a case of, 'Well, that's done. Move on.' I didn't have time to think about it anyway, as there was a seventh Tour de France to be won for my old roommate and the spearhead of our organization.

After Lance's record-breaking seventh Tour win and subsequent retirement, there was a necessary reshuffling of the pack. A lot of people thought that Discovery Channel without Lance would be like a Ferrari without an engine, and he certainly cast a huge shadow. It took a bit of time to find a new formula, but by the time we were getting ready for the 2007 Tour, there was a feeling that we were a force to be reckoned with again.

I'd repaid the favour to Craig by then, as Johan had asked me if I knew any English-speaking mechanics, and I said, 'I sure do.'

'We had Levi Leipheimer as leader,' says Johan, 'but we also had a Spanish kid from Madrid who had come to us from ONCE, called Alberto Contador. I sat down with him before the Tour to talk to him about his rivals for the white jersey of best young rider. He said, "I'm not interested in white. I'm here for yellow." I knew we had a trump card.'

Alberto was a great character to work with. Very professional, very determined, but nervous and edgy. We had some fun times, especially at País Vasco and Castilla y León, where he just wanted to take on the world. He'd won Paris–Nice already that year, blowing away Davide Rebellin on the Col d'Eze.

Going into the final time trial of that 2007 Tour, I recce'd the route in the morning with Alberto and Levi. The crowds were enormous, the pressure intense. It was something else. Alberto was on edge and not feeling well; he was tired after fighting tooth and nail for three weeks in what was only his second Grand Tour. Cadel Evans had ridden into absolutely great form in that final week and was breathing down Alberto's neck. Only three minutes separated Alberto, Levi and Cadel. He knew that he had to do the ride of his life, but he did it, winning the overall by just 23 seconds from Cadel, with Levi another eight seconds back.

Towards the end of 2007, I was contacted by Oleg

Tinkoff, the Russian businessman who had set up the Tinkoff Credit Systems ProTour team, about joining them for 2008. I spoke to Johan, as we knew that Discovery Channel's three-year sponsorship arrangement was coming to an end. Unbelievably, despite having the Tour de France champion leading our squad, we couldn't find another title sponsor to take over. Johan said he was trying to tie down a deal that would let the same organization carry on with a different sponsor. He was great, saying that I should push on with negotiations but that if things came off he wanted me to stay.

I was due to fly down to Forte dei Marmi, near Lucca, to meet up with Tinkoff to nail things down, while Johan was simultaneously negotiating hard. I rode my motorbike up to Stansted for my flight, but before I could board it, Johan rang and told me it was all systems go. I didn't get on the plane. Dmitri Konyshev was meant to be picking me up – he was Tinkoff's head *directeur sportif* – but I rang them and told them I wasn't coming. Tinkoff went crazy.

'Who are you signing with? Tell me!' he was shouting down the phone.

I knew he and Johan had fallen out. Oleg was a feisty character with a temper on him, but I couldn't lie, he'd find out soon enough.

'Errr . . . Bruyneel,' I said.

'*Bruyneel?* BRUYNEEL? Tell that bastard I'm coming for him!'

'The new sponsor was actually an existing team,

Astana,' explains Johan. 'They were piling in loads of cash to fund a Kazakhstan-based team, but it wasn't working out the way they wanted with the existing team management, mainly because the team were involved in a big doping scandal. I did a deal with them for Astana to assimilate with the team we had under the Discovery Channel banner. We kept the *service course* in Belgium, the staff, the management, the riders – except we were strengthened by the addition of the best Kazakh riders.'

2008 turned into a bit of a nightmare, however. ASO, the Tour de France organizers, decided not to invite Astana to ride because of the doping scandal of 2007. We were a bit put out as we had all gone there after that, but their position was that the sponsor was not welcome and should pay a penalty for cheating. It was tough on Alberto, who'd been beating those guys at the Tour. The news filtered through while we were at the Tour of Mallorca. Alberto was so enraged he flew up the big mountain there and absolutely battered everybody. He had a stellar spring, knowing he had nothing to aim at in July, winning everything in sight, then went off for a holiday.

Just before the start of the Giro d'Italia, the race organizers RCS contacted us and told us that only our strongest team would be welcome. In other words: no Contador, no Astana. Johan was minded to tell them where they could stick their race, but with Astana missing the Tour and the sponsors looking for some value from their massive investment, we had no choice. Alberto was called back from the beach and I went to Italy as head *directeur sportif* with a stronger team than we had intended.

There was some serious shit going down at that Giro. Teams who had been creeping all year were suddenly firing guys off up the road every minute of the day in a manner I would term 'not normal'. Two of the least normal were Riccardo Riccò and Emanuele Sella, who were ripping the race up. Both of them tested positive later that year, which solved a few questions. Some teams were putting four or five guys in the break which made life rather hard for us.

Alberto would have had his work cut out to deal with those guys at the best of times, but he'd come straight from holiday and was resigned to hanging in and trying to ride himself into some form in the final week.

'Alberto is such a proud rider,' explains Johan, 'that you never have a problem motivating him. The issue is the opposite: holding him back, making him realize that attacking all the time is not the best way to win. He needs to be persuaded to measure his efforts and time his moments. All he wants to do when he wakes up in the morning is murder the opposition.'

We were lucky to have Andreas Klöden with us. The big German was the most professional, dedicated rider I've ever come across as a *directeur sportif*, but he didn't suffer fools gladly. Riccò's trademark cobra victory salute particularly irritated him. He wasn't so keen on some of our Kazakh guys either and I had to step in to prevent an argument on the Astana bus from turning into a fist fight. I know whose side I'd want to be on.

That race was a lot of fun. I remember Faustino, who was Alberto's personal mechanic, taking the radio off me to talk to him in Spanish. I didn't know what they were talking about – French and English (just about) are my languages – but apparently Alberto wanted to take a layer off and Faustino told him to chuck it down at the side of the road and we'd pick it up. Alberto agreed and did so, but Faustino didn't think to tell me what was going on. He saw the Astana *gilet* at the side of the road and opened the door to get out and grab it, but I had no idea what was going on and didn't slow down. I nearly killed him! We were pissing ourselves laughing.

Alberto hung in and hung in, riding intelligently and recognizing the need to not expose himself too early. I was trying to tackle the race as we had with Savoldelli three years previously and Alberto was smart enough to stick to the plan. He took the jersey in the final week with a great ride in the mountains to Passo Fedaia and held it through the following day's time trial.

The day after that was a rest day, featuring a long transfer. I naturally used that as an excuse to ride my bike rather than travel in the team car, and rode the 250 kilometres through the mountain valleys from Plan de Corones to Sondrio. Beautiful. Not such a beautiful evening, though, as, at the team hotel, Alain Gallopin was waiting. He'd flown in to 'help' as *directeur sportif* when Alberto took the jersey. As soon as he arrived, he said, 'I'm driving the first car, you're in the second.' After I'd steered the team through those first two weeks through all the pitfalls to put us in a winning position, I wasn't too enamoured with somebody turning up and saying, 'I'll take it from here, sonny.' Bloody glory hunter. I had one of my 'sod-it' moments and went home. Alberto held the jersey through to Milan at the weekend to take an excellent hard-earned narrow victory over Riccò, but the race will always have mixed memories for me.

Alberto was untouchable as a Tour rider, but 2009 would be more interesting, as he was going to have a co-leader. Three years of retirement had been enough for Lance and he was coming back.

I didn't get to see much of Lance's comeback because of health issues which I'll go into in more detail in the next chapter, but they kept me away from the action for virtually the whole season. Johan was incredibly under-standing about my prolonged absence and looked after me. I wanted to be in there with the boys – I like bike racing – and I felt so out of the loop. If you miss two weeks on a break it feels like you've been away for a year, so to miss months was painful. I begged to do the Vuelta, just to be involved again, and he relented, despite saying I could take off as much time as I needed. I hadn't been involved since Romandie, had missed the Giro, the Tour and countless other races . . . I needed to be back.

The one race Lance and I did together was the Tour of Castilla y León – well, I say 'did': he fell off after 20 kilometres of the first stage and broke his collarbone. Some good came of it, though. Lance's personal chef,

Duffy, turned up with a huge cooler full of these choice cuts of meat and fish – beautiful, the best. Lance had already gone home and I had a week to kill at the hotel between Castilla y León and País Vasco, so Duffy left the cooler with me and buggered off. I ate like a king.

Lance's comeback didn't go as planned. I'm sure he thought he could still be the best or he wouldn't have done it, but it wasn't to be. It would be a while until the Armstrong legend started to unravel, but for the moment he was thwarted by one of his own teammates who was a better bike rider than he was in 2009. Alberto v Lance with them both at their best . . . I honestly don't know who would win that.

'If we were going to do it all again, I would make more of an effort for us to be liked,' says Johan in the aftermath of the huge USADA inquiry fallout. 'The thing was, the myth of Lance the invincible was powerful and had worked so well for us that it made sense to reinforce it, to show him as the imperious overlord who could not be challenged. For instance, there is no way we would have won the Tour de France in 2003 without that cloak of invincibility. The other riders just felt that they couldn't beat him, that he was untouchable, where in reality there were probably two or three guys that were stronger in that race if only they'd believed they could win. And you know that training story about Lance riding up Alpe d'Huez seven times in one day? Let me tell you something: that didn't happen. It was twice; and he nearly had to get off on the second one. One guy says, "I saw Lance on the Alpe." Another says, "I saw him too," and the next thing you know, he's ridden it seven times. We did nothing to stop these stories and Lance went into attack mode if anybody challenged him. It served us well at the time, but there were a lot of grievances and grudges built up over those years that waited a long time to come out.

'I'm struggling with this whole thing about wanting to write off a whole era,' continues Johan. 'Especially when others from that same era who have also been caught just carry on without anybody saying anything. It just doesn't feel right to me, the hypocrisy of it. There are people making good money out of the Lance industry. I'm out of the sport now. I didn't leave on my own terms, which is a regret, but I don't miss it. I'm glad I'm out.'

When Dave Brailsford got in touch with me about the Sky project that was going to spring out of the GB national squad organization, I rang Johan to see what he thought.

'I was hoping to finalize something for 2010 and I hoped Sean would be with us, but the Sky thing sounded like an unbelievable opportunity for him. I thought he should do it.'

I did it.

Chapter Fifteen

Heads up: boring bit of the story coming up. I don't think I'd want to read a book about how some old bloke's dodgy ticker kept tripping him up, but unfortunately I have to tell you about my heart problems if this whole story is going to make sense at all.

The short version: my heart is old and knackered and goes wrong sometimes. If that's enough for you, please feel free to skip directly to chapter sixteen.

After the 2003 Liège–Bastogne–Liège with CSC, which, as I mentioned, we'd won in a superb solo victory by Tyler Hamilton, I drove down to Switzerland for the Tour of Romandie, which we were using as our final staging post before the Giro d'Italia. Tyler won that as well, and there was a massive buzz around the team.

I, on the other hand, was struggling. That spring I'd been riding regularly back home with my dentist's son-in-law, an ambitious guy who wanted to better himself on the bike. I went from coaching him and coaxing him along to creeping up the hills far behind him in about a week. It was very peculiar; I couldn't get my heart rate up at all. It got worse all the way through Romandie (I was doing my usual trick of riding before breakfast every day) and I had to go and see the team doctor, a mightily unusual occurrence. We agreed that I had a chest infection and he prescribed a course of antibiotics which I started out on before driving back up through Europe for the Four Days of Dunkirk, the world's worst-named five-day race.

By the time I got there I could hardly walk up a flight of stairs. I'm used to having a low resting pulse, say, 30 when I wake up, but it was still 30 in the afternoon when I'd been working all morning. That wasn't right. The doctor sent me home and told me to get an ECG done.

I remember that day quite well, as I went to the clinic in the morning, and then I was meant to be going to see Black Sabbath that night with Pippa and Chris. I love a bit of classic rock, me, so I was put out when the doctor called back and said the readout was very abnormal and I had to go to hospital immediately. I found myself in a bed in Haywards Heath being fed warfarin, before being transferred to Brighton for a cardioversion.

They found that I have a condition called arrhythmia. In my case, the ventricles of the heart had gone out of time with each other. Instead of the double-thump heartbeat that most people get, I was getting one beat at half the pace, meaning that blood was only being pumped round my body at half the rate. No wonder I was knackered.

Lots of people suffer from arrhythmia, not necessarily sportsmen. One famous patient is Tony Blair. He was first diagnosed at around the same time as me and I remember reading about his cardioversion, the same treatment I had. Once they've thinned your blood out with warfarin – to be confident enough that it won't clot – they knock you out then give your heart a quick electric shock to set it back in sync. Wumph! And then you're back ten minutes later wondering what the hell has happened.

I got ready to leave and head back to work when the doctor dropped the bombshell that I couldn't fly or drive for six weeks. Six weeks! I thought I was bound to lose my job. Whoever heard of a *directeur sportif* without a driving licence? I concocted a plan with my brother Conall. He drove me down to the Alps and then the team arranged for our mechanic, Frédéric Bessy, to take over driving duties with me in the passenger seat. Fred was my chauffeur for the Classique des Alpes and then the Critérium du Dauphiné and the Route du Sud. We had a hoot, my health worries forgotten; an embarrassment I didn't want to discuss in the team. I was only 43 – what sort of loser has a busted heart at 43?

I got a call from Och and Max Testa, who'd been the doctor at Motorola, a smashing bloke who has the best name for any doctor in the history of sport. It was good to see that the old Motorola family spirit lived on years after the team had finished. Max talked to me for a while about my condition and gave me a better understanding of it, explaining that I could have an operation known as an ablation to fix it. I thanked him but carried on with life as usual, doing the Tour de France and riding my bike every morning just the same as ever.

Two years later, it snuck up on me again. It's a gradual thing over a few days; you start by feeling tired when you get to a hill, then it's all the time on your bike, then it's when you're walking upstairs. The doctor at Discovery, where I was working at the time, was a guy called Pedro Celaya. He's been deeply implicated in the USADA investigation into Lance and the US Postal Service doping programme, but I don't mind standing up and saying he is a lovely guy who would do anything for you. In my case, he took control immediately and agreed with Max Testa that an ablation was the answer. He organized the procedure at a hospital in Bilbao, so off I went.

An ablation is a pretty amazing thing. I've just been reading up on it and I see that Tony Blair has had one of these too. They go in through your groin then laser away all the extra material around your heart. You'll be aware that heartbeat is controlled by an electrical impulse – well, sometimes that 'spark' is messed up by too much flesh. Effectively, it shorts. This is more common in people with overdeveloped hearts. It's hard to say whether my problem had come about because of the extra strain I've put on my heart over the years with the extremes of racing and training that I've always enjoyed, or whether I naturally had an over-developed heart that made me a useful cyclist in the first place – or a combination of the two; or whether it's to do with something else entirely. Some people who've never been out from behind a desk in their lives have ablations, so who can say?

Anyway, for this one you're awake. I was lying there, listening to my heart rate going mental on the machine as they chipped away at it, vaporizing all these little extra bits of muscle. Then, almost miraculously, after about twenty minutes of blasting my heart with a laser, I heard the machine settle down to a steady beat. I was fixed.

After one night in hospital I flew up to Paris for the beginning of Paris–Nice and cadged a lift to the start off Kim Andersen who was at CSC. With Pedro's vehement instructions to take it easy ringing in my ears, I didn't ride my bike. Instead, I took to going for a walk each day. Within a few days I was running. By the end of the week-long race I was running for half an hour in the mornings. He told me I was the worst fucking patient he'd ever had.

I went home between races and started time trialling, doing the Antelope CC 3-Up Time Trial with Chris and Pete Tadros and then getting third in the National 50-Mile Time Trial, which pleased me no end.

'I was Sean's helper in that race,' remembers Brian Smith. 'I was on my way to the National Road Race Championships and the 50 was the day before in Teeside, so I stood at the side of the road holding up time checks. He was gunning for a medal, working on the assumption that Michael Hutchinson would have the title sewn up when he did. Sean was third, trailing Gethin Butler in second by a few seconds and was pumped to get a medal.

I followed him through the finish and he took a left turn up a side road. "Where's he off to?" I thought, following him round the corner. When I caught up with him he was vomiting at the side of the road, covered in sick. He'd gone up the side road because he didn't want anybody to see him. This is a 45-year-old man with nothing to prove to anybody, with a history of serious heart problems. He just can't help pushing himself to the limit. Beyond the limit, as it happens.'

In 2006 Michael Hutchinson and I set the competition record for 25 miles on a tandem when we clocked 43-44, which still stands today. I was glad I was on the front and not the passenger at that speed. I was still turning out 19-minute ten-mile time trials then, too. Anyway, it was obvious that the ablation was a success and I was totally cured.

Except that I wasn't. In spring of 2007, continuing my heart's unhappy run of screwing up every two years or so, I was hit by another bout of arrhythmia. I asked Pedro about another ablation, but it turns out that doctors don't like repeating it, as there's only so much extra tissue you can cut away before you start blasting into the good stuff. So it was my second cardioversion instead.

This time I was really hit for six. I remember being in bed at Mum's – Pippa and I were divorced by then – and being unable to get down the stairs, let alone up them. I eased back into work at the Giro but stayed off my bike like a good boy. A good miserable boy.

2007 was the year that the Tour de France began in

London, which was a really exciting time for all British cyclists. From England we headed for Dunkirk, and as we emerged from the Channel Tunnel, so did my sadly neglected bike from the inner depths of the Discovery team truck. From that day forward, it was back to riding every day.

To be honest, I was fairly confident my racing days were behind me. Or should I say my competitive days. The legs of 2006 and that tandem record were gone and seemed unlikely to return, but I still wanted to ride all the time, and if I was going to ride I might as well enter the odd event now and then, eh? What can I say: I like bike riding and I've never known any different. Those three months off my bike in 2007 are the only three months I've gone without cycling in my whole life.

'In 2008 he was still riding ridiculous miles every day,' reports Johan Bruyneel, my boss at the time. 'Our team doctor was Pedro Celaya and obviously he knew all about Sean's problems as he'd sent him for the ablation. "Please stop Sean from doing so much, Johan, he's going to kill himself," he would say. I tried, but it was like telling a river not to flow. On the rest day of the Giro, the photographer Tim De Waele came up to me in the evening and said, "I saw one of your riders out training today. He was outside a supermarket drinking water, he looked shattered." It was a hot day with a 250-kilometre transfer from Plan de Corones to Aprica in the Dolomites. It wasn't an Astana rider, it was Sean – he'd ridden the whole way. That's ten hours. What can you do with him?'

By 2009 I must have still been thinking about racing, as I was planning to ride the National Team Time Trial Championships with Pete Tadros and Hutch for In-Gear, my friend Pete Roberts's bike shop in Uckfield. Liam works there now. Where does the time go? Anyway, I was spending quite a lot of time down in Freiburg in the Black Forest with my girlfriend at that time, Judith. I was on my way out one day – I think I was going to race somewhere as I'd put my bike on the roof of the car rather than ridden from the house – poured a glass of water and sat down at the kitchen table before leaving. All of a sudden, the room began to swim around me, everything spinning like I'd just got off a fairground ride. I rested my forehead on the table in front of me and waited for it to stop, but it didn't, it just kept whirling around. I couldn't get up or move, Judith was talking to me, asking what was wrong but I couldn't reply. Another distant part of my brain seemed to be looking down on me and saying, 'Boy, you're really screwed this time.'

Eventually, mainly because I couldn't just sit there all day, I crawled into the bedroom and collapsed on the bed. I was throwing up and sweating almost as much, my vision was doubling, trebling at times, my body seemingly packing up altogether. I was vaguely aware of Judith arguing on the phone in German, trying to get an ambulance to come out to me. The ambulance arrived at some point in the afternoon and they spirited me off to hospital.

When I was fully conscious after various tests, examinations and medications, and beginning to feel almost human again, a doctor told me I had suffered a stroke. What's more, they could tell from the charts that I'd had one before. I thought back and realized, yes, something like this had happened at the previous year's Tour of Austria, but not as bad. On that occasion I'd been lifting my kitbag out of the truck when the spinning came on and I'd sat in the car for an hour to let it recede, not wanting to tell anyone.

They kept me on an intensive care unit for a week. During that time they explained that the stroke wasn't caused by arrhythmia, more that it was a separate conclusion reached by my weak heart. My resting pulse was so low – normally a sign of fitness and a product of all the training and racing – that it wasn't strong enough to propel my blood around my body, leading to a clot, leading to a stroke. My right arm ached and didn't want to work properly; I couldn't write and concentrating to read was difficult. My peripheral vision had disappeared and my speech was laboured and slurred. They moved me on to another ward where I was set puzzles and physiotherapy to try to recover. Judith managed to organize my care via the E111 NHS European scheme – typically I was worried about paying for it even though I was in a right state – and they moved me into a rehabilitation centre out in the Black Forest for three weeks' recovery.

I looked around at some of the poor old folk around me at the centre and counted my blessings. I'd had a scare, but I considered myself to be a fit and healthy guy despite everything that had happened. They had citybikes at the centre for pootling into the nearby village for a coffee. I used one to ride the 40-kilometre round trip to Judith's every other day, then I bought a football and amused myself by having kickabouts and doing shuttle runs like in the old days on the Ashdown Forest. I felt great by the time I got out, got straight on my road bike and did a threshold test with my power meter, discovering I hadn't lost much, then immediately entered a German national series road race. I got dropped, but I didn't die.

Despite the stroke, I kept up my training through the rest of the year and the winter before moving to my new job at Sky for 2010. The reason was that my old friend Brian Phillips and I had been planning a tour of the Dolomites for our fiftieth birthdays for about ten years and had pencilled in a slot after the Tour de France. In retrospect, my health had been deteriorating for some time. The workload at Sky was much bigger than I had been used to. At CSC and Discovery/Astana it was mainly a case of turning up at a race, driving the car, managing the boys on the road, then going home. At Sky, as head *directeur sportif*, there was a host of other responsibilities and functions, like riders' programmes, race reports, progress reporting, strategy meetings, etc. Writing was harder than it had once been, which made all those reports a bit of a pain. My speech hadn't really recovered from the stroke and I was aware of it, especially on race radio. I'd actually done some TV commentary for Eurosport at the World Championships in Switzerland at the end of the previous season and somebody had posted on a newsgroup, 'Sean Yates is drunk on TV!' Somebody else had replied with the news that I'd had a stroke, then somebody else again wrote that he could 'find no evidence' of me having a stroke. Seriously. Like I'm meant to write a letter to the nation saying I've been ill. These days, I do use Twitter, but, to be honest, I long for a simpler bygone age.

I did a lot of races with Sky and was scheduled to do all three Grand Tours. The most restful time was actually in the car during a race when you couldn't really do anything but drive and think. That's when I was most relaxed.

I drove the Sky team car to Paris in August and left it at Alain Gallopin's place, intending to pick it up after our holiday and drive down to the Vuelta a España. Conall, Brian and I headed from there to Bourg-Saint-Maurice, a favourite old stamping ground of mine in the Isère valley, deep in the Alps. From there we embarked on a ten-hour ride that took us up to Val d'Isère, over the Col d'Iseran into Italy and up the brutal unsurfaced slopes of the Colle delle Finestre. I'd always wanted to ride it since driving over it in the Giro five years previously, and I'd been talking to Brian for years about riding these roads together. The guys were waiting for me on all the climbs: I was completely shattered. When we got back to the car I couldn't get my sandals on, my feet were so swollen. I slept for hours, then the next day we went east to ride the Passo dello Stelvio, the second highest climb in the

Alps after the Iseran that we'd topped the day before. I was a wreck. Day three took us over the Classic Dolomiti ascents of the Mortirolo and the Gavia, but by now I was a ghost of a man. It took me hours to get up the Mortirolo, then we were ages in a café at the base of the Gavia, but we had to get over it because it was getting dark and the hotel was on the other side of the mountain. I remember lying stretched out for ten minutes at a time at the side of the road trying to muster my strength. There were two days left, the fourth stage taking us over the Marmolada and the Pordoi. The Pordoi probably remains the worst couple of hours I have ever spent on a bike in my life. Still, once we were over the top, I wanted to race the other two down to the hotel where we were spending that night. By that evening I was a yellowy-grey colour with cold sores on my face and bags under my eyes like black suitcases.

It may sound bizarre, but even with my history and the fact that my hands and feet were swollen like balloons, I didn't think there was anything seriously wrong; I just thought I was run down. It wasn't like my stroke, and it wasn't like my 30-bpm arrhythmia; I was just shattered. The other two were getting fed up with moaning at me and I had to concede that I looked pretty rough, so I drove the car for them on the last day instead of riding. We drove on back to Paris where we split and I picked up the team car late in the evening and pointed it down the *autoroute* towards Spain.

I pulled over outside Paris and phoned Pippa and

she pulled out the big old medical encyclopaedia while I described my symptoms. She diagnosed it as a serious heart problem. A couple of hours later, I stopped again and phoned one of the Sky doctors. I was a few hundred kilometres south-west of Paris by this time, so he directed me towards Bordeaux, where he knew the hospital had a heart unit. I walked into A&E around 2 a.m. and they put me on a trolley in a corridor, where my condition began to worsen. Fortunately, a nurse realized what was happening and rescued me from being ignored, and I was rushed across town to a specialist unit. A day later I woke up having had my chest opened up and a pacemaker fitted.

I had suffered a heart failure. The beat was so weak that it couldn't pump enough to flush my system and fluid built up and up until I either had the operation or died, as I certainly would have done in a previous era. I remember shuffling across the ward to the toilet, pushing a drip stand like an 80-year-old, and pissing for about fifteen glorious minutes.

By a stroke of fortune, my sister Ella was on holiday with her family at Arcachon, a few miles away. She was able to help me out, and Marcus Ljungqvist took over for me as *directeur sportif* at the Vuelta. Ella was amazed and delighted that the most obvious and unexpected benefit of having a pacemaker fitted was that it improved my speech immediately.

The pacemaker works by sending its own electrical impulse to the heart. Mine won't let my heartbeat go below 60, with the intention of never letting it get so slow as to provoke another stroke or heart failure. And yes, I do still ride my bike every day, but I'm thinking that you'd probably guessed that already. It hasn't stopped me needing another cardioversion – my arrhythmia was an unwelcome visitor again at the end of 2011 – but I've been generally more comfortable. I can ride aerobically without any bother indefinitely, but big efforts wipe me out. Gradual intensity is the key, which is why I can still put out a decent ramp test, as you build it slowly. I still love a time trial, but I don't think I'll be outsprinting anybody again any time soon.

Sky were very good and fixed me up with a consultant who ran all sorts of tests and gave a full report. He described my problems like this:

'Imagine your face when you were 18. Now look at it in your mid-fifties. It's not the same, is it? There are lines, cracks, scars, folds and blemishes. It's no different for your heart.

'Now, imagine that you have spent your whole life eating junk food, living outdoors, drinking booze and smoking a packet of fags a day. Because that's the equivalent of what you've been putting your heart through with the amount of strain you've put it under every day for twenty-five years.

'It's an old guy now, older than the rest of you, and you need to look after it.'

Some days I remember to look after it. At least I'm not a big drinker or smoker, I suppose, and I've always paid attention to my diet, though we won't go into what a dietician would say about my various food fads and obsessions over the years.

In 2011, a few months after our fiftieth birthday trip to the Dolomites, Brian headed back to Italy to race in an East Grinstead team in the Michele Bartoli Invitational Team Time Trial. Just one kilometre into the event, Brian collapsed and died. Something had caused a blood clot and he died instantly.

Brian had never had a moment's concern with his health in his entire life. He was as fit as a fiddle. He had been at my side, coaxing me over those hellish days through the Alps and Dolomites, watching with sympathy and understanding as I struggled with my failing body and my long-term heart problems. A few short months later he was taken away from us with no warning.

I wanted to go to Italy this year to take his place in the team in the race on the anniversary of his death. We all wanted to pay tribute to him in the best way we knew. Ironically, though I went to the event, I wasn't allowed to race because of the medical safeguards the race had installed in the wake of Brian's death. I expect that would make him smile and shake his head.

I really miss him.

Chapter Sixteen

I'd been chatting to Dave Brailsford during the 2008
World Championships in Varese. I was at Eurosport
in Feltham doing some commentary and I remember
popping outside to ring him. I'd heard that he was trying
to put something together to launch a British-based
pro road team. He ran the all-conquering GB national
cycling set-up that had done so much to transform the
medal table at the last few Olympics. It was no secret
that what he really wanted was to see a British road team
at the Tour de France: a pinnacle at which the young
riders in the national set-up could aim. A tilt, if you like,
at taking the successful approach that had been such a
revelation in the velodrome to the Champs-Elysées.

I said I'd be interested. It sounded good.

I was recovering in that Black Forest clinic in Germany
after my stroke when things began to get serious. Dave had
already mentioned that he had some big-name companies
interested, and he had a longstanding relationship with
Sky, as they'd been supporting the national set-up for a

while. I was in that clinic in 2009 when I got a call from Shane Sutton, who was working with Dave to set it up. Sky were on board and the whole thing was getting ready for lift-off.

I spoke to Johan about it. He thought it sounded like a massive opportunity for me and, although he was looking for a sponsor to take over from Astana and wanted me to stay, as a friend he thought I should go for it.

'It was more money than I could offer,' Johan explains, 'and it being a British team would be big for Sean. Plus, it wasn't certain we would carry on – Sky was in place before I had RadioShack's agreement to take over – and it wouldn't have been fair to string him along when he had a good offer on the table.'

Scott Sunderland had already been appointed as head *directeur sportif* and was fundamentally involved with getting the team on the road. Though I had a more complete *directeur*'s CV than Scott, that suited me perfectly as I wanted to continue what I'd been doing for the past few years with Bjarne and Johan: turn up, drive the car, help the guys race, go home.

Setting up a top cycling team from scratch is a massive undertaking. Tweaking things to make them run smoother or more effectively in a team that is already up and running is one thing; starting to build an empire from a blank sheet of paper is another altogether. Dave, Scott, Shane Sutton, Rod Ellingworth and Carsten Jeppesen moved heaven and earth in 2009 to ensure that there would be a Sky Pro Cycling Team on the road in

2010. It's well known that Dave is always striving for perfection, so it couldn't just be thrown together. I was getting over serious illness and working for Astana as soon as I was able, so I wasn't involved until the 2009 season was done and they'd already made massive strides – but there were inevitable teething problems. For example, I'd hate to have to count how many times the Jaguars we'd gone for as team cars broke down in that first season. It got to the point that you were crossing your fingers and saying a little prayer as you unlocked it in the morning. Jaguar were very supportive though; it was a learning process for both us at Team Sky and Jaguar, and they worked very hard to improve things. The fact that Sky still drive Jaguars is a testament to how far they've come and also shows that Jaguar are delighted with the amount of coverage that Team Sky brings them.

We created a huge buzz with our fancy bus and our black team kit. We took some stick for having nice gear, nice bikes, nice cars, or just for looking good sometimes. I felt that there was no rule about having to put up with crappy old second-hand buses that had been sold off by AG2R or somebody just because we were a new team . . . Why shouldn't we strive for the best? In fact, if you're starting from scratch, that's the best time to do it, isn't it?

There was something very swan-like about those first few months at Sky: we looked elegant and smooth to the outside world, but below the waterline we were just keeping beyond a state of panic.

In keeping with our imperious image, we won our first race: the criterium preceding the Tour Down Under in Adelaide in January, Greg Henderson and Chris Sutton taking a one-two. We followed more Australian success with a win in the Tour of Qatar's team time trial, a sure sign that Sky was beginning to gel as a unit. Men who would become stalwarts of the team – Bradley Wiggins, Edvald Boasson Hagen, Juan Antonio Flecha, Geraint Thomas – were already making their presence felt as a force to be reckoned with.

Behind that, things weren't running all that smoothly – understandably so, with such an ambitious agenda. There was a bit of moaning, and I was inevitably caught in the middle of it: as the management's representative, the riders and staff would complain to me about various niggles at races; then the management would express displeasure to me if a race hadn't gone how they would have liked. There were all sorts of little power struggles going on as various people at all levels tried to assert their own position in the food chain.

It was against that background that Scott Sunderland left by mutual consent in the spring. I had only seen Scott at the team presentation and our first get-together in Manchester, so I can't say exactly what went on. He had done a hell of a lot of work in setting the team up and had not been afraid to speak his mind, which seemed to isolate him a little bit from the riders on one side and the management on the other. He had been butting up against the operations side of the management for a while

and some kind of shakedown was inevitable – not everybody could get their own way. Scott's son was unwell
too, and my guess is that he didn't need the grief of Sky,
and Sky felt they didn't need the grief of Scott.

Things settled down a bit after he left as there were
fewer divisions in the rank, but there was a lot more work
for me. As you know, I like to get on with my work and
be left to do it, but now I was head *directeur sportif* more
by accident than design, and suddenly it felt like I was
spending my life writing reports, having meetings, setting programmes, resolving disputes . . . the only time
I could relax was when I was behind the wheel in a race. I
honestly thought about leaving, pretty much every day,
but, equally honestly, the main reason I kept pushing my
way through the paperwork and the workload was the
excellent salary. I knew I was worth a lot less elsewhere –
to Sky, I was valuable as a British *directeur sportif,* which
wouldn't make a difference with other teams – but also,
cycling was all I knew. It wasn't like I could just stroll off
and get a job managing a branch of Barclays or something. I felt under pressure to provide the very best level
of financial support to Pippa and the kids, so I couldn't
really turn my back on the team.

One of the problems, while we're being honest, was
dealing with British people all the time. I wasn't used to
it. I was used to European teams, where things ran like
clockwork. Cycling just isn't ingrained in British culture
like it is in, say, France or Belgium. The Sky masseurs
and mechanics were mostly European, but given the

nature of the team, there was no core of experience of the European pro scene in the operation, so things I regarded as simple ended up being complicated. After Scott's departure we were a very inexperienced *directeur sportif* line-up, too. I had a good bit of experience under my belt, but Marcus Ljungqvist and Steven de Jongh were learning on the job and needed help. I'd had plenty of experienced guys around me at CSC and Discovery, so I knew how much help they could be just in practical things, let alone how to read the race from behind it rather than in it.

My job, as I saw it, was to worry about the guys at the races. I wasn't interested in stories that Brad's private life was chaotic or that he was upset by things written about him in the press. I was interested in getting the team together at a race and calling the shots. That was the job description given to me by Shane Sutton when I joined the team and, although it had changed a little (whether I'd liked it or not) when Scott had left, I still felt that was the bit I was good at.

A big budget doesn't automatically mean everything is going to be OK – I only had to look back at that Fagor farrago to know that. My biggest issue with the Sky hierarchy was that I felt we were often sacrificing substance for style. For instance, we went to Paris–Nice looking to put down some building blocks for the Tour de France and provide a platform for Brad to perform later in the season. We got a great result when Greg Henderson won the first stage, but then they wanted us to pull out all the stops on all the other stages too. I was looking at the bigger picture of preparing for the Tour de France, but the press guys wanted something to write about every day. I didn't agree with that.

We went to that first Tour in 2010 with a huge amount of expectation on Bradley Wiggins's shoulders. His fourth place with Garmin the year before had led many to see him as a genuine contender for the yellow jersey, and he had been a natural target to lead the nascent Sky team, especially as he too was a product of the GB national track squad that had led to the formation of the team. There were horrible, protracted contract negotiations to bring him from Garmin to Sky, and then the numerous teething problems in our first few months of racing had led to Brad not being in the right place mentally or physically for his first Tour as a team leader. He didn't enjoy being thrust into the limelight and he started to get a reputation for being truculent and difficult when being asked the same question for the umpteenth time at a press conference or in an interview. He wasn't ready for that stuff – he didn't like it, and it got him down. The perceived arrogance of Sky – the fancy bus and fancy kit nonsense again – didn't help, as people tried to draw a parallel between what they thought was an aloof approach from the whole team organization and a distant persona in Brad. It just wasn't like that, but journalists have pages to fill, websites have click-through sponsors to satisfy, and these stories tend to take on a life of their own.

The problem with Brad was that, as a thinker, it wasn't just his demeanour at the races that was affected by this depressive cloud, it was his training too. He couldn't switch his brain off enough to really train hard in the way he needed to if he was going to match, or even surpass, his performance of 2009.

We tried to replicate his programme of the year before by using the Giro as preparation, but taking the leader's jersey by winning the prologue didn't really help as it heaped a bit more pressure on him to perform there rather than prepare for the Tour, our real goal. It started brilliantly though; when we turned up for the first stage with the pink jersey, we were so excited that we were the first bus in the car park. We had Ludacris blasting out on the bus and everybody was singing along. We had some shit luck with crashes in the first few days of that Giro, then lost the team time trial by a handful of seconds after losing CJ Sutton just after the start to a puncture then getting caught in a hailstorm. It should have all been written off as good prep, but instead it just mounted pressure on to Brad to perform. When he got back into the overall picture at the Giro, despite that bad luck in the first week, I wanted him to ride steady, but senior management wanted us to push for results for the rest of the race. Goalposts were being moved and I didn't like it.

At the recon camp arranged to tune things before the Tour and check out some key stages, Brad wasn't switched on. He would abandon planned efforts in training because he 'didn't feel right', and it was clear he wasn't in the form of 2009, but we hoped he could ride into something like it during the race.

Sky's first negative Tour story landed on the very first day of that 2010 race. We used the weather forecast to try to avoid the predicted heavy showers and give Brad a dry start time by sending him out early on the Rotterdam course – but instead he got caught in a sharp shower and couldn't push it as hard in the many corners as he would have liked, and came in half a minute or so down on the main contenders. It wasn't a major blow, but it gave the commentators a good chance to expand on their general point of Sky being too clever by half.

I thought the criticism was harsh. With the information available to us – the forecast was for heavier showers later on – we made an informed decision. If we'd have ignored that, we would have been belying our own principles of attention to detail and marginal gains, using everything we can to be the best we can be. Just because it didn't work out that day didn't make it a mistake, or mean that the philosophy was flawed.

It was clear that our determination to do things our own way, to ignore tradition unless it was proven to be useful and not to be ashamed of aiming to be the best, wasn't winning Sky many friends in the pro cycling circus. It was around this time that we began to realize that trying to be a bit easier to like might help a little in the overall plan. François Lemarchand came up to me at the Dauphiné. He'd been a teammate of mine back in Fagor days, but for the past few years he has been Christian Prudhomme's right-hand man as Tour de France organizer. At Sky, we were warming up and down before and after stages behind closed doors – tinted-perspex walls, in fact, which were very private – and he said, 'You're not planning to do that at the Tour, are you? That won't go down well.' We tried to project a more friendly public image that included mixing with the fans a bit more at races. Instead of the Eastern Bloc Terminator image, we resorted to Plan B: the Friendly Face of Sky.

The sarcastic flak followed Brad and Sky throughout that Tour. It was always going to be difficult to get near to his 2009 result. He'd been largely ignored as unimportant by the favourites in that race until the last week, he wasn't even leader of his own team, and now he was leading a very inexperienced brand new team. Of course, like everybody, I was disappointed when he dropped away from contention, but the sniggering coverage – 'It's all part of their plan,' was supposedly the in-joke in the press room whenever Brad lost contact with the front group in the mountains – was snidey and unjustified.

I didn't think Brad's final placing, 24th, 39 minutes behind Alberto, was a disgrace. It wasn't brilliant, but was no great mystery. Also, I was buoyed by his performance in the final time trial, when he put out 450 watts at the end of a three-week race. His position of 9th on the stage was a bit false, because Tony Martin and Fabian Cancellara had gone off early and the wind had turned around to buffet the later starters, but Brad put serious time into all the guys who had ridden in the same conditions as him, and all the favourites who had started behind him, including taking a whopping seven minutes or so from Cadel Evans, who was close to Brad in the GC.

The mood around the team was very flat, with various senior figures describing the race as a 'nightmare' for us, but I disagreed. Plus, I appreciated the way we were working. The teething troubles that were bound to afflict a big team setting up from scratch in a country with no history of running professional cycling teams were methodically being dealt with. I didn't like all the extra reports and planning that I was having to do, but I had to admit that the team's painstaking approach to racing was definitely beginning to pay off. Our winning percentage was good, the squad was gelling, and young riders like Edvald Boasson Hagen and Geraint Thomas were showing they had real quality. In fact, Edvald's attacking victory on the last stage of that year's Dauphiné was such a great achievement it sticks in my mind alongside many higher-profile wins during my three seasons with Sky. Having been at smaller teams like Linda McCartney and iTeam Nova, I know that success doesn't come easily and is always worth celebrating. The way the team persisted and never gave up trying was really gratifying. Trying to win the Tour in 2010 would have been like building a house in a day. I couldn't see it happening beforehand, so I wasn't gutted when it didn't happen. The team behind Sky had come from track racing. They hadn't succeeded at that overnight either; it had taken a little time and so would this. Step by step, two forward, one back, learning from our mistakes. It wasn't reasonable to expect so much from Brad either, but he'd be back, and he'd be better.

The story of the 2012 Tour de France actually begins in 2011. Brad and I were chatting near the start of the season and I tried to encapsulate my advice as briefly as possible. I just said, 'Brad, you've got to enjoy it.'

We had a much more considered approach towards success in 2011 after the rush to get off the ground in 2010. There were two really key signings. The first one was a highly visible move when we managed to bring in Mick Rogers from HTC. He'd been a tour team leader in his own right for the previous few years, at HTC and before that at T-Mobile. His experience, approach and general demeanour were fantastic, and he relished his new role as tour hopeful's right-hand man. Less pressure but a clear target. Mick's ready smile and calm state had a massive impact on Brad.

The second signing of importance wasn't really a signing as such – because Australian sports scientist Tim Kerrison had been with us from the start. He'd spent 2010 studying the new sport of cycling – he'd come to us from swimming – but in 2011 he was appointed head of performance support. Tim was 'The Numbers Guy'.

It might be worth giving you a quick background in what The Numbers Guy does. It's a role that has increased in importance since the early days of applying scientific theory to cycling, in the eighties and nineties, until it would appear impossible to succeed in today's big tours without one.

After the USADA report, we all know who Dr Michele Ferrari is. He is the man whose methods were so in demand by riders in the pursuit of glory in the nineties and beyond. Ferrari has been accused of having advised, authorized, organized and condoned widespread, illegal, performance-enhancing drug use in cycling, which he continues to deny. He was smart, though, and a lot of the science he applied has changed cycling for ever. It was Ferrari's methods of determining racing success that enabled us to make sense of the numbers.

To explain, we, or rather Tim, can calculate a rider's body weight, power output, the distance he needs to cover, what the gradient he's climbing is, and what speed he is travelling at. What's more, he can make these calculations with nearly as much accuracy on our opponents too. The phrase 'power-to-weight ratio' has been bandied about for pretty much as long as I've been a cyclist, but it's only recently that we would routinely be able to quantify that number. It varies a little from rider to rider, but Lance, for instance, knew that if he could put out 6.9 watts for each kilo of his weight, he would be virtually unbeatable. There is no cheating in that, in itself; the cheating comes when you decide to cross a line in how you're going to reach that number. It doesn't mean you have to take drugs. It can be done with hard work, fantastic natural ability, and a supremely skilful head of performance support.

So, for instance, we know that if Mick Rogers is sitting

at the front of the peloton on the Croix de Fer in the Tour de France putting out say 440 watts and Vincenzo Nibali attacks him, we can roughly estimate the likelihood of that attack succeeding and what we need to do about it. In the old dirty days, when somebody attacked like that, we wouldn't know if we'd see him again.

Tim is now rightly recognized as the leading figure in this branch of science and is much sought after by teams in many sports across the world. He certainly made a big difference to Sky, and the riders warmed to him.

The 2011 season began well for Brad, with third overall in Paris–Nice, and our focus on Tour general classification success looked well suited to pay off.

The first knockback of an otherwise comfortable start to 2011 was when Mick Rogers was laid low by glandular fever. He'd had it before and it was totally debilitating. The unfortunate conclusion was that Mick would miss most of the year recovering from the insidious illness.

Bradley Wiggins, like any leader, is high maintenance. I'm sure he wouldn't dispute that. When things are going well for him he's unstoppable. The trick is getting him in the right frame of mind for that to happen. We had our differences that spring.

Everything came to a head at the Tour of Romandie. We were using it as our springboard towards the Tour and were approaching it as a dry run for the big one. Preparing for the first big mountain, we laid down a plan that would see the team working together to set things up for Brad there. It was a horrible day, raining hard, cold, and when we hit that climb Brad sat up and drifted back through the peloton almost immediately. When the leader fails to follow through on a plan that the team has been working towards it has a massive detrimental effect on the other riders, too. I was pissed off and I told Brad that he had amazing physical ability and that, if he wasn't careful, he could waste it. It was a little tricky to fully speak my mind as Shane was there too, and his job a lot of the time is to keep Brad happy, so I didn't want to tread on his toes.

On another stage, everybody had got blasted from the front group except Brad and Ben Swift, our sprinter. I spoke to Brad on the radio and asked him to help out Swifty if he could for the sprint. In the last couple of kilometres Brad worked his way up to the front then swung off almost immediately in what I saw as a really half-hearted effort. Ben won the sprint anyway – it was for third, as two riders had got away – but I was very un-happy and questioned Brad's commitment. If he'd really committed to it, he might even have dragged the bunch up to the late breakaway and Ben's sprint would have been for the win.

The next day, during the team talk on the bus, I again asked the team to help Ben in the sprint if they could. Brad stood up and said, 'If we're going to help Swifty go for the sprint, I want us all to commit now, not agree to help if we can.'

I bristled at that after the events of the day before. 'Help if you can doesn't mean help if you fancy it,' I replied. 'The only time you should not do it is if you absolutely can't. It's not a choice.' We obviously had different views of what constituted commitment. The team all agreed to support Ben and he won the stage on the back of some excellent teamwork.

I must have spoken to a journalist and given some indication that I wasn't happy with Brad, and it got back to him, as he rang me to say he wasn't happy about it. He had a point – I should have spoken to him directly – but it gave us the opportunity to talk through the disagreement properly. 'It's not my job to be your psychiatrist, Brad,' I said. 'I expect you to always try your best, no matter what. I don't care if it's raining. If you're fucked, you're fucked; otherwise I expect you to always give it one hundred per cent.'

Shane and I had a talk on the phone to discuss Brad. 'I'm just so frustrated,' I said. 'If I had Brad's talent, I would have loved the rain. I would have said, "Bring it on, bitches!" and caned everybody. Instead, he's letting everything get to him. Everything is a reason not to succeed.'

Shane was very attuned to Brad, having known him for years and understood his background and what makes him tick, and he always had a knack of getting through to him.

That Tour of Romandie was the turning point. On no other occasion during my whole time with Sky did I ever again have to question Brad's approach or commitment. He turned up in top condition for every race; he was obviously training supremely well. He won our last race before the Tour, the Critérium du Dauphiné, and rightly went into the race as one of the favourites.

We've seen time and time again that the best of plans can go astray with a crash, and so it proved again. We'd avoided serious mishap in the first week, when most crashes occur before the general classification order begins to settle down a bit. We won stage six thanks to a daring bit of riding from Geraint and Edvald, with our Norwegian winning a hard sprint, and Brad was looking like the great, confident leader he had become. Stage seven, on the way to Châteauroux, was a straightforward day, but a touch of wheels brought our Tour to a standstill. Brad landed smack on his left collarbone and that was that.

What really impressed me was his response. Something had clicked inside Brad and he now understood what it was going to take. He knew where he had to get to, and he knew what he had to do to get there. He went to the Vuelta in the autumn and regained his great summer form, got a silver medal in the time trial at the Worlds, trained perfectly over the winter, opened the year with a great Volta ao Algarve, won Paris–Nice, won the Tour of Romandie, won the Dauphiné, and arrived in Liège for the Tour in supremely confident shape.

Chapter Seventeen

I was just looking back through all my bits and pieces to remind me of that great 2012 Tour de France and I came across this. It's Bradley's pacenotes from the first long time trial in the race, stage nine, Arc-et-Senans to Besançon. What we do is go over the course together beforehand and note down corners, hazards, rises, drops, places to take care and places to go flat out. I can then feed that information back to Brad via radio from the following car and let him concentrate on pushing his legs round as fast as he can. It's in Yatesish, so I don't know how much will make sense, but I hope it will give you a little insight into our approach:

LEFT 1.2 – OK – into flat for 2 kms – till km 3.5

3.5 – drag up 700 metres – till 4.2 swing round to the right at top then down into little village

4.5 – village – new tarmac into left OK down 4.8 into another left OK (CARE) into flat onto bridge

5.2 – exit bridge into drag top 6.2 = 400 metres
  dragging

6.2 swing left FULL-going into DOWN then flat 1.2
  kms to right hander into climb

7.4 right OK into climb = 2.5kms 6% big road power
  on 9 top = flat 500 metres

9.8 down for 2 and 5 kms to start of steep climb
  fly!!!!!

10.6 long left full 11 long right full 11.2 down 12
  BOTTOM into 2 kms of FLAT

14 enter village small hump 14.3 LEFT OK!!! 14.5
  hump climb ahead

14.7 start climb, gets progressively steeper over
  next 500 15.2 HARD LEFT climb

15.2 1.1 kms at 6%

16.3 top turn right into a 900-metre drag 4% 17.2 top
  village then DOWN

sweeping turns left-right-left-right look at
  MOTORBIKE

19.4 CARE left into LONG right then into tightish left
  19.19 DOWN

20.4 RIGHT full if good line so enter corner from the
  LEFT and cut apex GO

21 start 5% 800 metres drag though feed zone then
  into village follow *moto*

22.7 top-push on DOWN

23.9 long left full 24.2 hump then up round to the
  right down onto bridge

25.3 RIGHT then 400 metres LEFT into climb 1 km

6-7% *ALLEZ!!!!!!!!!!!!!!!*

26.7 TOP then DOWN fast

27.2 RIGHT – care then left then GO end of campers
little right up then down GO!

28.7 left DOWN into left OK go

29.4 RIGHT onto big road 12 kms to go – 1 climb
left

31.4 ROUNDABOUT narrow STRAIGHT

31.6 RIGHT OK swing left OK

5 kms to last climb

HANG TOUGH – *ALLEZ!!!!!!!*

33.5 slight LEFT – RIGHT = straight

36.6 LEFT UP GEARS!!!! 7-8% 1.1 km eases then
kicks up near top

37.7 TOP DOWN

38 DOWN into left OK FULL lines! 800 metres to left
take inside islands

38.8 LEFT go

39.5 ROUNDABOUT take left side drift right to take
traffic islands on right

40 left full enter from RIGHT then DOWN – 700
metres to CARE point!!

40.8 LEFT – RIGHT down CARE straight then swing
right up to FINISH

The 2012 Bradley Wiggins was an altogether different beast to the one who joined Sky as the team's inaugural leader in 2010. He was a happy, contented, relaxed person, but he was also more serious. The mickey-taking and comedy impressions were put away. Food, drink and sleep were meticulously thought through and planned. If there needed to be a sauna at the hotel, then we would only stay in a hotel with a sauna. If we needed a tough climb to train on, we'd only stay near a tough hill. If it benefited him to take a private jet to a race rather than queue for hours at an airport, he took a private jet. It was all about maximizing his chances. It was all about winning the Tour de France.

Brad realized that he had reached a glass ceiling in his previous persona and had broken through it. He was adhering to one of Dave Brailsford's most well-known maxims: he was being the best he could be. He trusted everybody around him: Dave, Tim, Shane, Rod Ellingworth, me, the other riders. We had a hardcore of Brad, Chris Froome, Mick Rogers, Richie Porte, Edvald Boasson Hagen, Kosta Sivtsov and Christian Knees that would go through the spring together as much as possible.

Our plan was to keep the same squad of people together right through the year, from the beginning to the Tour. Not just riders, but *directeurs sportifs*, mechanics, *soigneurs* – everybody. We felt that if you knew everybody in the team, everybody knew their role and everybody could predict what their teammates would do in a given situation, then that would be a tremendous advantage. This is one of the great benefits of having somebody like Dave Brailsford. It sounds obvious – a football team has a first-team squad with their own physios, coaches, bus driver, et cetera. – but to my knowledge it had never been done in cycling before. Dave's broad thinking always produces ideas. I'm not much of a thinker, I just do things. It needs somebody like him to get you to do things differently.

In the old days of cycling, back when I rode a bike for money, when everybody rode the same races together instead of there being thirty-man squads split over any number of events, much was made of the reciprocal nature of teamwork. Andy Hampsten would help me at Paris–Roubaix and I would pay him back at the Tour de France. That doesn't work so much these days, because the guys you see at Roubaix will be somewhere else entirely come Tour time. That wasn't the case with the Sky 2012 Tour team. We went everywhere together, building confidence in each other, building trust and building performance. When Brad buried himself for Richie Porte to win our first European stage race in the Algarve, he knew that, come July, Richie would be pulling himself inside out to repay the favour.

We liked Tenerife to train. There's a hotel at 2000 metres up on Mount Teide where there's nothing to do except ride your bike. Perfect. He rode and trained so hard there that racing came as a break sometimes. We were there in April before Romandie, and the workload that Brad was taking upon himself blew me away. Few people that I've ever worked with could train with that intensity. He was doing everything he could to maximize his talent.

The team for the Tour wasn't hard to set. The *directeur sportif* team at Sky at the 2012 Tour was myself and Servais Knaven. Servais had recce'd all the flat stages, so he and I were to sit in the first car for the week before the race ramped up to La Planche des Belles Filles, while Marcus Ljungqvist would be in team car two. Servais sat in the passenger seat with his iPad on his lap, pointing out all the hazards we were likely to encounter, and we'd pass them on to the riders. Dave would be with me in the car on other occasions, but he also liked to watch from the bus at the finish, as he could follow the action more easily from there on the mountain stages.

Rod Ellingworth worked with us to set the programmes for everybody. His job title is performance manager; he helps the riders organize their lives in a professional way, something which is especially useful for a guy like Mark Cavendish. Cav isn't a natural trainer in the way someone like Brad is. When Brad is focused, his appetite for training puts others in the shade. Cav, on the other hand, though he recognizes the importance of training, doesn't relish it in the same way. That doesn't bother me too much: I've seen plenty of sprinters lose their out-and-out finishing speed over the years in an effort to become better all-round cyclists. But not everybody can transform from bunch-kick winner to be a Kelly or a Jalabert or a Museeuw. If you protect your main asset – raw speed – you can have a career like Cipollini, winning sprints the whole time he was a pro. Cav can do that. He is the only rider I wouldn't be pissed off with for turning up at the Tour and not being super skinny, because he gets faster as the race goes on. Those four consecutive Champs-Elysées final-stage victories aren't a coincidence.

Cav had joined us for 2012. He was already World Champion, after one of *the* great team performances by the GB squad in Copenhagen, and the winner of countless Tour stages. He was a long-term mate of Brad's and the two of them had been in countless national teams since they'd been kids. Shoehorning the world's best sprinter into a team that hoped to win the Tour de France wasn't straightforward, however, and Cav's needs would be very different to Brad's. We decided that it would be crazy to go to the Tour without Cav, but Brad's quest for the yellow jersey would come first. If Cav came, his wingman Bernie Eisel came too. I had to argue for the inclusion of Christian Knees – it was impossible for me to envisage controlling the race without the lanky German. We needed somebody to be at Brad's side at all times and do whatever was asked of him. His ability to sit on the front of the bunch unquestioningly for literally weeks on end would be invaluable if we did find ourselves in possession of the yellow jersey.

So that was the team: Brad, Edvald, Cav, Bernie, Froomey, Christian, Richie, Mick and Kosta.

Apart from the differences between Cav's and Brad's targets, there was also the conundrum of Chris Froome. Froomey is an unbelievably talented climber who has become a brilliant Tour rider in his own right, but was still something of a wildcard in 2012. He had bouts suffering from bilharzia, a nasty tropical illness that he'd picked up in his native Africa, which had made it appear that he'd landed on the scene at Sky out of nowhere – but he'd been progressing with the team since we'd begun, culminating in a storming performance in the 2011 Vuelta, where we'd faltered in trying to support both Brad's and Froomey's chances of victory. His 2012 had been a broken year, not just because of his illness, but because Froomey, one of the nicest people you could meet, was a trouble magnet.

He'd attracted attention at his first Worlds when, competing as a junior for Kenya in the time trial, he'd crashed off the start ramp. In 2012 he'd already tried to drive his car into a multi-storey car park with his bike on the roof, and run over a septuagenarian pedestrian on a training ride. In the spring, when he'd disappeared from view, getting ill, falling off, going back to Africa for family weddings and this, that and the other, he'd looked an unlikely Tour starter, but I was always confident he'd come good in July. For a guy like Brad, who loves his cycling history, winning Paris–Nice with all the great memories of bygone editions – Kelly's seven back-to-back wins, Merckx, Poulidor and Anquetil – would always be a glorious thing. In Kenya the only bike race of any note is the Tour de France. I knew Froomey would be focused on the Tour and wasn't surprised when he arrived in Liège for the start in amazing condition, even when he rode the prologue with cotton wool stuffed up his nose, as I said earlier. He's that sort of bloke.

That's why there was no immense surprise when it was Froomey's race number that was broadcast on race radio as being a puncture victim when the racing was very hot at the business end of stage one. If it was going to be anyone, it would be him – that's just how it was, no fault of his. Richie Porte waited for him – the rest of the team were protecting Brad in a nervous, frenetic stage finale – and the two of them came within seconds of getting back on. They chased and chased, finally barely making contact just as the race negotiated a roundabout. That concertinaing of the line was enough to snap the elastic and they lost a minute to the front of the race. If they'd got back on just ten seconds earlier, they would have been further up the line and not got caught behind the split. The stage finished with a three-kilometre climb, and when I checked the classification, I saw that Froome had passed numerous other riders. I made a note that he was clearly in great climbing form.

If I'm going to be frank, in the charmed Tour de France we had just begun, even this seeming misfortune turned out to be good luck. When we reached the mountains and there was some discussion as to who would be best placed of our riders to win the Tour, Brad or Froomey, that lost minute was decisive. It had always been our plan to win the yellow jersey and Brad was our spearhead for that, but Froomey's incredible form, not just in the mountains but his blistering time-trial speed, demanded that the question be asked. In that Besançon time trial, I had been following Brad and giving him the pacenotes that we were looking at earlier, and kept being amazed by the time checks I was getting from Froomey. Here was Brad, one of the world's best time triallists, in the undoubted form of his life, racing with utter dedication to win the yellow jersey, yet he was only putting 35 seconds into Froomey.

The sublime double where Brad took the jersey and Froomey the stage at La Planche des Belles Filles that I spoke about at the start of this book set the tone for the race.

Froomey wanted to win, but not at Brad's expense. He would have liked us to have two leaders, to let the two of them duke it out; but for me that meant weakening our overall ability to win the race. Opponents like Cadel Evans and Vincenzo Nibali would seek to exploit any rift in our ranks, and we were, after all, in complete control. I thought riding full on for Brad with Froomey in reserve was definitely our best bet for victory.

Things came to a head on the Alpine stage to La Toussuire over the Madeleine and La Croix de Fer. I had actually previously had a discussion with Froomey about the Croix de Fer when I'd pointed out that it would be possible for him to win the Tour if he attacked there. It was unlikely the other teams would chase if he did attack, as they would follow Brad. I wasn't suggesting it as a real plan, more a discussion about what could happen, so I may have been guilty of sowing the seeds of dissent in his mind. There was a meeting the night before the stage with Dave, Brad, Froomey and myself, where all the various options were discussed and the air cleared. Froomey was keen to establish himself in second place overall and have a free hand. Dave and I wanted to stick to the original plan of Brad taking the yellow jersey all the way to Paris. Brad was obviously supportive of that, but wary of what could happen if Froomey was to ride off. The upshot was that we decided without any ambiguity that Froomey would stay at Brad's side until the last 500 metres, when he would be free to attack if he wished, the idea being that he could take time out of Nibali and Evans in the race for second without endangering Brad's lead. Even after that, right up to the morning of the stage, when we were on the bus, he was asking, 'What about five kilometres out?' No. 'Three kilometres?' No, Froomey.

Cadel Evans attacked on the Croix de Fer, a monster of a climb, but too far from the finish to put us in any serious trouble and we reeled him in. More intent was shown by Thibault Pinot, Jurgen Van Den Broeck and Janez Brajkovič when they attacked continually as Richie Porte tried to set the pace for Brad on the last climb up to the finish. When Nibali joined them it was clear that we had to react, and Froomey upped the speed to bring Brad back up to the front. He then pulled over and I assumed he was done – if he still had something left under the bonnet, his job there would have been to keep the pace high to the finish and put more time into Evans, who had cracked under the acceleration. With Froomey done, Brad concentrated on time-trialling the final five kilometres to the finish at a steady speed. However, as we went inside 4 kilometres, Froomey suddenly reappeared and attacked.

For a moment I couldn't believe it. 'What the fuck?' I said, followed by something like, 'Froomey, what the fucking hell are you playing at?' or, as the cartoonist Marty McCrossan has it, 'Froomeeee!' God knows what Brad thought, as he had been riding pretty close to his limit for the previous kilometre, believing that Froomey was spent and had already given his all as his last team-mate left at the front.

I made it pretty clear on the radio that this was NOT the plan and he had better wait. He did. There was no damage done in practical terms. We finished the stage with Froomey having moved up to second overall following Evans's drop from contention. However, I'd seen Brad's reaction to Froomey's attack and it was clear his head was spinning.

There was pandemonium at the team bus, with the press surrounding us. Dave and I agreed not to talk to anyone, let the situation calm down and discuss what had happened later.

That process was accelerated when I got back to my room and received a text from Brad, saying:

'I think it would be better for everyone if I went home.'

I went straight to his room to talk to him. He was upset, disappointed with what had happened, and felt like Froomey had stabbed him in the back after the

discussion we'd had before the stage. He couldn't understand why he'd gone back on the agreement, especially
when everything was going so well, dropping Evans and
covering the moves of the other challengers with ease. I
sat down and chatted with him for a while, explaining
that I thought this was his time. His condition was
unbelievable, he was at the head of one of the most
focused Tour machines ever brought to the race, and
nobody could challenge him. I texted Dave to tell him
what was going on, looking for a bit of support. Brad's
room was up on the third or fourth floor of the resort
hotel. I glanced out of the window at the view and was
surprised to see Dave, Tim and Rod heading out for
a stroll! I texted Dave again and said he'd better turn
around fairly sharpish as there was some shit going down
and he needed to get up here. A few minutes later he
arrived at Brad's room and gave him a great talk about
how the Tour was his destiny, that his whole life had
been leading up to this moment and it was within his
grasp. Now was not the time to turn his back on it.

Dave and I had a swift discussion in which he said
he would also talk to Froomey, and I headed off. Riders
usually go to bed around 9 or 9.30 p.m. on the Tour.
Indeed, Bobby Julich, who was working as a coach with
us in 2012, likes to tell people a story of how we were
rooming together when he was a new pro and I was an
old lag at Motorola. It was 10 p.m. and he was sitting up
in bed reading a book when I abruptly said, 'Goodnight,'
and switched the light off, leaving him staring at the

pages in surprise in the black. So I was surprised to pass through the dining area at 10 p.m. and see Froomey sitting there on his own.

'Has Dave spoken to you, Froomey?'

'No, nobody's spoken to me.'

Shit. I sat down and went over the big talking point of the day with him. We disagreed on the main point, which was that he had done nothing wrong. I couldn't accept that, and said that he shouldn't have signed up to the plan before the stage if he didn't agree with it.

He sloped off to bed a bit down and I texted Dave, wondering where the hell he'd been.

Dave Brailsford's foresight in setting up the team and having the ideas to see it to such a high level are phenomenal. Without Dave, there is no Sky team, and British cycling fans would still be mumbling to each other on cold Sunday-morning rides about how nice it would be to get all our decent riders together on one team. But he's not perfect, and not alone in his occasional dislike of confrontation. However, sometimes it has to be done. Somebody has to say the hard word, to deliver bad news or say what somebody doesn't want to hear.

People often ask me what would have happened if Froomey had persevered with that attack. Brad was in as good a shape as any Tour rider had been in 2012, a condition he may never make again. His numbers were amazing, his results that spring and the way he performed in the time trials and in the reduced amount of climbing-mountain mileage in that Tour showed that he had the physical measure of anybody. There were only four kilometres left at that point, and Brad went on to win the Tour by three minutes, so the maths says that he would still have been comfortably on top in Paris. However, his mental state was always fragile, and that psychological blow could have been a knockout one.

I mentally compared Brad's reaction to what might have happened if one of Lance's US Postal teammates had tried something similar in his glory years – there were riders on that team talented enough to challenge him, if not fierce or strong enough to do so. I think he would have most likely snarled like a pitbull and chased them down before beating them to a pulp.

There was no animosity between Brad and Froomey as the race rolled on, but there was perhaps a slight mistrust, a worry that Froomey might just pull something. However, the lack of sustained, long, steep, climbing stages still meant that Brad was in the box seat, especially with another long time trial to come on the penultimate day. Brad smoothed things over by letting it be known that he thought that Froomey's time would come, that he was grateful for his support, but that it would be his turn to help Froomey soon enough.

Attention began to turn back to our other soap opera: Mark Cavendish's desire to win stages and take the green jersey. Cav's open commitment is fantastic, just the sort of leader a team desires. He would stand up on the bus at the morning's team meeting and say, 'Get me there and I will win.'

For me, as a *directeur sportif* trying to win the Tour de France, having Cav on the team was frankly an inconvenience. But he's the greatest sprinter in the world, who wouldn't want him? It was clear that the objective, above all else, was to win the yellow jersey. If we were in a position to win stages through Cav then great, but I was not prepared to risk the jersey to make it happen. He won stage two to give us and himself a great opening to the race. After I got caught up for the best part of five minutes behind the massive crash on stage six, Cav and I had a major falling out. He was three minutes behind the bunch because of the crash and livid that I hadn't waited for him and helped to bring him back up to the front of the race for the sprint that was certain to decide the stage. I, however, was not prepared to isolate Brad in the bunch to make that happen. We'd already lost Kosta the day before to a freak accident, when a soft crash was followed by another rider hitting Kosta on the ground while he was still clipped into his pedals, breaking his leg. I just couldn't risk waiting for Cav: what if Brad crashed? I had his spare bike on the car, and he was the only guy in the team using Speedplay pedals. What if the bunch split in front of him because of another crash? That was happening every day: who would drag the race back together? I felt that I had to leave Cav to his own devices and get back up to the front as soon as possible. I floored it, the Jaguar got up to 190km/h, with the bikes threatening to rip themselves off the roof, and made it up to the back of the peloton after ten minutes of flat-out driving. Cav would live to fight another day, but the Tour could have been lost for good. Stage six would just have to be written off.

Marcus Ljunqvist had been behind Cav in team car two and let me know that Cav was none too pleased with me. I went to Cav's room that night, but he was so angry that he wouldn't speak to me, just looking at the floor and obviously very emotional. I didn't know if he was going to punch me on the face or start crying. Rod Ellingworth came up to me the next day and spoke to me. 'Sean, will you talk to Cav?' I wasn't interested. 'We're here to win the Tour de France, Rod.' I had total tunnel vision about the yellow jersey. I couldn't understand why Cav couldn't see that and thought it would blow over. At the next day's meeting, in front of everybody, I said, 'Cav, I know you're pissed off with me, but we're here to win the Tour de France.' In hindsight, I should have listened to Rod and sorted it out there and then, as Cav sulked for days. Eventually, he came up to me and we shook hands.

I wish I'd ridden for more people like Cav in my career. His will to win is as great as anybody who has ever ridden a bike, and his willingness to wear his heart on his sleeve makes him an extremely popular teammate. But his involvement in a team with other priorities just wasn't ideal for him or anybody else. The most gratifying aspect of Cav's monumental strop was the emergence of Bernie Eisel. The Austrian had come to the team with Cav from HTC in the winter and had been briefed to be his sidekick for the year, and the Tour in particular.

When Cav went into his shell, though, Bernie came out of his to take a leading role.

I say Bernie came out of his shell . . . anyone who has met Bernie will know that there is very little of the retiring nature about him. On training rides, it is always his voice you can hear. He knows the best routes. He knows where all the cafés are. He knows which ones sell the best cakes. And everybody had better pay attention. Far from following Cav's lead as we left the flat stages of the first week, Bernie grew more and more vocal, helping marshal things on the road, reiterating tactics, encouraging his teammates. You'd hear him on the radio all the time: 'Good job, Christian,' when Knees was doing one of his massive turns; or 'Nice one, Eddy!' after Edvald had hauled in a break. Halfway through the Tour, Bradley said to everybody, 'Can I just say what a pleasure it is to have Bernie Eisel as part of this team,' and got a rousing reception.

The Cav problem reared its head again as we headed to Pau before the Pyrenean stages. He was desperate for us to chase hard and bring the race back together to give him a chance of winning the stage, but I wasn't keen. You could see just by the way that people were pedalling and the bunch was stretching that it was a hard day, up and down all the way. Frankly, it didn't make much difference to me if we won five stages or ten, the overall was everything. If we could do it, great, but I wasn't prepared to put the whole team on the front all day to make it happen. I wasn't on my own in thinking that; it was generally the view of most of the team. I was covering my own arse to some extent: it was my decisions on the road that would define whether we succeeded or not, and I needed to prioritize what we were aiming at. It was an unnecessary load on guys who had been burying themselves for weeks as far as I was concerned.

Also, it's not a great idea to rub the other teams' noses in it. We had been so dominant in the race – first and second overall, big time gaps, setting the pace all the time, stage wins – that it was smart, in my opinion, to share it round a little bit. Another few riders get in a break, another rider wins a stage, another sponsor gets some TV time, everybody benefits. It's good for the race. We'd seen what harm the animosity of other teams could do to us in that first difficult season. I'd had first-hand experience of it at the sharp end at that awful Vuelta in 1985 when Roland Berland had pissed off the Spaniards and turned the whole race against us. When you ride alongside other competitors for a hundred days a year, you get to know each other. Friendships and rivalries develop and it's easy to fall out with somebody. Let them have a slice of the cake and we all stay happy.

I remember Stephen Roche being asked about LeMond's 1989 victory and how incredible it was, considering he had no help from his team. Roche disagreed, saying that LeMond had the best team in the bunch: his teammates were his leading competitors. They didn't go out of their way to attack him because he hadn't pissed them off.

Edvald Boasson Hagen is a star; one of the greatest riders I've ever had the pleasure of working with. The day before the final time trial was a rolling long one through the Lot and the Dordogne to Brive, and at the team meeting I said, 'OK, it's going to be an easy day today.' I didn't want everybody on the front all day again. They were tired. Cav put his hand up and said, 'Please, just give me a chance, I know I can win today.' Brad said OK, and everybody else followed suit. The team spirit in that squad was so strong you could almost touch it. We all appreciated Cav sweating through a difficult couple of weeks in support of his leader. It's not often you see the World Champion going back to the team car for bottles for everyone. 'Right . . . but I don't want us to have to ride on the front all day. We need to put somebody in the break so that we're not the ones chasing,' I said.

'I'll do it,' said Edvald.

The day before had been the last real chance for anyone to unseat Brad and Froomey at the top of the tree; a difficult Pyrenean stage. The first climb of the day was the Col de Menté, a beautiful road in the middle of the Pyrenees, and there was a break up the road. It wasn't dangerous in itself, but could be used by dangerous climbers as a springboard to put us under pressure. I'd spoken to Edvald: 'Eddy, I want that break brought back at the summit. Not before the summit, at the summit.' He went straight to the front, tapped out 430 watts all the way up, then accelerated at the top just to make contact.

That's the sort of performance that makes a *directeur sportif* purr.

On this next day into Brive, we knew that we had to get somebody into the break – something we hadn't really done all race as we'd been massing for Brad – or Cav's tilt at the stage would be off the menu. There was a small climb coming up and the break of the day had already formed without any of the guys making it. Edvald saw the climb and bridged the gap like a bat out of hell. As expected, the race settled down and everybody was able to ride calmly in the bunch in the knowledge that we had somebody in there and other teams would have to chase. Chase they did, and brought the gap down until it looked likely that the break might be captured in the last few metres. At that point, we massed at the front to pull as hard as we could, Brad putting in a massive turn at the head of the race in the yellow jersey, setting things up for Cav to take his second stage. There was a pretty good atmosphere on the bus that night.

If anybody needed convincing that Bradley Wiggins was a worthy winner of the 2012 Tour de France, they only have to look at his incredible performance in that final time trial on the penultimate day. His roaring salute as he crossed the line in his yellow skinsuit remains the enduring image of the race for me. I had James Murdoch in the car next to me, so the people at the top of the Sky tree were taking notice of what we were doing.

Paris was just surreal. When you've spent three weeks in your own little bubble, just concentrating on the job you've been planning for months – years – you don't take in much of what's going on. When we hit the Champs-Elysées to be met with an unending sea of Union Jacks, all of that changed. After Cav had inevitably won his third stage, following another fantastic Skytrain lead out, there was an incredible urge to soak it up, to truly appreciate the moment. We'd won the Tour de France. We'd got second as well. In amongst a clutch of stage wins, we'd won the last three in a row. It was hard to take it all in.

Who knows what will happen in the future? Perhaps British winners of the Tour de France will become commonplace? Perhaps British *directeurs sportifs* will rule the roost? But you can only be the first to do something once: Brad will always have that.

And, I suppose, so will I.

Chapter Eighteen

Kids today, eh? Don't know they're born, some of them.

I know that makes me sound like an old git. And I know that people born in the forties were saying it about my generation, and people born in the twenties were saying it about them. It's as old as age itself, I suspect.

Johan Bruyneel and I found ourselves talking about how much things have changed since we got involved in cycling in the eighties. A recurring theme is a lack of respect for those who have gone before you. Is that purely a cycling thing? I don't think so, it's more of a general malaise in society, a lack of wanting to take responsibility for your own actions. I hope my kids aren't like that. I don't think they are.

One of the problems as you get older is that you're putting more and more chronological distance between yourself and the kids that are coming through, taking the sport up, turning pro, looking for guidance. What neo-pro is going to be impressed that I won a Tour de France time trial in 1988 when he wasn't born until 1993? It's understandable that that's not going to rock his world, especially if he saw the sort of bike I was riding to do it.

'That's one of the advantages of Sean riding his bike as a *directeur sportif*,' says Johan. 'The young guys would be looking at some fat guy driving a team car, unable to conceive that he might have won some big races. They were probably on black and white TV. But then Sean rides up alongside them as they're sweating up some hill in the middle of nowhere and says, "You're not making an effort, boy!" and rides off into the distance. They know he knows what he's talking about.'

It's true: the fact that I'm still riding my bike does make people look at me in a different way. Amongst my peers, the guys I was a pro alongside all those years ago, there's a general disbelief that I spend my Sunday mornings racing my sons and my brothers in time trials on the old Q10. The ones that know I've been ill are horrified.

There's another group of people, younger than me but old-timers in cycling terms, who do a little double take when they pitch up on the start line of a Surrey League road race at Dunsfold Aerodrome and see me alongside them on the grid. But there's a much bigger group of riders in those races, and elsewhere, who simply haven't a clue who I am: I'm just another old bloke who spends too much time and money on bicycles. One with particularly bad legs, though.

Looking through the pictures in all of those cuttings for this book, I had a little laugh to myself when I saw a shot of my legs that Phil Ashley took a couple a years ago for a profile in *Ride*, the Australian magazine. 'That's not me,' I said to him, when he showed me the image – a gnarled and pitted contour map, or a roughly carved tree trunk, not the body of a former professional athlete. They must have got a bit worse over the years, but, amusingly, my legs looked well on the way to that state when I was a 17-year-old at East Grinstead Cycling Club, according to the older pictures.

I got used to people knowing who I was at bike races, but that level of fame was never an issue because I was always one of the supporting cast, a *domestique*, a team helper. There was always a Roche, an Armstrong or a Wiggins to take the limelight. The one time in recent years when it felt like that wasn't the case was during the London Olympics.

I was on my way to Hampton Court to help Brad in the time trial. We were basically trying to replicate the format for his Tour success, so that meant me driving the car behind him, feeding him the pacenotes, making sure he was on top of his game. I'd been advised to avoid getting there by car because of the traffic and road closures, so I hopped on the train from Uckfield. I got up to Victoria and got embroiled in a discussion with a ticket inspector because, being a bumpkin, I'd gone the wrong way and didn't have the right ticket. 'You've got to let him through, mate!' shouted a passer-by. 'He's a legend and he's going to help us win the Olympics!'

When I got out at the front of the station, I was looking around for where I should be heading when a guy in a suit rode past me on a Boris Bike. 'Legend,' he said out of the corner of his mouth.

What a day that was. If there has ever been an athlete in more supreme condition than Brad was that day, I've certainly not been around to witness it.

In the 2011 Tour de France, Brad went in at about 70 kilograms, as lean as he could be, and much, much skinnier than his 2010 shape. For 2012, Tim decided that he could afford to carry a little more weight as there were fewer high mountain kilometres, and he would benefit from the increased power that it would give him in the time trials, so he started the race at 72 kilos. He came out of the Tour with not only the yellow jersey that he'd dared to dream of, but two immense time-trial victories, and the small matter of nearly ninety hours of racing in his legs. Ten days of restive training meant that he was as ready as he'd ever be, and that proved to be a lot more ready than anybody else.

I'm so pleased to have been part of the London 2012 experience. The wave of euphoria that swept over the country during those two weeks was unforgettable, and we were lucky enough to have been in on it at the start, as the road cycling events were amongst the first, well before the athletics got underway. I felt like I had come full circle: from clearing toothpaste off my pillow with Terry Tinsley in Moscow, thirty-two years later here I was following the first British winner of the Tour de

France to an Olympic gold medal within riding distance of my home.

Finishing off my *directeur sportif* career at Sky with a Tour de France yellow jersey and an Olympic title was a pretty good moment to bow out. My record as a *directeur sportif* in 2012 might stand some comparison, too. The races I went to were the Volta ao Algarve, Paris–Nice, Tour of Romandie, Tour of Catalunya, Critérium du Dauphiné, Tour de France and the Olympic Time Trial. The only one we didn't win was Catalunya, after getting caught out by a snowstorm. That's a winning percentage I can look back on with some satisfaction.

So it's back to the forest. I did some hedge-cutting in the winter. I'm working with my friend Jon Sharples and his coaching business, helping other people to enjoy getting the best out of themselves. I love the riding – every day, naturally – and I love seeing people giving it their all on the ramp tests.

I've bought a new van. I've put a second row of seats in, and there's room for all the bikes and kit, and I'm off to the Tour almost as soon as I shut the lid on this laptop. As I write this, Liam is taking wheels on and off bikes and Jesse is loading them into the van whilst I hurl instructions and insults at them. My life in a nutshell really: it's always been all about the bike.

My twenty-first Tour de France won't put many expectations on me, though: it will be the first one that I'll be going to with no job to do. I'm just going on holiday with my boys. We'll be on the slopes of Ventoux and Alpe d'Huez to cheer on the men I used to ride with and drive behind. It'll be the first time I've ridden for fun in the mountains with my sons.

Don't expect it to be fun for them, though.

Author's Note

As I said earlier, when I decided to write this book I was worried that I wouldn't remember enough about my life. Having written it, my concern now is that this book may not be how I envisaged it. How can a book possibly cover everything that has happened in my life? It can only be a snippet. The reality of my life is so much more than the words in this book. Still, I hope they're entertaining.

I also thought it would be amusing to list a few of the things I'm particularly proud of, a sort of career highlights, without going into the detail of every last race (even if my younger self would be horrified, having kept all those records about our races in the forest).

So here they are. Sean Yates the Superstar: some achievements and how they make me feel now.

♦ Breaking the 10-mile time trial competition record twice in one day in 1979 (I don't think it has ever been done before or since)

- National 25-mile Champion in 1980 (my first big win)

- World and Olympic Team Pursuit record holder in Moscow in 1980 (nice to be a World and Olympic record holder, even if it was only for ten minutes)

- Leader's jersey in Paris–Nice in 1988 (made me feel like I had arrived)

- Tour of Spain stage win in 1988 (it was close but I hung on)

- Tour de France time trial win in 1988 (nice because of my testing background)

- Philly US Pro win in 1994 (the best finishing straight there is)

- Tour yellow jersey in 1994 (everybody knows what that is)

- 5th in Paris–Roubaix in 1994 (it was an epic battle in the toughest of conditions, which I loved)

- World Masters Individual Pursuit Champion and World record holder in 2000 (showed I was keen)

- Silver Medal in the World Masters Road Race in 2003 (showed I was still keen)

- Competition record in the 12-hours Tandem (304 miles) with Zak Carr in 2005 (showed I still can take the pain; I didn't touch my bike for six weeks after that one)

♦ Bronze medal in the National 50-mile champion-ships in 2005 (26 years after my National 25-mile bronze medal in 1979 – is that some kind of record?)

♦ Competition record in the 25-mile Tandem (43.44) with Michael Hutchinson in 2006 (27 years after my first competition record – that's definitely a record in itself)

♦ 281 miles in the National 12-hours championships in 2011, aged 51 (competition record for a rider fitted with a pacemaker, I think!!!)

So, yes, I can definitely say I'm proud of the many years I've been on a bike, and I hope there's still lots more to come. After all, I was quoted in *Cycling Weekly* in 2008, under the headline 'Yates wins last race', that 'It's out of my system and I'm not going to do it again.'

I was clearly not myself that day. I'm still racing.

Acknowledgements

Without the input of some special people, this book would have been very short indeed.

Dag Otto Lauritzen, John Herety, Craig Geater, Johan Bruyneel, Sean Kelly, Allan Peiper, Brian Smith and Terry Tinsley have all brought back memories of good, bad and funny days. Thanks for everything.

So many people have helped me with my career, and put up with my idiosyncrasies, that it would take another book to list them, so I hope each of them knows that I don't forget people's kindness and generosity. I must say a special thank you though to Tony Mills, for his support and belief before anybody else had seen my potential; and to Vic Haines, Michael Hutchinson, Bjarne Riis, Paul Sherwen, Jim Ochowicz (the best time and the best team), Jean-René Bernedeau (that was a turning point of my career) and finally the late Tony York and Zak Carr.

I would also like to thank all the medical staff who have helped take care of me over the years, especially Pedro Celaya, and all those unsung heroes on cycling teams – the mechanics and masseurs, in particular Txema González, who died so tragically in 2010 at the age of just 43.

My uncle Michael was an immense help when I started racing, and still is a great help, and of course Mum and Dad backed me from the day I was born. With the addition of Chris, Ella, Conall and Oriana, I couldn't have wished for a better family growing up.

Pippa, Liam, Jesse, Bathsheba: you're the guys that motivate me every day. You make it all worthwhile.

Graham Watson's timeless photos, Phil Ashley's cover shot, my agent Kevin Pocklington and my editor Giles Elliott are all responsible for the book you hold in your hands. But mostly, that title goes to my friend John Deering, who has listened to my rants, written down my tales, crossed them out and written them down again for months on end.

Thanks.

Picture Acknowledgements

All images have been supplied courtesy of the author unless otherwise stated. Every effort has been made to contact the copyright holders. We apologize for any omissions in this respect and will be pleased to make the appropriate acknowledgements in any future edition.

Section 1

1984 Het Volk, 1984 Tour de France, 1985 Vuelta, 1986 Tour (climbing), 1987 Tour (x2), 1988 Vuelta all © Graham Watson.

Section 2

Pages 1–7 all © Graham Watson except Page 3 (National road race championships; Tour de Trump) courtesy of the author and Page 7 (Froomey) © Marty McCrossan. Page 8 both © Phil Ashley.

Index

IT'S ALL ABOUT THE BIKE

ABOUT THE AUTHORS

Sean Yates was born in 1960 and started riding as a pro for Peugeot in 1982 after graduating from the famed ACBB team in Paris, like Stephen Roche and Robert Millar before him. During a highly successful cycling career, he became the first British rider to win a time-trial stage of the Tour de France, in 1988, and then, six years later, only the third ever to wear the yellow jersey.

After his twelfth Tour de France in 1996, Yates retired to pursue a career in team management. At the Discovery Channel team, he was the architect of Paolo Savoldelli's win in the Giro d'Italia in 2005, and then became head sporting director at Team Sky. Among his many triumphs in three years at Sky before his retirement in 2012 were Bradley Wiggins's Tour de France and London Olympic Games victories.

John Deering, who collaborated with Sean Yates on this book, is an author, journalist and musician who has known Yates since 1998, when they worked together at the Linda McCartney Pro Cycling Team, a period he documented in his acclaimed book *Team on the Run*. His other books include *Bradley Wiggins: Tour de Force* and *12 Months in the Saddle*, with Phil Ashley.